The Simon and Schuster

POCKET GUIDE TO

The Wines of BURGUNDY

BY SERENA SUTCLIFFE

With an Introduction by

—HUGH JOHNSON—

AUX BOURGUIGNONS

Simon & Schuster, Inc.
New York

Serena Sutcliffe's Pocket Guide to the Wines of Burgundy was edited and designed by Mitchell Beazley International Limited, Artists House, 14–15 Manette Street, London W1V 5LB

Published by Simon and Schuster
A Division of Simon & Schuster, Inc.
Simon & Schuster Building
Rockefeller Center
1230 Avenue of the Americas
New York, New York 10020

ISBN 0 671-61695 1
Library of Congress Cataloging Information available upon request

Maps by Eugene Fleury
Typeset by Servis Filmsetting Ltd, Manchester, England
Reproduction by Gilchrist Bros. Ltd, Leeds, England
Printed and bound in Hong Kong by Mandarin Offset International Ltd.

Editor	Elizabeth Hubbard
Designer	Sheila Volpe
Production	Androulla Pavlou
Senior Executive Editor	Chris Foulkes
Senior Executive Art Editor	Roger Walton

CONTENTS

INTRODUCTION

Access to the personal files of a top professional is surely the most that any serious amateur of wine could ask. The new generation of wine books represented by Serena Sutcliffe's *Pocket Guide to the Wines of Burgundy* and David Peppercorn's companion volume on Bordeaux amounts almost to such a privileged snoop.

The situation reports and critical opinions that form the basis of buying decisions are normally classified information. But wine literature has moved with quite startling speed from the phase of enthusiastic generalization to that of precise wine-by-wine commentary. In these two books it drops its sixth, if not seventh, veil. Now we are allowed to know as much as the most experienced professionals.

Serena Sutcliffe has earned a formidable international reputation as a wine-taster of authority and decision. She and her husband David Peppercorn are partners in their own much-respected broking house in London. From London she travels constantly throughout the wine world, but makes a speciality of Burgundy – partly, one suspects, because it is such an enigmatic, volatile and controversial area. Everyone knows that burgundy, both red and white, can be sublime. Yet it so often fails to meet expectations. What greater challenge for an unprejudiced taster and writer than to track down the authentic and commendable, and to warn us about the rest?

Serena Sutcliffe learned her impeccable French as a translator for UNESCO in Paris. She learned her wine in the London wine trade, being one of the first women to pass the stiff examination and become a Master of Wine. Her writing is a natural gift, which was made plain to the world in 1981 when she was responsible for a totally new edition of André Simon's *Wines of the World.*

These attributes together make her a highly qualified guide. Her day-to-day dealings with Burgundy and Burgundians give her an up-to-date insight such as none before her has tried to pack into the convenient compass of a pocket book. It is a remarkable privilege to be able, as it were, to look over her shoulder at the sometimes hypnotizing complexities of the most enigmatic of all the great wine regions.

Hugh Johnson

HOW TO USE THIS BOOK

This book has two main sections. The Introduction gives a general picture of the Burgundy region and its wines, including the history, geography and climate of the region, moving on to the appellations, the grapes and how the wines are produced and marketed. The Introduction concludes with a section on enjoying burgundy, followed by a run-down of the merits of recent vintages.

The main section of the book is Wines and Villages, a guide to the Burgundy regions and their wines. The Côte d'Or section, which is naturally the largest, is followed by an A–Z directory of Burgundy producers. Sections on Chablis, the Côte Chalonnaise, the Mâconnais and Beaujolais follow.

Within the Wines and Villages section, each village/appellation entry gives the following information: 1983 production figures where available for red, white and rosé wines, a list of Premiers Crus for the appellation(s), and notes on soil and topography and their effects on the wines. Then follows the author's personal selection of the appellation's producers.

For more detail about a wine producer, consult the A–Z of Burgundy producers which begins on page 77. Here producers are listed alphabetically giving name and address, the total area of land cultivated and details of vineyard holdings and production figures, where applicable. This is followed by the author's assessment of the wines.

To look up a particular village or appellation, turn to the area section first and then the village e.g. Beaujolais, Fleurie. Individual producers and their wines may also be listed here under the author's personal selections.

To save space, certain abbreviations have been used. Vineyard areas are expressed in hectares (ha), and yields are expressed in hectolitres (hl) and hectolitres per hectare (hl/ha). Symbols at the beginning of each area/village/appellation indicate whether red, white, or rosé wines are produced (red ●, white ○, rose ◕).

GAEC Groupement Agricole d'Exploitation en Commun
AC (AOC) Appellation d'Origine Contrôlée
km kilometres
cm centimetres
mm millimetres
1 hectare (ha) = 2.47 acres
1 hectolitre (hl) = 100 litres = 22.02 gallons (Imperial) = 26.45 gallons (US). 1 hectolitre = approx. 11 cases of wine (12 × 75cl bottles per case).

Introduction

THE REGION & THE WINES

To many people, French and foreigners alike, the word Burgundy is synonymous with wine and rollicking good living. It conjures up visions of gastronomy, bonhomie and rosy cheeks, berets and cellars and baggy trousers. Quite how this image came about is lost in the alcoholic fumes of time, but there is no doubt that it is there. Whether it has actually helped or hindered historic Burgundy to find its rightful place amongst the truly great wines of the world is another matter.

There is nothing homogeneous about the term Burgundy. "Burgundy" is a good chunk of eastern France, and to many who live there its frontiers are often the limits of their travels. The region covers the area from Chablis down to Lyon, encompassing much beautiful, rolling countryside which will not be of immediate interest to the wine lover. But what will attract anyone who has ever lifted a glass of good burgundy to his lips is the diversity of tastes emerging from such a disparate landscape.

Viticultural Burgundy consists of the Yonne, chiefly known for its Chablis, the Côte d'Or, the Côte Chalonnaise, the Mâconnais and the Beaujolais. Chablis is an island, isolated from the rest and logically more a part of Champagne than Burgundy, but the other four defined areas form the Burgundian corridor which leads into the Rhône valley and on down to the Mediterranean.

History of the Region

Camille Rodier, writing from the fastness of Nuits-St-Georges in 1920, pours a certain amount of scorn on the theories of Pliny and Plutarch as to the origins of the vine in present-day Burgundy. The ancients would have it that the Gauls invaded Italy for its wine (a somewhat chauvinistic point of view) and when they turned tail and returned over the Alps, they took Italian vinous habits with them. The Burgundians of our days have, incidentally, made a brave attempt to illustrate Gallo-Roman living conditions by erecting a model village of that era by the Beaune service station on the Autoroute du Sud. What does seem likely is that the vine came to Burgundy via the Greek settlement of Marseilles about 600 years BC, considerably predating the arrival of the Romans and their need for the grape. In the following centuries, in spite of Roman protectionism, safeguarding the Italian home product, and barbarian invasions in the 5th century, the vine flourished – so much so that in the 6th century Gregory of Tours was singing the praises of the wines produced near Dijon.

The history of the vine in Burgundy is unalterably linked with the Church. From the end of the 5th century, monasteries were established throughout Burgundy, and the rise of what are now some of the grandest appellations of the area became inextricably bound up with royal or aristocratic gifts to the abbeys. The vastly powerful religious centre of Cluny in the Mâconnais was founded in 910 and Cîteaux, in the plain near Nuits, followed in 1098. The harsh order of the Cistercians did much to discipline vine production and ensure the fame of the local wines, and they were, of course, the founders of the Clos de Vougeot. It is worth pondering the austerity of the Cistercian order as one dines now in Bacchanalian fashion with the Chevaliers du Tastevin at Vougeot.

Secular power in Burgundy was held from the 14th century for more than 100 years by the Valois Dukes. At their apogee, their empire and influence included large chunks of France and Flanders; and, in the absence of a competent King, Duke Philip the Bold of Burgundy was certainly the most powerful man in the whole of France. Four Dukes, Philip the Bold, John the Fearless, Philip the Good and Charles the Bold, presided over a state characterized by military strength, material wealth and artistic splendour, perfect conditions for the vine to flourish. It was at this time that the Low Countries became such good clients of Burgundian winemakers, a tradition which has continued to this day. A key figure was Nicolas Rolin, Chancellor to Philip the Good, who was able to amass considerable wealth while holding this post. In 1443 he atoned for his excesses by founding the Hôtel-Dieu in Beaune, later to be supported by vineyards donated to the charity.

However, in the end, the scattered nature of the Burgundian empire proved to be its downfall, and with the death in battle of Charles the Bold in 1477, Burgundy became truly French under Louis XI.

The first great Valois Duke, Philip the Bold, had in 1395 declared war on the Gamay grape by ordering that it be pulled up and replaced by the nobler Pinot. This was a recurring theme in Burgundian viticultural history, and the first shot in what was to be a long battle between quality and quantity. But the pendulum always had a tendency to swing towards the "generous" Gamay. In 1855, of the 26,500ha of vines on the Côte d'Or, 23,000ha were planted to Gamay, a state of affairs which needs no commentary. However, in mitigation, it must be said that yields varied between 15 and 20hls per ha. It should also be remembered that Burgundy was ahead of Bordeaux in the selection of grape varieties.

Taking the Côte d'Or, it is interesting to note the fluctuations in the area under vine:

1816	24,000ha
1875	33,745ha
1929	12,112ha
1955	8,825ha
1982	8,600ha

The 1982 figure included 7,621ha of vines producing AC wine, with a mere 979ha producing *vins de table*. In 1929, hybrid vines were planted on 1,723ha of the region, while in 1955 there were 5,048ha of Appellation Contrôlée wines.

One of the keys to the whole enigma that is Burgundy is the multifarious ownership of the vineyards. This was originally brought about by the French Revolution of 1789, when the religious estates were broken up with all the ferocity of a zealous Henry VIII of England 250 years earlier. Aristocratic domains were also dispersed, rarely to come together again, whereas in Bordeaux the returning emigrés were able to carry on as before. This fragmentation of the vineyard area has been exacerbated by the French laws of succession, whereby all the children inherit instead of just the eldest son.

Burgundy did not escape the two natural disasters which hit the whole of viticultural France in the 19th century. The first was oidium, or powdery mildew, which began seriously to affect yields until the remedy of dusting the vines with sulphur was discovered. This method has been used, in one form or another, ever since.

The second disaster, phylloxera, was to have far more devastating effects, as shown by the dramatic drop in the area under vine between 1875 and 1929. This vine louse, or aphid, came originally from the United States, and vines simply died under its attack. In the absence of accurate scientific methods growers often resorted to superstitious folk remedies, and much time and money were lost in experiment and deliberation. Flooding, one suggested remedy, was hardly practicable on the slopes, and injecting the soil with carbon bisulphide was not a permanent solution to the invasion. Only grafting on to American vine rootstocks, immune to the activities of the pest, guaranteed complete safety and gradually, as the 19th century turned into the 20th, this technique was adopted. But the economic ramifications were enormous. Many growers could not afford the cost and either gave up vine-growing or left the region, and the area under vines shrank irrevocably. It was the better sites on the slopes that survived and yields leapt forward, so the picture after the phylloxera was in many ways a good deal healthier than in the past. At this time high-yielding Pinots made their appearance. It is a distortion, however, to attribute the increase in yields entirely to new clones. Better and more intelligent vineyard husbandry played a part. The comparatively tiny yields of the past were as often the result of disease as anything else.

The Geography

Burgundy is in eastern France, far away from maritime influence and "enjoying" a continental climate (although sometimes that is perhaps not quite the word to use in the Siberian conditions of many a Burgundian January). What rivers there are do not make their mark on the microclimate in any significant way – the Serein in Chablis is far too tiny, and the Saône of the Côte Chalonnaise too far from the vineyard slopes. River and vineyard are closest in the Mâconnais, where the Saône breaks its banks with monotonous regularity – however, crops other than the vine usually bear the brunt of this.

Chablis, 136km (85 miles) to the northwest of Dijon, lies stranded on the way to Paris, only about 70km (44 miles) to the south of the Aube, the southernmost classified area of Champagne. Chablis forms part of the Auxerrois, with the Yonne valley vineyards west of Chablis producing somewhat earthy wines from the communes of Saint-Bris-le-Vineux, Chitry, Irancy and Coulanges-la-Vineuse. Chablis' claim to fame is its subsoil of Kimmeridge clay/limestone, to which Chardonnay is ideally suited. Nowadays, Portlandian limestone, found in some of the outlying villages around Chablis, is considered by the authorities to be just as special. Unfortunately, this island of vines is subject to particularly severe winters, with spring frost a hazard right up to the end of May. The great hill of the Grands Crus, close to Chablis itself, is a particular frost trap, while the plateau areas of Chablis are often swept by snow during the winter. Indeed, in 1985 Chablis was hit by an isolated snowstorm as late as March 16, a final flurry after an especially bitter winter.

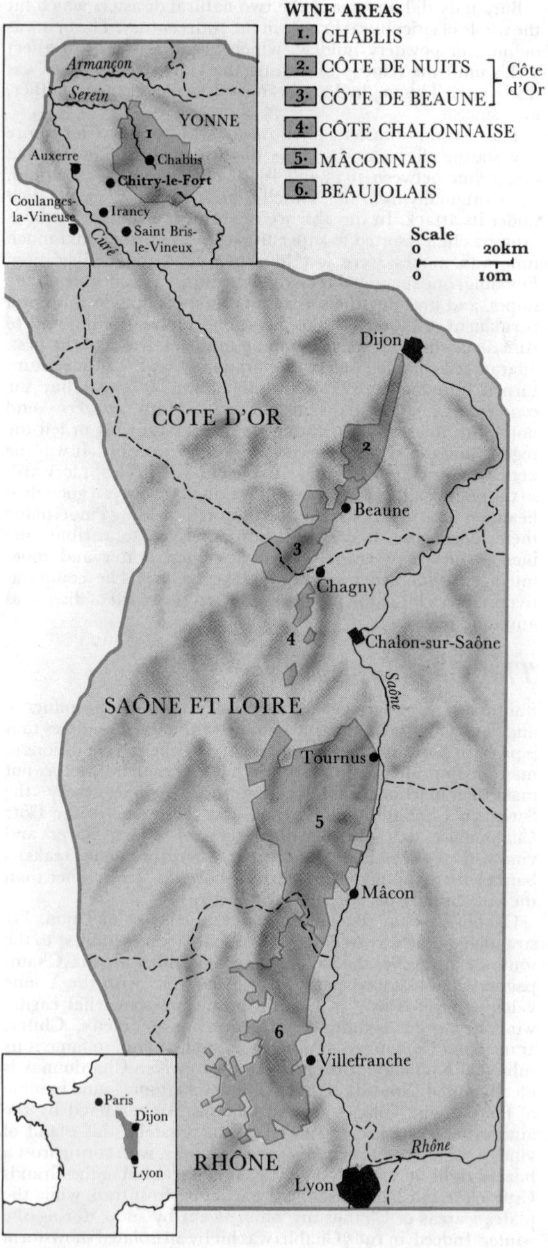
WINE AREAS
1. CHABLIS
2. CÔTE DE NUITS
3. CÔTE DE BEAUNE
Côte d'Or
4. CÔTE CHALONNAISE
5. MÂCONNAIS
6. BEAUJOLAIS
Scale
0 20km
0 10m
Armançon
Serein
YONNE
1
Chablis
Auxerre
Chitry-le-Fort
Coulanges-la-Vineuse
Irancy
Saint Bris-le-Vineux
Cure
Dijon
CÔTE D'OR
2
Beaune
3
Chagny
4
Chalon-sur-Saône
Saône
SAÔNE ET LOIRE
Tournus
5
Mâcon
6
Villefranche
Rhône
RHÔNE
Lyon
Paris
Dijon
Lyon

The Côte d'Or, or *la Côte* as it is known locally, stretches from Dijon 50km (31 miles) down to Dezize-les-Maranges in the department of Saône et Loire, in a southerly direction until Beaune, but then veering more to the southwest. The Côte is, in fact, the eastern edge of a calcareous upland plateau which ends with the Saône river plain. The "Golden Slope" is so described because of the fiery colours of the vineleaves in autumn. When gazing at this splendour, it is easy to forget that only 2% of the agricultural surface of the department of the Côte d'Or is covered by vines, but this supports 2,300 growers and 30% of salaried agricultural labour.

The vineyard area of the Côte d'Or can be divided into three distinct parts: the Côte, which comprises the Côte de Nuits and the Côte de Beaune; the Hautes Côtes; and the plain of Beaune. The greatest wines come from the Côte and the vine here reigns supreme. The domains are very small, averaging 5ha, mostly family-owned and often with plots of land in several villages.

The Hautes Côtes, frequently ignored in the past but now worthy of serious consideration, are in the hinterland, with vines planted on the slopes of small valleys called *combes*. Here the vine is mixed with other fruit production such as blackcurrants and raspberries, but, as the growers find more economic ways to run their vineyards, confidence in wine is returning. The family properties in the Hautes Côtes tend to be between 10–15ha in size and, for economic viability, the vines are mostly high-trained and wide-spaced. Some of the slopes are not as well exposed here as on the Côte itself, so good weather is needed for optimum ripeness.

The plain around Beaune is, again, not specifically viticultural, but there are now some noble grapes, Pinot Noir, Chardonnay, Aligoté and Gamay, amongst the mixed farming.

The Côte Chalonnaise is not a continuous, visible escarpment, but a series of hills, stretching southwards from Chagny, with fine slopes ideal for vine-growing. The vines are usually grown at heights of between 300 and 335 metres (985 and 1,100 feet), higher than the Côte d'Or and therefore usually vintaging three or four days later. The vineyards of Rully and Mercurey are close to each other, but Givry stands on its own to the south, and to the southwest of Chalon-sur-Saône, Montagny and Buxy are responsible for some fine white wines. The vineyards appear between fields and woods, not as predominantly eastward facing as those on the Côte d'Or.

Much of the Mâconnais vineyard area lies to the northwest of the town of Mâcon, but the finest area of the "Pouilly satellites" is found to the southwest. To the north, where the "bulk" Mâcon is made, the slopes are gentle and undulating, with patches of vineyard where the slope is favourably placed and white cattle grazing on rich grass where the site is not so propitious to the grape. To the south, the slopes and escarpments become more dramatic, and this is where the grandest wines are made.

The Mâconnais runs into the Beaujolais – more accurately, into the granite hills which make up the nine Beaujolais *crus*, the best area. Vines here are intensely planted, to the virtual exclusion of anything else, making up about a half of the total AC surface area of viticultural Burgundy. The steep hills and peaks of northern Beaujolais give way to different soil and flatter land south of Villefranche, clay and limestone rather than sand over granite, Beaujolais rather than Beaujolais Villages.

Soil in Burgundy is a geologist's dream, or a layman's nightmare. The Burgundian vineyards perch on the edge of the

Massif Central and the Morvan. On the Côte d'Or, we are looking at a limestone base interspersed with marl, which is itself a calcareous mudstone, or clay and carbonate of lime, with admixtures of pure clay, sand and gravel. Of course, limestone varies considerably in consistency, from the exceptionally hard Comblanchien "marble" to something much softer and less resistant.

The limestone scree from the top of the hills has, over the years, been regularly washed down over the surface of the slopes to mix with the marl. This is all to the good, for marl on its own is too rich for even the most powerful red wines. But there is no doubt that without this marl, great red wines could never be made in such a northerly area (for who but the most chauvinistic of protagonists would call Pinot Noir from Alsace or a Spätburgunder from Germany "great"?).

The basic rule is that where the limestone is dominant and the soil chalky, the Chardonnay is planted for white wine. When the Pinot Noir is planted too near the top of the slope, where the soil is significantly more chalky, the resultant red wine is thin indeed. Over the last 20 years on the Côte d'Or, much land on the upper slopes which was scrub and forest has been cleared for vineyards. No one can pretend that the wine produced at these extremities is of top quality.

The Côte de Nuits is narrower and more sharply sloping than much of the Côte de Beaune. Most of its vineyards clearly face east, with variations of east-south-east and east-north-east. Rich alluvial deposits tend to be lower down the slope on the Côte de Nuits than on the Côte de Beaune, with the best growths correspondingly lower down. Alluvial deposits also gather in folds in the slope, or in *combes*, which can explain why there are sudden pockets of top *climats*. The wider Côte de Beaune faces east or southeast, according to the various valleys, with softer, rounder hills and vines growing closer to the summits. The marl "strip" is wider here than on the Côte de Nuits, and higher up the slope.

All this soil has been worked for centuries, and it consequently suffers from erosion, countered at certain times by extra additions of earth from the foot of the slope or elsewhere. When comparing wines from the so-called New World with the Old, it is worth remembering the often thin, meagre soil of historic vineyards, where the vine has to delve deep for goodness, in comparison with the fertile, "virgin" soil of some new plantations in America and Australia.

Who is to say that an element of soil exhaustion does not contribute to finesse? On the other hand, really tired soil in Europe is now helped by judicious fertilizing or mineral additions. Drainage on the slopes is not a problem, and the process is facilitated by gravel and particles of broken-up stone, an important element in vineyards producing top quality wines.

Climate

The most vital month in the whole year, from a climatic point of view, is September. In Burgundy, the weather's performance in this crucial month can make or mar a vintage. Whereas the *size* of the crop is largely decided (with last-minute variations possible due to rain) either by the presence or absence of spring frosts, or by the relative success of the flowering, the *quality* of the crop is determined in September. Catastrophic rain in September ruined the 1975s on the Côte d'Or, whereas a superb September saved the situation in 1978 and thus made the wines great.

Clearly, making red wine in such a northerly region is something of a risk, and Burgundian white wines will always show less vintage variability than reds or, to be more accurate, they will plumb the depths less often than the reds. There is a basic north-to-south difference in temperatures, with Chablis cooler than the Mâconnais, especially in the summer months. However, during this period, the temperatures on the Côte Chalonnaise are lower than on the Côte de Nuits, while the Côte de Beaune suffers fewer extremes of cold and heat than the Côte de Nuits, so there is no straightforward pattern.

December, January and February are the coldest months, July and August the hottest. The strongest frosts are in January and February, but March and April frosts are usually more to be feared since the vegetation is further advanced. Snow cover is always a protection against frost damage, but unfortunately there was no snow in the severe cold of February 1985. One way to combat frost is careful selection of vineyard sites – facing east and south in the Beaujolais, Mâconnais and the Côte Chalonnaise, east-south-east (generally) in the Côte d'Or, and southeast and southwest in Chablis. A warm June is critical for flowering. August and September are always hotter in Bordeaux than in Burgundy, which goes a long way towards explaining the more consistent record of Bordeaux vintages compared with those of Burgundy.

Light and sunshine are also vital to successful grape-growing and Burgundy, situated around 47° latitude, enjoys long periods of daylight in the growing season. With its inland continental climate, Burgundy hardly lags behind Bordeaux in hours of sunshine. July is the sunniest month, followed by August, June and May. Humidity is remarkably similar in both areas during the time of the vine's development.

Rainfall is often the cause of Burgundy's undoing. The crucial factor with rain is not so much the *quantity* which falls, but *when* it falls. Regular light rain is always more desirable than storms, and when rain is interspersed with sun, the earth can warm up relatively quickly. Persistent rain in summer brings with it the risk of grey rot, the Burgundians' bogey. However, even after a seemingly lethal bout of rain in August, a dry September and early October can completely save the situation. The Côte d'Or is drier than the regions to the south, and certainly less wet than the Hautes Côtes, partly because the climate is drier and more continental towards Dijon, and partly because the slope of the Côte affords a measure of protection from the rain-bearing winds from the west.

However, the drawback of this favoured position is that northern Burgundy is more susceptible to hail than elsewhere, and the Côte de Nuits seems particularly vulnerable, with significant damage in 1983, 1981, 1979 and 1971 (the Côte de Beaune was even worse hit in the latter year). But hail is always highly localized, and part of a commune can be hit while the rest remains untouched.

As in every viticultural region, the microclimate of his particular area (or plots, in the case of Burgundy) will concern the grower far more than the general picture. Factors like position on a slope, proximity to woods and the neighbouring topography (for instance, a dip in the hill causing a current of wind) all serve to temper or aggravate an overall tendency, and can make the difference between wild success or only moderate performance.

The Appellations

To set the scene, it is as well to keep in mind the amount of wine produced in Burgundy which is covered by the Appellation Contrôlée laws. These AC figures for 1983, both a very good and a generous year, are broken down between the regions thus:

THE 1983 CROP IN BURGUNDY

Area	White (in hectolitres)	Red and Rosé (in hectolitres)
Regional Appellations	102,524	114,035
Chablis	141,567	—
Côte de Beaune + Grands Crus	39,418	114,771
Côte de Nuits + Grands Crus	147	138,584
Chalonnaise	9,316	32,704
Mâconnais	175,140	60,989
Beaujolais	5,817	1,264,256
TOTAL = 2,199,268	473,929	1,725,339

The comparable 1982 figure was 2,582,000hl, but these were two large years – 1984, 1981 and 1980 were the opposite.

The first known attempt to define burgundy wines and guard their origins was made by King Charles VI of France in 1416. He defined the area of "Vin François", by which he meant wine made in the region of Paris, and that of "Vins de Bourgogne", which were the wines made above the bridge at Sens, including the Auxerrois and the Beaunois, and which were transported on the Yonne river. Things have become a little more sophisticated since then. However, at the outset, it should be reiterated that the AC system in France (and not just in Burgundy, although this region seems to receive more criticism than most) is not a *guarantee* of quality, much as we would like it to be. For that to happen, controls would have to be more stringent and, in the case of Burgundy, the arrangements regarding tasting dramatically overhauled. But that would be Utopia. What one could realistically hope for would be rules and regulations created by men of integrity with great practical knowledge of growing vines and making wine in a capricious area, rather than by desk-bound bureaucrats, however worthy their motives.

What the AC laws do endeavour to do is guarantee the geographical origin of the wines, and lay down viticultural and vinification precepts which *should* lead to better quality. The specifications cover:

- Area of production
- Grape varieties permitted
- Minimum alcohol level before chaptalization (Page 15)
- Maximum yield per hectare
- Methods of planting, pruning and treating the vines
- Vinification
- Maturation and *élevage*

Four organizations carry out between them the work of controlling the quality and marketing of French wines:

- The INAO (*Institut National des Appellations d'Origine*)
- The ONIVIT (*Office National Interprofessionnel des Vins de Table*)
- The SRFCQ (*Service de la Répression des Fraudes et du Contrôle de la Qualité*)
- The DGI (*Direction Générale des Impôts*)

The basis for today's laws has been laid down during this century, with refinements and improvements at each stage, culminating in the 1974 revision, which offers the chance of real progress. The two 1974 Decrees stopped the "cascade" quality rating system and ordered that all AC wines be analysed and tasted.

Before 1974, a grower who made well over the permitted yield from a Grand Cru site could obtain the Grand Cru AC for up to 30hl/ha of what he had produced, and baptize the excess yield with more modest names (Premier Cru, straight "village" wine, and right down the line to Bourgogne Rouge and *Vin de Table*) in descending (or "cascading") order. All the wine was the same, but the prices changed. *Génial!*

Now the grower has to opt for the classification he wants for his entire crop at the time of the *déclaration de récolte*. The system starts with a *rendement de base*, or basic yield, which can be adjusted each year by the fixing of a *rendement annuel*, or annual yield for that vintage, to allow for fluctuating climatic conditions. After 1974, a *plafond limite de classement* (PLC), or classification ceiling, was also introduced, allowing a further quantity (usually 20%) to be accepted. As this involves obligatory tasting, and distilling of the entire production if the PLC is refused, many growers (especially in the Beaujolais) hold back from making this request, through a profound dislike of "busybody" visits to their cellars.

In any case, it has to be said that, given the variable Burgundian climate, this kind of yield is often a pipe-dream. In many domains, especially where there is a good proportion of old vines, growers often do not achieve the maximum allowed for their Grands Crus. Consequently there is an argument for widening the gap between these very special wines and the Premiers Crus and village wines. These can stand an increase in the allowed production in good years, whereas the Grands Crus will not and should not be so prolific. A move towards a lighter hand on the rein was made in a Decree just before the prolific vintage of 1982, but perhaps at the wrong end of the quality scale, because red Grands Crus like Corton had their *basic* yield increased from 30hl/ha to 35hl/ha, while the whites jumped further, Chablis Grand Cru from 35 to 45hl/ha and Montrachet from 30 to 40hl/ha. Montrachet's 1982 *rendement annuel* was increased to 60hl/ha, which, plus a further 20% PLC, gave a total of 72hl/ha. In 1983, the comparable figures were 50hl/ha plus 20%, giving 60hl/ha. Large yields affect the quality of white wine less than that of red, especially with the sensitive Pinot Noir, but these very generous yields for Grand Cru wine must impair concentration and extract. But again one knows of producers who did not reach these permitted yields, to their credit.

As an example of how the *rendement annuel* can alter the *rendement de base*, the table overleaf shows those fixed for 1983. Unusually, certain Grands Crus such as Echézeaux, La Tâche and Romanée-Conti, and communes like Vosne-Romanée, had their basic yields greatly reduced by the *rendement annuel* – in this case because of hail damage. But they were given very high PLC limits, which allowed for more AC wine to be declared, after tasting.

The tasting requirement in Burgundy, supposedly operational since 1979, works quite well in the Côte Chalonnaise (with a certain amount of self-regulation) but not on the Côte d'Or. It has proved impossible in this immensely complex and fragmented area for every wine in every grower's cellar to be tasted every year. This, of course, does not worry the majority of growers, but logistically the scheme does pose genuine problems. In any case, the plan was to taste in growers' rather than

ALLOWABLE YIELDS PER HECTARE IN BURGUNDY			
APPELLATIONS	**Rendement de base**	**1983 Rendement annuel**	**Plafond limite de classement**
COTE D'OR GRANDS CRUS COTE DE NUITS Chambertin, Chambertin Clos de Bèze, Clos de la Roche, Clos St-Denis, Clos des Lambrays, Clos de Tart, Clos Vougeot, Musigny Rouge	35hl/ha	35hl/ha	+20%
Chapelle-Chambertin, Charmes-Chambertin, Griotte-Chambertin, Latricières-Chambertin, Mazis-Chambertin, Mazoyères-Chambertin, Ruchottes-Chambertin	37hl/ha	37hl/ha	+20%
Musigny Blanc	40hl/ha	37hl/ha	+20%
Echézeaux, Grands Echézeaux	35hl/ha	26hl/ha	+60%
La Tâche, Richebourg, La Romanée, La Romanée-Conti, Romanée-St-Vivant	35hl/ha	15hl/ha	+100%
1ER CRU COTE DE NUITS: Same figures apply as for communes below			
AC COMMUNES COTE DE NUITS Chambolle-Musigny, Côte de Nuits-Villages, Fixin, Gevrey-Chambertin, Morey-St-Denis, Nuits-St-Georges, Vougeot	40hl/ha	40hl/ha	+100%
Vosne-Romanée	40hl/ha	24hl/ha	+100%
GRANDS CRUS COTE DE BEAUNE Corton Blanc, Corton-Charlemagne, Charlemagne, Bâtard-Montrachet, Bienvenues-Bâtard-Montrachet, Chevalier-Montrachet, Criots-Bâtard-Montrachet, Montrachet	40hl/ha	50hl/ha	+20%
Corton Rouge	35hl/ha	35hl/ha	+20%
1ER CRU COTE DE BEAUNE: Same figures apply as for Côte de Beaune-Villages			
COTE DE BEAUNE-VILLAGES Vins rouges: Aloxe-Corton, Auxey-Duresses, Beaune, Blagny, Chassagne-Montrachet, Cheilly-les-Maranges, Chorey, Côte de Beaune, Dézize-les-Maranges, Ladoix, Meursault, Monthélie, Pernand-Vergelesses, Pommard, Puligny-Montrachet, St-Aubin, St-Romain, Sampigny-les-Maranges, Santenay, Savigny, Volnay	40hl/ha	40hl/ha	+20%
Vins Blancs: Aloxe-Corton, Auxey-Duresses, Beaune, Chassagne-Montrachet	45hl/ha	45hl/ha	+20%
Cheilly-les-Maranges, Chorey, Côte de Beaune, Dézize-les-Maranges, Ladoix, Meursault, Monthélie, Pernand-Vergelesses, Puligny-Montrachet, St-Aubin, St-Romain, Sampigny-les-Maranges, Santenay, Savigny	45hl/ha	55hl/ha	+20%

négociants' cellars, meaning that an enormous amount of wine would have to be tasted in the few months after the vintage, before many wines "disappeared" into blends. What happens in reality is that random sampling is done in growers' cellars, which acts as a mild deterrent.

But even if the tasting is done to the letter of the Decree, there is still room for switching and deception if the producer is determined enough. The INAO controls the amount of burgundy sold in relation to what is harvested, but obviously there is room for manoeuvre here, given the fact that major roads pass through Burgundy. The INAO reputedly tastes a producer's wines at least once every three years, but it is worth stressing that there is many an AC and VDQS wine from other regions in France that has jumped through all the tasting and analytical hoops and come out disgusting! Strict adherence to all the rules in the world will not ensure delicious wine at all times – it comes down to the integrity and intelligence of the producer and the demands of an enlightened consumer.

The Répression des Fraudes does make periodic prosecutions, which sometimes even bite, at least financially. Where the AC system falls down in Burgundy, at least as a credible institution, is in the hypocrisy of some of its edicts – for instance, chaptalization (the addition of sugar to the must, or grape juice, to increase alcohol). The legal limit is clear: 1.7kg of sugar added to 100 litres of must, increasing the alcohol in the wine by approximately 1%. It is not permitted to go over the addition of 9kg of sugar per 3hl of must and 200kg per ha. Above all, the wine must have naturally attained the minimum alcohol level for its AC before any sugar can be added to the must. It is widely known that in 1984, for example, there were many wines (especially reds) which did not attain the minimum level and were consequently chaptalized way beyond the permitted amount – for they have all finished up around 12.8–13% as usual. There has been a string of years with a similar problem.

Another aspect of the AC laws that indicates that they are somewhat removed from the realities of wine-making in Burgundy is the virtual banning of acidification. Many Burgundies need additions of tartaric acid in order to keep well. There is nothing wrong in this: low natural acidities are a problem in other parts of France, especially recently. A recognition of this would inspire more confidence that the AC system is designed to improve the wines rather than just forming rules and pushing paper.

The hierarchy of the ACs is as follows:

Grand Cru
Premier Cru
Village Wine (*AOC Communale*)
Generic or Regional

The last category includes Bourgogne and Bourgogne Grand Ordinaire, Bourgogne Rosé Marsannay, Bourgogne Passe-Tout-Grains, Bourgogne Aligoté, Bourgogne Hautes Côtes de Beaune and Bourgogne Hautes Côtes de Nuits.

Nomenclature

No one can be in Burgundy for long, or read a book on the subject, without noting the number of hyphens in the place names. The simple explanation is that the wily Burgundian, at some stage, tagged the name of the best-known local vineyard on to the name of his village – hence, Gevrey-Chambertin, Morey-St-Denis, Chambolle-Musigny and right on down the Côte.

Vineyard names, or *climats*, often give an indication of their soil: Les Chaillots (siliceous pebbles), Les Crais (pebbles), Les Grèves (small pebbles or gravel); or the vegetation once found there: Les Charmes (yoke-elms or hornbeams), Les Genevrières (juniper bushes), Les Chênes (oaks); or even of the wildlife one met there: Les Cailles (quails), Les Perdrix (partridges), La Combe aux Alouettes (the valley of the larks). The walls built from stones collected in the vines are even cited – Aux Murgers. Yes, Burgundian place names are picturesque, designed to lure and to allure.

Burgundian spelling is often what the French would call *facultatif* – you have a choice. Thus, Dominode and Dominaude, Véroilles and Varoilles, etc. They also seem uncertain as to whether to put an "s" on the end of Passe-Tout-Grains, and Chablisien spelling can appear positively anarchic. Mercifully, none of this affects the taste of the wine. A vagary of Burgundian pronunciation is to say "ss" for "x", i.e. "Fissin" (Fixin) and "Aussey-Duresses" (Auxey-Duresses).

THE GRAPES

The grape scene is relatively simple in Burgundy although, given the difficult climatic conditions, continuous work is being done on clones in order to develop resistance to misfortunes such as grey rot. These are the principal varieties:

Red

Pinot Noir

This is perhaps the most tantalizing of the world's noble red grapes. In Burgundy, the Pinot Noir is the red grape of the Côte d'Or and the Côte Chalonnaise, with only a tiny amount grown in the Mâconnais. It achieves heights unsurpassed anywhere when at its best in Burgundy, but it travels only tentatively. The finest examples outside Burgundy seem to come from Oregon and Australia, with California in the running, but they tend to be isolated cases, created by brilliant winemakers. Pinot Noir is also grown in Alsace, Jura, Germany (where the wines are very light), Switzerland, Eastern Europe, northeast Italy, and is a vital part of classic champagne.

The Pinot Noir both buds and ripens early, and it is susceptible to spring frost and winter cold, as well as cold temperatures during flowering. It likes calcareous, marly soils, but dislikes unduly hot climates, where the wines lack finesse – hence its lack of success in the Napa Valley of California. The dark green leaves are thick and of medium size, with small, cylindrical bunches. The grapes are close together in the bunches, which facilitates the spread of rot given the right humid circumstances. The berries are blue-black in colour, slightly oval, with relatively thick skins, although less thick than in the early part of this century due to clonal selection. All the colour in the wine comes from the skins, as the flesh and juice of the grape are colourless. It is encouraging that in a thin-skin year like 1984, many growers still managed to produce wines of good colour, showing improved vinification techniques.

Considerable experimentation on Pinot Noir clones is being done, especially at Echevronne in the Hautes Côtes de Beaune. The work is carried out under the auspices of the regional department of the Association Nationale Technique pour l'Amélioration de la Viticulture (ANTAV), which is composed of representatives from the INAO, the Syndicats et Associations Viticoles, the Coopératives, the Chambres d'Agriculture and the vine nurserymen. A vast array of Pinots are grown under controlled and identical conditions, and the resulting wines are tasted blind against each other. There are Pinots from the Côte Chalonnaise, the Jura, Champagne and Switzerland, and Pinots fins, moyens and gros, as well as the high-yielding Pinot droit. Some Pinots are named after villages on the Côte, some after growers.

Work is being done on resistance to grey rot and virus diseases such as fan leaf and leaf curl, and on the relationship between yield, alcohol and quality. It is difficult to see great red wines being produced at over 35hl/ha, but good wines, in a healthy year, can certainly be made with a yield of 40hl/ha. After all, not *every* village burgundy should be made for lengthy laying down – just as not all Bordeaux should play the role of a classed growth. But growers should be persuaded to adopt the most successful quality clones, even if they have to renounce the highest-yielding examples. There is no excuse not to, with the prices their wines command nowadays. Good results have been seen on the Côte d'Or from three Pinot fin clones, numbers 113, 114 and 115, if they are not grafted on to excessively productive rootstocks.

Gamay

Although this is the grape *par excellence* of the Beaujolais, it probably originated in the hamlet of this name next door to St-Aubin on the Côte d'Or. It is at its best on the granite-based, sandy-schisty soil of the northern Beaujolais, where the nine *crus* are to be found. It is also successful on the richer clay and limestone soil of the southern Beaujolais (though the wines should be drunk very young). Here, overlarge yields can make the wine a pale imitation of the "real thing", but very good Beaujolais can be produced at 50–60hl/ha.

The Gamay covers about one-third of the Mâconnais AC area, and is a significant grape in the Côte Chalonnaise, where it contributes to Bourgogne Passe-Tout-Grains, which is made of two-thirds Gamay and one-third Pinot Noir. It has very little importance on the Côte d'Or. The Gamay can be found scattered around France, in Savoie, the Loire, the Ardèche, as well as in California.

The Gamay Noir à Jus Blanc, or Gamay Beaujolais, yields well, even after spring frosts. Its juice is white, as the name implies, so the colour comes from the skins. The compact grapes are grouped in cylindrical bunches encouraging the spread of grey rot under humid conditions. The grape ripens early, but the optimum picking time must be judged carefully if the must is to have a good natural sugar content, especially if the yield is high. If rain swells the grapes near or at the vintage, it is difficult to get good colour and extract.

Two other grapes, the César and the Tressot, are allowed in the Yonne for Bourgogne, Bourgogne Ordinaire or Bourgogne Grand Ordinaire. They are earthy varieties, even a bit "foxy". The César has more merit than the Tressot, but both are rare and invariably mixed with Pinot.

White

Chardonnay

This is probably the most magic grape name in the whole world in the 1980s, eliciting cries of joy from consumers as they drink it, but groans of pain as they pay the bill. The name Chardonnay may have come from a village of that name in the Mâconnais, or it could have been the other way round. The Chardonnay makes all the best white wines from Chablis to the Mâconnais. It is one of the classic grapes of Champagne, and has recently appeared in the Ardèche, thanks to the efforts of a leading Beaune house. It is also grown successfully in California and Australia (including Tasmania), with Bulgaria and northern Italy knocking at the consumer's door (and at a more reasonable price).

The Chardonnay adores limestone soil and, in most cases, its wine ages beautifully in bottle. The vine has large thin leaves and the bunches are not so tight as other varieties, allowing air movement and reducing the risk of rot. The early budbreak makes spring frost a danger, but relatively early maturity makes it a good choice for areas of shorter growing seasons. It is a generous producer, but is susceptible to fan leaf, or *court noué*. It is not a member of the Pinot family, as was originally thought – the erroneous name is even enshrined in a Burgundian AC, Pinot-Chardonnay-Mâcon. Two Chardonnay moyen clones which have proved successful on the Côte d'Or are 95 and 96.

Aligoté

This is the second white grape variety of Burgundy, but not in the same league as Chardonnay. However, it yields well and ripens early and, in sunny years, the wine can be most appetizing. In less ripe years the results are too acid. It has no potential for ageing in bottle and should always be drunk young. The best Aligoté wines tend to be produced in the northern part of the Côte Chalonnaise and in villages like Pernand-Vergelesses and St-Aubin on the Côte d'Or.

Pinot Blanc

For a long time this variety was confused with Chardonnay, and not only in Burgundy (northeast Italy often got it wrong also). It seems rather a waste to grow it in Burgundy in the place of Chardonnay, as it does not have the zest of Pinot Blanc in Alsace. The wines can be rather heavy and plain. It is probably a mutation of the Pinot Noir. There are one or two good examples on the Côte de Nuits, but it is a rarity.

Pinot Beurot

This is the Pinot Gris, or Tokay d'Alsace. Although in the same Pinot family, the wine is really more stylish than the Pinot Blanc when planted in Burgundy. It is rare indeed, but occasionally appears in the Hautes Côtes de Beaune.

The Melon de Bourgogne is still allowed for Bourgogne Grand Ordinaire, but I have never consciously drunk it. It is the same grape variety as the Muscadet of the Loire, but that is another story. The Sacy is grown in the Auxerrois, where it is usually made into sparkling wine because of its high acidity and low alcohol, essential prerequisites for transformation into bubbly. The Sauvignon appears here too, in the VDQS wine Sauvignon de Saint-Bris.

Rootstocks

Since phylloxera the European grape varieties must be grafted on to American or American/French rootstocks. Vine and rootstock must be well matched. Just as research and experiment with grape clones has been improved and extended, so has work on rootstocks. A particular rootstock on unsuitable soil can cause the grafted vine to overcrop, produce unripe or low sugar-grapes, or create *coulure* (failed flowering).

Successful combinations have been, for example, Pinot Noir clones 115 and 114 on rootstocks SO4 and 161–49, but 115 is also recommended on another pure American *porte-greffe*, Téléki 5BB, on very dry slopes. However, some growers have found that 161–49 is particularly good on calcareous soil, giving grapes which ripen well, while SO4 can produce too much wood and grapes of less sugar content on the Côte de Nuits. A Franco-American hybrid is 41B, very good in high limestone soils and on high ground. Chardonnay clones 95 and 96 have done well on 161–49 on pebbly soil.

Most of these same rootstocks are found in Beaujolais, but there is also the Vialla on granite soils, probably of pre-phylloxera origin, and the pure American 420A, which thrives at high altitude in *crus* like Chiroubles. In Chablis, with high lime and accompanying risk of chlorosis (disease causing loss of colour in leaves, due to lack of iron in calcareous soil), the most common rootstocks are SO4 and 41B.

GROWERS AND MERCHANTS

There is a tendency nowadays to "pigeon-hole" growers and merchants into "Goodies and Baddies". Of course, like everything else in Burgundy, it is far more complicated than that. There are good and bad in both camps, and there are merchants (négociants) who are also important domain owners. The traditional role of the négociant was to buy a multitude of different lots of wine, blend them, bring them up (*élevage*) and bottle them. Now, even that is changing, with some merchants (notably Bouchard Père et Fils and Moillard, with others following or already doing it on a smaller scale) buying in grapes and vinifying themselves.

Growers often sell part of their crop to négociants, in order to improve their cash flow, and "domain-bottle" a proportion, which involves 18 months to two years of stock-holding on the Côte d'Or. The domain-bottling is done either by the grower himself or by a mobile bottling unit, such as Ninot of Beaune. There is also a good deal of *métayage* in Burgundy, a rather feudal practice which can work well. Basically, an owner who does not want to tend his vines or make wine passes this responsibility to a *métayer* or farmer, who divides the crop with the landowner. It is a system which can be successful, but naturally it further confuses the issue of wine identification in Burgundy, as two differently labelled wines can be made by the same person. It is also frustrating when long-term arrangements cannot be broken and a really fine winemaker cannot reclaim control of some of his vineyards due to *métayage* contracts.

The négociant business first started to flourish in the first half of the eighteenth century; some of those companies are still well-known today. In 1984 there were 156 négociant-éleveur businesses in Burgundy, belonging to the Fédération des

Syndicats de Négociants Eleveurs de Grande Bourgogne, with 84 of them in the Côte d'Or, 32 in Saône-et-Loire, 35 in the Rhône (which covers Beaujolais) and 5 in the Yonne. The export market took 60% of their output, France 40%. The négociant-éleveur is equally important in Bordeaux and Champagne, with near identical turnovers in terms of millions of francs. His role is therefore fundamental both to the health of the Burgundian economy and to the supply of large quantities of wine as required around the world. The small grower, with a handful of casks to sell, is not going to be able to supply chains of hotels or shops with enough burgundy to win friends and influence people. There is a place in the mosaic of international customers for both the small grower, with "hand-made" quantities of wine to sell, and the négociant with important lots available.

The Burgundian négociants-éleveurs sold 3,650,000 hectolitres (or the equivalent of 490,000,000 bottles) in 1984, of which 42% was AC wine from Burgundy, 9% other ACs (mostly Côtes-du-Rhône), 1% VDQS wine, 2% *vins de pays*, and a whopping 46% *vins de table*. It is this which gives the slightly dubious reputation to the Burgundian merchant. Here he is, in Beaune or Nuits, selling this vast amount of ordinary table wine. Is it never possible for him to mix his *ordinaire* with his AC names? Of course, nowadays the two categories of wines have different *acquits* (certificates of origin), as stipulated by the INAO, but it would be a hypocrite who did not admit that a well-known Burgundian house name on a label can give an impression of quality to a *vin de table*. The only answer is for the consumer to become more knowledgeable in reading a label – if there is no Burgundian Appellation Contrôlée on the label, then he is not drinking burgundy. Of course, to the purist, it would be better if a Burgundian house did not combine the two functions of supplying burgundy and *vin de table*, and certain respected houses

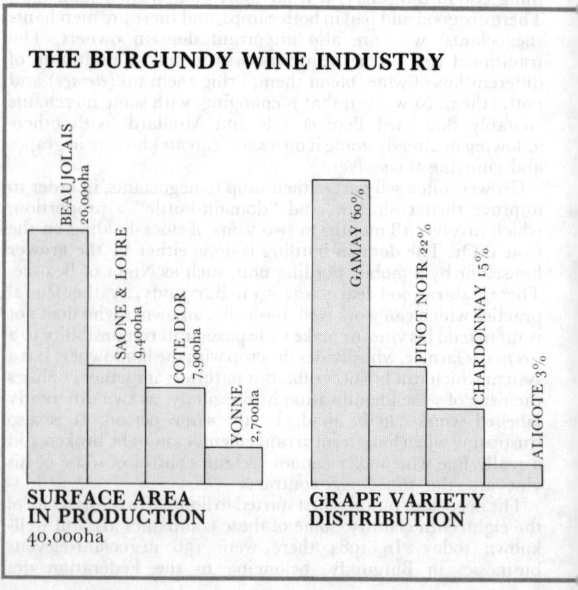

have never been in the *vin de table* market (for example, Joseph Drouhin, Louis Jadot and Louis Latour). But there is the argument that healthy sales of *vin de table* can help to finance the costly business of buying and maturing fine burgundy.

Taking an average over the last three years, 72% of the Burgundian harvest is sold by *le commerce bourguignon*, or the négociant houses, and 28% directly by the domains or properties. Among the latter category there are some who are very new to the business of maturing and bottling their own wine, and others (like Gouges, d'Angerville and Rousseau) who have been doing it for 50 years. Of course, even old-established domain-bottlers and direct sellers sometimes sell part of their crop to the négociants, for fiscal or quality reasons, and occasionally they will take the really dramatic decision not to domain-bottle at all, in a particularly poor year. In this case, the négociant, with his ability to blend from many, varied lots has a far better chance of producing at least a palatable wine than a grower who can use only his own produce and who may have been particularly badly hit by, say, hail or rot.

There is no doubt that a fine domain wine, whether owned by a grower or a négociant house, can have all the individuality, excitement and character that we seek – among these are surely the best wines of Burgundy. Equally it is not in doubt that, just as there are some boring and lacklustre négociants' blends, there are some really appalling domain wines, individual only through their glaring faults. We, buyers and consumers, have to pinpoint the successes and lambaste (figuratively at least) the dismal failures until we raise the general standard and have a more happy "strike rate". We should be grateful to those who first encouraged domain-bottling, people like Frank Schoonmaker and Alexis Lichine, and support those Burgundians who do it really well.

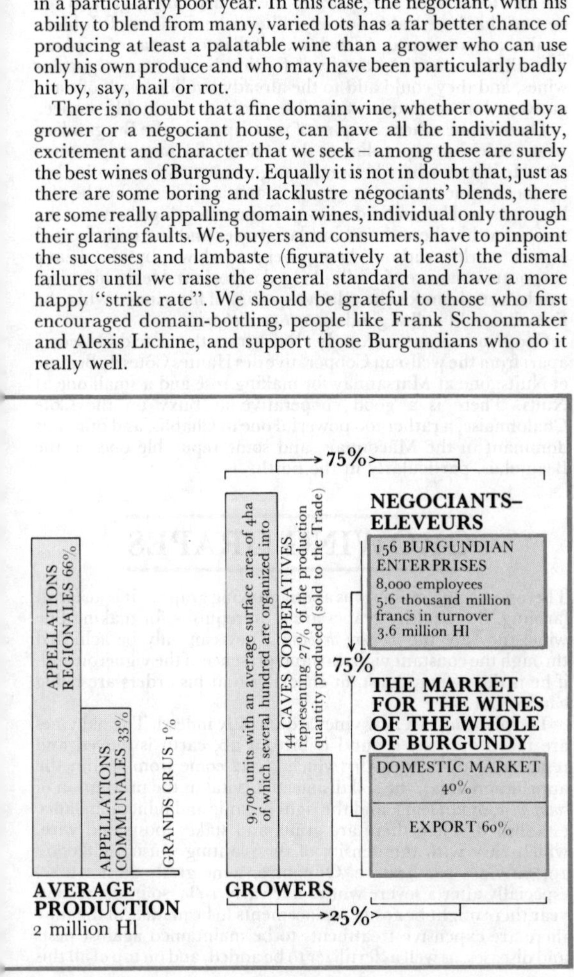

With all the wine which passes between grower and négociant in Burgundy, brokers play a vital role. They submit the samples to the négociant, and row upon row of small bottles on the laboratory shelves of any merchant house is a familiar sight. Sometimes one wonders how long it takes for the samples to be tasted, but there is no doubt that the négociant who wants to get the best of a vintage has to make up his mind early. The broker, or *courtier*, will receive a 2–3% commission from the buyer and up to 3% from the grower. He never holds any stock, but it is his responsibility to ensure that the wine subsequently delivered is identical to the sample accepted.

There are also a few brokers in Burgundy who specialize in finding good domains, grouping them together and offering a choice to foreign buyers. This is especially useful to those who do not like to wrangle over price in the French language, and the best of this breed also act as a filter where wines of dubious quality are concerned. A few brokers fall into the trap of thinking that all domain wines are by definition better than négociant wines, and they could add to the already swollen heads of some growers, but the most responsible perform a valuable service.

There is one other category of participant in the Burgundian wine trade that is peculiar to the region – the *commissionnaire en vins*. He is somewhere between a négociant and a *courtier* in that he does engineer sales between domains and clients, but he also keeps stocks. He can hold a key position as a bridge between the somewhat hidebound and insular grower and the multifaceted export world, without being weighed down by the heavy corporate structure of a fully-fledged négociant. Hence his prices can be very keen for the relative quality of his wines – what the French would call a good *rapport qualité-prix*.

Cooperatives are singularly absent from the Côte d'Or scene, apart from the well-run Coopérative des Hautes Côtes de Beaune et Nuits, one at Marsannay for making rosé and a small one at Nuits. There is a good cooperative at Buxy on the Côte Chalonnaise, a rather too powerful one in Chablis, and others as dominant in the Mâconnais, and some reputable ones in the Beaujolais, particularly in the north.

GROWING GRAPES

There is nothing mysterious about growing grapes – it is just fruit farming. But healthy grapes are a prerequisite for making fine wine; they are the *matière de base*. They can only be achieved through the constant vigilance and presence of the vigneron and, if he is the owner, constant checking that his orders are being carried out.

The planting of a new vineyard is costly indeed. The old vines are taken out, the ground is broken up, earth is moved and replaced with new earth (which *should* come from within the appellation area), the soil disinfected (vital in the prevention of *court noué*, or fan leaf), and the right organic and mineral balance established. Then there are grafts and stakes, posts and wire, which vary with the density of the planting – usually 8,000–10,000 vines per hectare. Of course, some grafts do not take, especially after a severe winter like early 1985, so in the second year there might be costly replacements to be made. All the time there are expensive treatments to be maintained against pests and diseases, as well as fertilizer to be added, and on top of all this are the labour costs. Not until the "fourth leaf", or fourth year, can AC wine be made from the new vineyard.

Soil analysis is relatively new for some vignerons, and there is no doubt that there were periods, for instance, when too much potassium was added – one grower on the Côte de Nuits says he has not added any for 20 years. Nitrogen must also be added with measured care, otherwise too much vegetation is produced, causing increased humidity around the vine and therefore increased risk of grey rot. Dehydrated manure is often used. As for weedkiller, some would not touch it, others insist on it, but what clearly emerges is that it should never be used over-enthusiastically – who knows what is being stored in the soil for the future?

Infectious degeneration of the vines, *court noué* or fan leaf, has been a problem in Burgundy, and the only cure is grubbing up a vineyard and disinfection, as well as the planting of resistant clones. Sometimes growers talk proudly of their small yields, but the telltale yellowish, deformed leaves give the game away. Not all small crops are healthy!

Grey rot is the bogey of Burgundy and it has by no means been mastered. It is ironic that this disease is welcomed under certain conditions in Sauternes/Barsac and in Germany, for it is none other than *Botrytis cinerea*. But it is a disaster when it spreads amongst Pinot Noir or Gamay grapes, destroying the colour cells and imparting an unpleasant taste to the resultant wine. Burgundian growers took to regular spraying against grey rot after the shattering experience of 1975, and for a few years it looked as if the situation was under control, but 1983 on parts of the Côte de Nuits proved that it was not. One answer seems to be to vary the chemical formula of the spray every two years, and certainly the grower has to be there to spray at *exactly* the right time. One spraying too few is often a false economy. Were the Septembers of the past 20 years more rainy than previous ones, or are there other factors, such as thinner grape skins and bigger grapes packed close together, which foster the conditions conducive to grey rot? Mildew, the downy variety, and oidium, the powdery type, are often now treated with fungicides, whereas in the past a copper sulphate and lime spray (Bordeaux mixture) effectively controlled downy mildew, or *peronospora*. This had the side-effect of hardening the grape-skins, probably making them more resistant to the spread of grey rot. It may or may not be significant that Beaujolais still widely uses Bordeaux mixture and suffers far less from rot than the Côte d'Or – but it is also less humid in summer in the Beaujolais, so it is not an entirely fair comparison.

Red and yellow spider and various kinds of moth all need careful and regular treatment at the critical times. The grape caterpillar which seems most to worry the Burgundian, especially in recent years, is the *ver de la grappe*, also known as *tordeuse de la grappe*, *cochylis* or *eudemis*. The most dangerous period is mid-July.

This is an outline of a Burgundian viticultural year:

January

It is usually too cold and the ground too frozen to do much in the vineyard and, in any case, it is often unwise to prune too early. Those who had made a precocious start were caught by the extreme cold of 1985. Snow cover, of course, can act as protection for the vines if the temperature falls really low.

February

February and March are when the main pruning takes place. This sets the whole scene for the eventual quality of the wine, because one can prune either for indiscriminate quantity or for reasonable cropping. It is the most skilled job in the vineyard, and good pruners are highly prized. Each vine must be treated individually, bearing in mind its strength, how it may have reacted to a previous big yield, hail or cold. An experienced pruner has a feel for each vine, something almost instinctive which guides his pruning clippers.

The following types of pruning are used in the region:
Guyot pruning. This is the most common form found on the Côte d'Or and on the Côte Chalonnaise, with double-Guyot in Chablis. The main, fruit-bearing cane, pruned to six buds, is attached to the lowest of three wires supporting the shoots and vegetation. A short cane, with two buds, is also left to produce fruit but especially the shoots which become the next year's two canes – hence, poor pruning can affect not only the current year's crop, but also the following one.

Vines are trained low in Burgundy, about 30cm from the ground, so that any warmth in the soil from daytime sunshine can continue to help ripen the grapes at night. High training is practised in the Hautes Côtes, which is more economical and carries less risk of spring frost.
Goblet pruning. This is the classic method of pruning in the Beaujolais. The vine is really a free-standing bush, with three or four "spurs" of wood, each producing a fruit-bearing cane cut back to two buds. The vigorous vegetation is tied up around a post, or occasionally trained between wires, resulting in a less bush-like appearance.
Cordon-de-Royat pruning. This spur-pruning is found at the southern end of the Côte de Beaune, especially in Santenay and Chassagne-Montrachet. The vine is trained horizontally, with the spurs producing fruit-bearing canes pruned to one or two buds. Skill is needed to start off the horizontal training, but once set up, the vegetation is well spread out between wires.
Taille à queue. This is what is seen traditionally in the Mâconnais, with the producing branch bent over in a semicircle.

One of the most evocative Burgundian sights in winter is the smoke from the wheelbarrow braziers where the vigneron burns the prunings as he works up and down the rows. The smoke mingles with the frosty mist and the effect is a blue haze. It also warms freezing fingers, and the soil is enriched by the ashes.

March

The pruning is completed during this month, followed by bending the fruit-bearing canes under the lower wires, avoiding damage to the buds. If earth has been piled around the roots to protect them from severe frosts, it is dug up and spread out. This airs the soil and helps distribute fertilizer. The fertilizer options here are: manure (probably still the best choice), nitrogen for the vegetation, phosphoric acid for successful fruit development and healthiness, and potassium for increased yield, improved must and to help the vines resist disease and frost. Getting the recipe right is a difficult task. Tractors for ploughing have been used for 30 years in Burgundy now. This is also the month for grafting, using the *greffe anglaise*, a z-shaped cut which fits the French vine graft to the rootstock. In these northern climes, there is no such thing as grafting "in the field", and these successful grafts will be planted in the vineyard the following year.

April

Grafting continues, usually requiring about two to three weeks to take at a temperature of 20°C in sand or sawdust. The vigneron fears spring frost, as by this time the vine is really vulnerable and it is often this fear which causes him to prune "generously". The red spider can also make a first appearance at this time. The main cane is fixed to the lower wire and, now that the sap has risen, the wood is more pliable. New vineyards are planted out this month. There will be grapes after three years, but AC wine only after four.

May

The frost threat continues during the first week. Weeds are dealt with by weedkillers or ploughing, and treatments against spiders, moths, mildew and oidium are applied – frequently these can be combined in one spray. The timing of these treatments is critical, and a *station d'avertissements agricoles* issues advice based on the meteorological conditions. It is a frightening thought that mildew fungi can remain incubated for several years – those of 1975 survived the dryness of 1976 to reappear alarmingly in 1977. The successful new grafts are planted out in the nursery for their year's sojourn there. In the vineyard, unwanted, non-fruit-bearing shoots are removed.

June

This is the month when the vines flower. Ideal conditions include sun and warmth, with minimum rain and wind. Good, quick, regular flowering ensures a healthy crop, barring later calamities like hail storms. However, if the weather is poor, *coulure*, or flower abortion, occurs, substantially reducing the size of the harvest. Any straggling branches are placed between the double wire in the middle and new shoots are attached to the upper wire by metal or plastic clasps or clips. Treatments continue, although preferably not during the actual flowering.

July

Treatments continue as before, with growers totting up the cost. Ploughing along the rows is often effected, as well as the mechanical trimming of excess foliage at the end of the branches, which only takes away nutrition intended for the grapes. This is also the time when an altruistic grower might remove excess bunches in an effort to improve quality. This could give as much as a 2% increase in natural alcohol if a crop is reduced by a third. Understandably, growers are reluctant to do this, on the assumption that quantity equals cash (if not reputation) but if more had done so in 1982, we would not have seen the excessive yields and resultant over-chaptalized wines so often encountered in this vintage. Hail is a risk during this month, and both rockets and aircraft have been used to disperse clouds or to make the hail fall as rain. However, as hail often happens at night, disasters still occur – parts of the Côte de Nuits in 1983 bore witness to the fact that nature is still not completely tamed.

August

There will be more foliage trimming, or *rognage*, plus general maintenance, such as repairing walls, and cleaning around the periphery of vineyards. This is the month of the *véraison*, or the process of the grapes softening and changing colour. In the nursery, any rootlets which have appeared on the graft are removed. All the equipment for the vintage is cleaned, with all wooden vessels being soaked and rendered watertight. Bacteria can take a real hold on equipment lying fallow for a year, and there is no doubt that the arrival of stainless steel or enamel-lined equipment has simplified this work.

September

General maintenance and preparation for the vintage continues, with one eye on the heavens. Grape ripeness depends on so many things – the weather, the age of the vine, where it is planted, how much it has been asked to produce, how it has been cared for. The optimum moment for picking is when there is the right balance between sugar and acidity, but it is usually the former quality which is deficient in Burgundy, hence the need to chaptalize. But acidity has been on the low side if one takes a general view of the past 15 years, a phenomenon noted also in Bordeaux. Pick early and the risks from inclement weather are reduced, but there is more sugar to make up. Pick late and the acidity can go even lower and the resultant wine can lack balance and be without much projection of fruit.

The Côte Chalonnaise usually picks a few days after the Côte d'Or, probably due to vineyards at a higher altitude, with the Mâconnais starting before them both, usually in company with the Beaujolais. To show how widely the start of the harvest can vary, here are the dates when the *Ban de Vendanges* was called on the Côte de Beaune in recent years:

1973	22 September
1974	23 September
1975	25 September
1976	30 August
1977	9 October
1978	7 October (*except for Crémant*)
1979	25 September
1980	6 October
1981	23 September
1982	16 September
1983	22 September (*the date for Crémant 19.9.*)
1984	29 September

It can be seen at a glance that there is no neat correlation between date of picking and quality, with a fine year like 1978 being late, and another fine year, 1983, early.

Picking is still done almost entirely by hand in Burgundy, in sharp contrast to Bordeaux. In 1983 the Gironde topped the list with 1,050 machines, while the Yonne had 27, the Côte d'Or 25, the Saône et Loire 16, with the Rhône (Beaujolais) right at the bottom with just one. No doubt the machine will come to Burgundy, but at the moment there is no pressing socioeconomic need for it, and much of the vineyard does not lend itself easily to machine picking, either on account of its topography or because of the way it is divided into small plots.

October

The vintage finishes this month and the grower gets down to making the wine – unless he sells his grapes to a négociant or a cooperative. This is also when old vineyards are grubbed up, with deep ploughing, manuring and disinfecting.

November

Winter deep ploughing is accompanied by replacing any earth which might have fallen to the foot of a slope. Pre-pruning starts, cutting off the fruit-bearing main cane and leaving two shoots on the short cane for the main spring pruning. Some growers plough a furrow of earth around the feet of the vines to protect them from winter frosts, but others aver that the process is detrimental to the vine's root system.

December

This month sees a repetition of the activities of deep ploughing, pre-pruning, preparing new vineyard land and earth adjustments. Pre-pruning is held up if the temperature drops below freezing.

MAKING THE WINE

Winemaking in Burgundy is as idiosyncratic as one would expect from a region of individualists. If you make a tour around any given group of winemakers, you will hear almost as many theories and views on the best way to make either red or white wine. A variety of different systems coexist, particularly with regard to procedure at vinification, or fermentation, and there is no absolute blueprint for success. However, the main themes are clear. It is also worthy of note that both a particularly brilliant maker of white wine and one of red have cited cleanliness as being the most important element in the whole process.

A brief look at the structure of the grape will give a clearer idea of the raw material. The stalk or stem accounts for 3–5% of the whole, the skin 10–20%, the pulp or fleshy part of the fruit 70–80%, and the pips 2–4%. Within these component parts are distributed water, cellulose, minerals such as sulphates, potassium phosphates, lime and soda, sugars (glucose and levulose), acids (tartaric, malic and citric) and tannin. The stalks contain tannin, which, in excess, can give a bitter taste, and water, which can dilute the alcohol level. A small quantity of stalks can, however, give a wine backbone. The pips contain even more tannin, so great care must be taken with crushing and pressing, otherwise far too much astringence will appear in the wine.

But the flesh and the skins provide the basis of both the must (the unfermented juice) and the wine. The colourless juice which comes from the flesh contains the sugars and the acids, while, during fermentation, the colouring matter in the grape skins of both the Pinot Noir and the Gamay is dissolved by the alcohol and distributed in the must.

Red wines

The Pinot Noir grapes (for Gamay in the Beaujolais there is a different method) are brought into the *cuverie* and put through a crusher-stemmer. Many winemakers put back a proportion of stalks to strengthen the structure of the wine – perhaps from 10–20%. Fermentation vats vary considerably, both in size and material. The traditional open wooden vats are still seen in many cellars and, whereas this type of vat poses problems in Bordeaux, the coolish Burgundian Octobers rarely result in temperature-control risks. Sometimes the temperature can go briefly over 30°C at the beginning of the fermentation, but it is usually not too dangerous and at night the temperature drops sufficiently for it to be a brake. In fact, it is much more usual to have to heat all or part of the must (in steam-heated, double-lined, copper bowls), in order to get things going, for a "stuck" fermentation is dangerous – either because of the risk of oxidation (in spite of judicious addition of sulphur dioxide) or because of contamination by bacteria. Sometimes, when the must heating has been excessive, the wine can have a slightly "jammy" taste.

Fermentation vats in Burgundy can also be of concrete or steel; some are lined with enamel or glass; and there is even a limited amount of stainless steel, especially with the largest houses. Nearly all vats, of whatever material, are open, but there are some advocates of closed vats. In many cases, the cap of skins is kept in contact with the juice, for good colour extraction, by means of wooden poles, or *piges*. There is also a certain amount of treading by men, which surprises those who think this practice is now confined to the Douro valley of Portugal. *Remontages*, or pumping the must from the base of the vat and spraying the top, is another means to the same end. There is a fair amount of tannin in the skins and the potential for aroma, so this process is vital if a quality wine is to be achieved. The yeasts are thus also spread well, essential when reliance is almost entirely on natural yeasts for turning the sugar into alcohol. Open vats can have a system of a permanently submerged cap, attained by the use of a perforated lid, but *remontages* are still necessary.

Chaptalization can be effected with a *remontage*. There are those who like to do this at the beginning of the fermentation, and others who like to do it in small doses as the fermentation progresses, but great care has to be taken that no residual sugar remains at the end. For red wines, cane or beet sugar can be used, with cane sugar for white wines. Chaptalization, or the adding of sugar to the fermenting must, of course, raises the alcohol level, but it also slightly lowers the fixed acidity of a wine. The ratio of alcohol to extract is higher in chaptalized wines, and excessive chaptalization also tends to mask fruit and aroma. So, the conundrum remains – what to do in Burgundy when natural alcohol is deficient, owing to a sunless year. My own inclination is to settle for less alcoholic wines, destined for young drinking, and rigorously to declassify Grand Cru and Premier Cru wines to village level when the modesty of the year warrants such action. In poor years in Burgundy these grand-sounding names often fail to reflect the real nature of a top *cru*, so let us cease to pretend and simply say that, in some years, this level of achievement is not possible. Is it so shaming when we are the victim of nature? After all, there was hardly a single 1972 Bordeaux Cru Classé worthy of the name!

As for length of fermentation, or vatting time, this varies between winemakers, and it certainly varies between years. In an excessively tannic year like 1976 (an admittedly rare occurrence – but nevertheless an example), some meticulous producers actually *reduced* their vatting time so as to avoid an imbalance of tannin. Some people also believe in shorter fermentation when the grapes are less than healthy. On the other hand, the wines produced in a year of high production or only moderately sunny conditions can often benefit from a long fermentation.

However, all the main colour extraction is achieved in the first three or four days, although the extraction of tannin continues throughout the vatting. Increased body and extract can be added to a wine which is perhaps light owing to high yields (as in 1982) through the process of drawing off a quantity of juice during the fermentation, thereby increasing the ratio of solids to liquids. This results in a good deal of non-AC rosé wine, but it is a financial sacrifice which can pay off by greatly enhancing the quality of the remaining red wine. So, vatting times in the Côte d'Or generally vary between 8 and 14 days, and there is no set of rules in this respect which will guarantee automatic perfection each time.

When the wine is run off the lees the remaining skin and pips are pressed and the first pressing is almost always added to the free-run wine. Nowadays, horizontal presses are in use – Vaslin, Mabille and Willmes. More press wine can be added if the vintage is completely healthy. The solid matter left after the pressings is later distilled into the spirit called *marc*. The malolactic fermentation follows, either in vat or barrel. The malic acid is transformed into lactic acid and carbon dioxide gas by this process, softening the wine and preventing a later fermentation in bottle, a misfortune which sometimes happened in the past in Burgundy. Often a cellar has to be warmed to about 17°C to enable the malolactic fermentation to take place – very cold Burgundian cellars create difficulties. I would go so far as to say that some growers' wines are bottled too late, way after the optimum point, just because they have had to wait so long for the malolactic fermentation to be completed.

Red wine is then taken off its lees and aged in oak barrels of approximately 225 litres for anything between one year and two, depending on the type of wine, the nature of the vintage and the whim of the producer – judgment might be a kinder word. Every type of oak seems to be in service, with wood from the Allier and the Vosges often favoured for red wine, as well as the Jura and the Limousin. However, oak from the Tronçais and the Châtillonais, the plateau of the Côte d'Or north of Dijon at Châtillon-sur-Seine, are also seen. The proportion of new wood in a cellar varies with the financial strength of a house and the needs of a year, although that is difficult to judge since the new casks have to be ordered well in advance of the harvest. In 1985, a new oak barrel, or *pièce*, cost 1,700 francs. The Pinot Noir cannot take excessive new oak, with its overpowering tannin and vanilla flavours, so the balance of new oak against old has to be just right. It is also possible to season new casks, often using water, to remove excess astringence.

Racking, or the periodic transfer of wine from one barrel to another, thereby separating it from any stale solid matter which may have fallen to the bottom of the cask, is usually done three times before bottling – in the spring after the vintage, before the following vintage, and before bottling. The tendency is for less rather than more, as excessive racking can tire and dry out a wine. Burgundian cellars are usually cold and humid, so less evaporation takes place here than elsewhere in France. Nevertheless, topping-up is a regular operation, especially as in Burgundy the bung-hole is always on top, and here there is obviously some room for personal expression. Of course, the wine used for topping-up should be similar, but often one suspects it might be inferior. If it is done too enthusiastically, it could contribute to the "house style" of certain négociants' wines, but, as usual, conscientious winemakers will do their honest best.

A fining to clarify the wine is usually carried out before bottling, using whites of egg, gelatine, casein (a milk protein), isinglass (a fish product) and bentonite. Whites of egg seem to be favoured for red wines, but gelatine can be used to remove excess tannin (as in 1976). These substances bring about a coagulation of any suspended matter, which then falls to the bottom of the barrel or tank, leaving the clear wine to be racked off. Usually, the wines receive a light filtering before bottling, but some domains feel this can affect quality (less flavour, body or extract?) and avoid filtering, often signifying this by a small slip label to warn the consumer that there might be some haze or deposit in the wine. Personally, I feel that super clarifying can detract from maximum character in a wine, but when wine is shipped around the world, deposit is disliked. However, it is ironic to note that it has always been more accepted in a Bordeaux than in a Burgundy, for no valid reason, unless it is that sediment in Burgundy can be more hazy and less solid than it is in Bordeaux.

Bottling is of vital importance, because it is tragic when a winemaker falls at the last hurdle, and there are still too many bottling faults in Burgundy – oxidation and uncleanliness being the two chief culprits. Nowadays, the wine is assembled in tanks before bottling so as to achieve homogeneity and avoid the cask-to-cask differences of the past. Nearly all burgundy is cold-bottled, although a few houses pasteurize. It seems to me that absolute hygiene, a great deal of running water in the cellar, and limited but sensible use of sulphur dioxide should provide all the precautions needed by a careful winemaker.

White wines

With these wines the whole process takes place in a different order, with pressing before fermentation. The stalks are not removed, and they help "drain" the juice from the horizontal presses, which can be pneumatic or screw type. Oxidation is a great enemy of white wine, so a speedy but gentle pressing and a judicious use of sulphur dioxide are both desirable. The murky juice is then immediately run off into vats to stand and clarify – the *débourbage*. In large concerns, centrifuges are sometimes used, as the aim is to start with a very clean must.

Fermentation then takes place, either in barrel or vat. Nearly all fine Côte d'Or wines are fermented in oak, often new – Limousin oak seems to be very successful in many cases. The ideal temperature is between 15° and 20°C and the fermentation should be lengthy in order to extract maximum flavour and bouquet, with periodic rousing of the lees and yeasts to keep the process moving regularly. The cask also needs to be filled to the right level, to allow some air for the yeasts to work, but not too much to cause oxidation. The wine stays on its lees until completion of the malolactic fermentation, which could be late spring, but is then run off into clean barrels for the rest of its ageing. Here again, Limousin oak is often used.

Chaptalization is usually effected right at the beginning of fermentation. The most usual finings for white wine are casein, isinglass and sometimes bentonite for excess protein, and for fine white wines only a light filtering should be necessary. Some of the best wines are bottled at 18 months of age, others before that time. Some Côte Chalonnaise wines are bottled in the spring after the vintage. In the Mâconnais, the more modest wines are kept in tank and bottled when needed, usually a matter of months after the vintage, and the wines are cold-stabilized by refrigeration to avoid tartrate deposit. On the Côte d'Or, allowing very cold air into the cellars usually brings this about naturally, and it would be a travesty to overtreat very fine white wines intended for ageing. A few tartaric crystals are a sign that a wine has been treated gently, which brings joy to the heart of a committed burgundy lover.

Rosé wines

Rosé does not mean much in Burgundy, except for the Rosé of Marsannay. The *vin gris* method is to press the red grapes in order to give a light colour, and then to ferment as for white wine. Or the grapes can be macerated for a day or two and the juice drawn off when the colour is right – fermentation follows.

Sparkling wines

Ever since 1822, *méthode champenoise* wines were made in Burgundy, but in 1975 a superior appellation, *Crémant de Bourgogne*, was created. Pinot Noir or Pinot Blanc, Chardonnay and Aligoté grapes are used and very gently pressed, with only the first pressings being retained for *Crémant de Bourgogne*. Fermentation is carried out and a *cuvée* is made which must be approved by a commission chosen by the INAO before it can be admitted for bottling and the *prise de mousse*, which is a secondary fermentation in bottle created by adding a dose of sugar and yeast to the wine. The wine has to age for 9 months and goes through riddling, or *remuage*, and then *dégorgement* to eliminate the dead particles of yeast.

This is now done by freezing the necks of the bottles to solidify the sediment, which can then be removed easily. The bottles are then topped up, their sweetness adjusted to correspond to the type of *crémant* required (Brut or Demi-Sec), recorked and "dressed", and rested before sale. *Crémants* can be blanc, blanc de blancs (only made from white grapes) or rosé.

It is a pity that *Crémant de Bourgogne* is not better known and distributed, because the wines are fruity and fine, and of a generally very high standard.

Bourgogne Mousseux Méthode Champenoise does not have such strict conditions as *crémant* as concerns the base wine (grape varieties, which can include Gamay and Sacy, ripeness at vintage, yields, methods of transport, pressing and vinification), but the wines are still most honourable, be they white, rosé or red, the latter rather a Burgundian speciality.

THE TRADE IN BURGUNDY

Historically, Burgundy was at a disadvantage in comparison with Bordeaux when trying to sell its wines abroad, as there was no port and no direct river to the sea. The Yonne was used to some extent, and wine was also taken both to Paris and Rouen for onward transportation on the River Seine. Nowadays, road tankers and container lorries leave Burgundy for destinations all over Europe, and France's fine system of autoroutes provides speedy travel. The hold-ups occur at frontiers, and even more so at Channel ports, but that is the fault of bureaucracy, not transportation. Wine for the United States is usually taken to Le Havre, while exports to the Far East and Australia are usually sent via Marseilles.

AC exports in Burgundy in 1984 reached a value of 2,730,000,000 francs and 1,136,000 hectolitres in volume, of which 77% was in bottle and 23% in bulk. This total is steadily rising, with bottle sales on the increase and bulk exports falling. In 1974 the exports were to the value of 592,000,000 francs and 689,000 hectolitres in volume, of which 50% was in bottle and 50% in bulk.

The principal customers for AC burgundy around the world are broken down as follows:

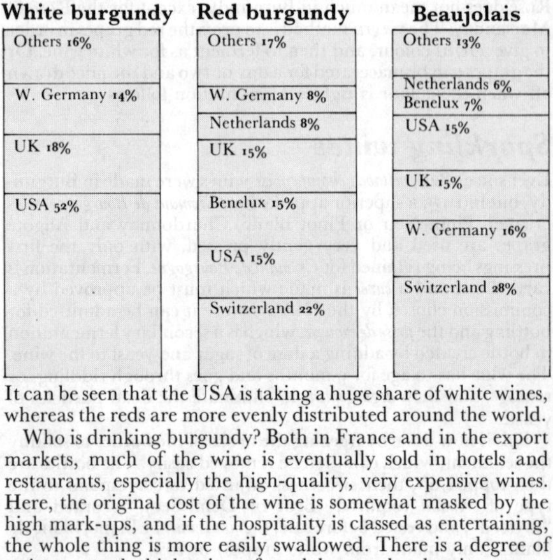

It can be seen that the USA is taking a huge share of white wines, whereas the reds are more evenly distributed around the world.

Who is drinking burgundy? Both in France and in the export markets, much of the wine is eventually sold in hotels and restaurants, especially the high-quality, very expensive wines. Here, the original cost of the wine is somewhat masked by the high mark-ups, and if the hospitality is classed as entertaining, the whole thing is more easily swallowed. There is a degree of resistance to the high prices of much burgundy when it comes to the "take home" trade, and burgundy is more likely to be sold by a fine wine merchant than a high-volume supermarket.

The upward trend in exports shows signs of continuing steadily, but only if unacceptable price increases are avoided. America, particularly, can fall out of love with a region just as fast as it can become enamoured of it, and the Burgundians should take care that they do not kill the golden goose. Many of the larger houses and domains are aware of this, but some estates, relatively new to exporting, might feel that the trend can only go upwards and that the market will absorb any wine at any price. This is not so, as numerous defections have shown in the past.

As long as Burgundy really delivers the quality behind the bottle, at a price which is not exorbitant for what the customer is getting, it will continue to keep old friends and find new ones. But greed and inconsistent quality are a certain route to failure in the long-term.

ENJOYING BURGUNDY

Bottles, labels and glasses

All burgundy is in sloping-shouldered bottles, never the square shoulders of Bordeaux. The traditional colour is a yellow-green, which the French call *feuilles mortes*. It is especially pleasing with white wines when matched with a yellow capsule – for red wine, the capsules are red. It is very rare to find magnums in Burgundy, in spite of the fact that this is the ideal size for laying down: Burgundians should be encouraged to use this large format in great years. There was a brief experiment in the early 1980s with a "Burgundian bottle" for AC wines, with "AOC de Bourgogne" imprinted in the glass under the neck label. It was an aesthetic disaster and, happily for all, it died an early death.

Labels are comparatively simple in Burgundy:

Joseph Drouhin

PULIGNY-MONTRACHET

Appellation Contrôlée

Mis en bouteille par

JOSEPH DROUHIN

Négociant à Beaune, Côte d'Or

75cl

Wine from a Négociant
The name of the négociant.
The name of the wine.
Confirms AC status.
Bottled by Joseph Drouhin.
Address of the firm.
75cl, the standard EEC and USA content.
The vintage in this case appears on the neck label.

Mis en bouteille au Domaine

GEVREY-CHAMBERTIN

1er Cru Aux Combottes

Appellation Gevrey-Chambertin
1er Cru Contrôlée

1982 DOMAINE DUJAC

Morey-St-Denis (Côte d'Or)

75cl

Wine from a Domain
Bottled at the domain.
Name of the wine.
The fact that it is 1er Cru is mentioned in this case.
Confirms AC status.
Vintage and name of the domain.
Address of domain owner.
75cl, the standard EEC and USA content.

All the folklore and drinking songs of Burgundy might lead one to believe that the *tastevin* is the only vessel from which to drink its wine! But in reality, this dimpled, silver tasting cup (actually, it is more like a small saucer) is only useful for seeing if a wine still in cask is clear of haze. With the *tastevin's* wide surface, the bouquet of a wine is immediately lost, and tasting is difficult against metal. So, for serious tasting and assessing, a glass is better.

The classic tulip-shaped glass is suitable for all wines, whether red or white, as is the approved tasting glass created by the INAO. But there are a few shapes widely used in Burgundy which seem to suit the particularly heady nature of the wines. It is as if burgundy needs more room in a glass to breathe and develop than Bordeaux; great burgundy has something slightly unrestrained about it, requiring space to express itself.

(**a**) The shape most favoured by Burgundians both for red and white wine, is the *ballon*, a Cognac-type squat glass, with short stem and a huge bowl narrowing at the top to catch and hold the bouquet. It is extraordinarily reassuring to grasp a *ballon* in the hand, swirl the wine around, deeply inhale and then, finally, take a good mouthful and let it roll in over the palate. The wine has every opportunity to explode in the mouth, with all the exciting, sensual tastes and flavours to be found in fine burgundy.
(**b**) In restaurants in Burgundy, particularly, one is quite often given a kind of elegant goldfish-bowl, on a long stem. Provided the size is not too exaggerated, this can be extremely effective in showing off the qualities of red burgundy.
(**c**) There is another shape which I have not seen elsewhere, a large glass with a long stem, and a generous bowl which tapers in only slightly towards the rim. This is a very traditional glass, and can allow a red wine to expand and open out.

Serving burgundy

Burgundians almost never decant their wines. Their attitude is usually one of great simplicity: bring up bottle from cellar, draw cork, pour into glass. As their cellars are very cool this eliminates the need for a refrigerator for the whites, and the reds are left to do their developing in the glass.

There is much to be said for this approach. Decanting is a controversial subject anyway, and experiments do not seem to have proved conclusively that the process is beneficial or otherwise. However, I have had young burgundy poured into a glass carafe and served soon afterwards, with delicious results. The perfume seemed to be even more heady than usual. With old wines it can also be sensible to separate wine from deposit, but the particles in suspension can be tricky to handle and, in this case, decanting needs a steady hand and a keen eye.

Outside Burgundy, the most common fault associated with the serving of its wines is to offer the red wines too warm and the white too cold. Over-warm reds can be "soupy" and really disappointing, while white burgundy, over-chilled or left too long in a refrigerator, can completely break up, taste flat and lose its flavour. Red burgundy is at its best served at 15–16°C (about 60°F), with young Beaujolais cooler, at about 13°C (55°F).

White burgundy can have a bigger variation. The very finest, especially if they have some bottle age, can be served at around 13°C (55°F), but a simple Mâcon Villages could be served a great deal cooler, at around 9–10°C (just under 50°F). But even then, don't kill it with cold – you will miss so much.

Tasting burgundy

Tasting fine burgundy is like unlocking a Pandora's box of flavours and smells. Trying poor burgundy is a deadening experience, with no impression of clean fruit on the palate, and either a tainted or over-alcoholic "mask" preventing you from seeing something true and frank.

Both red and white burgundy possess a multitude of perfumes and tastes, and the more you find, the better the wine is likely to be. More modest wines should be attractive, straightforward and fruity, while wines from fine sites, in ripe years and made by gifted winemakers will keep you searching for adjectives to describe them until the last drop has disappeared from the glass.

All the following flavours have been ascribed to burgundy, more especially to the bouquet of fine bottles – they are not fanciful, just an attempt to try to pinpoint those heady sensual aromas which assail the lucky drinker of good burgundy:

Cherries, Raspberries, Strawberries, Redcurrants, Cassis, Apricots, Peaches, Figs, Prunes, Plums, Greengages, Quinces, Apples, Loganberries, Blackberries, Hazelnuts, Vanilla, Cinnamon, Acacia, Mayblossom, Hawthorn, Blackthorn, Honey, Liquorice, Laurel, Truffles, Chocolate, Tar, Grilled almonds, Roses, Violets, Hay, Toast, Wet fur, Wet leaves, Farmyards, Leather, Cocoa, Honeysuckle, Hung game, Oatmeal.

This is by no means a definitive list and the more one tastes, the larger the experience and vocabulary become. In addition individual tasters differ in the qualities that impress them and the similarities that they perceive. There are other aromas, occasionally fleetingly encountered in burgundy, but which seem to me to occur much more frequently in Bordeaux – tobacco and mint are examples (the influence of Cabernet, as opposed to Pinot Noir, or is it more complicated than that?).

Some descriptions are used far more often with reference to white wine than to red. Mayblossom, acacia and hazelnuts are more often associated with Meursault than with Pommard, for instance, while cherries, farmyards and raspberries are firmly in the red camp. But it would be misleading to categorize all these descriptions rigidly into red and white columns, because they do overlap and surprises have a habit of creeping up on even the most experienced taster – this is one of the joys of wine.

When starting to taste burgundy, it might be less confusing first of all to try to impress the basic scent and flavour of Chardonnay and Pinot Noir on the mind and senses. Then treat this as a canvas upon which to splash all the other sensory perceptions which present themselves. Let us hope that most of them will be positive, attractive and appetizing, but inevitably there will be some less appealing odours and tastes too – maybe dirty wood, vinegar or nail varnish. Discard those wines, but not without complaining to the supplier, and concentrate on finding those burgundies which astonish with their range of bouquet and savour. They are easy to recognize and difficult to forget!

Burgundy with food

There is a burgundy to go with virtually every type of food, with the exception of the dessert or pudding course, as there is no sweet white wine of the region. However, some of the most perfect meals finish with cheese and nuts, and this gives great scope.

Burgundian red wines, particularly the great growths of the Côte de Nuits, are superb with game, especially if it is well hung. One of the greatest gastronomic partnerships I ever experienced was in the company of that respected burgundy man, Harry Yoxall, at what was to be our last dinner together. We had roast grouse, *bien faisandé*, with a bottle of Grands Echézeaux 1952 from the Domaine de la Romanée-Conti. What was incredible was that the Grands Echézeaux had the rich, gamey smell of the grouse! Venison, hare and wild boar are also magnificent with ripe burgundy from a good year.

The combinations, of course, are infinite – mixed *charcuterie* with Beaujolais, Chablis with *andouillettes*, Meursault with *jambon persillé*, that splendid green-speckled Burgundian ham galantine. It was in Burgundy that the myth that eggs "do not go with wine" was finally put to rest – what is better than a young Côte de Beaune with *oeufs en meurette*, lightly poached eggs with a red wine sauce? With the garlicky snails of the region, an Aligoté is ideal, while something like a plain sole or piece of turbot deserves a Chevalier-Montrachet or Corton-Charlemagne.

Robust dishes like *boeuf bourguignon* or *coq au vin* are more than welcome after a morning's tasting in cold cellars (or pruning on a February day), and a vibrant, even earthy burgundy is best here – perhaps a Santenay or a Mercurey. Unfortunately, some regional recipes which require a long cooking time are rarely found in restaurants, such as *potée bourguignonne* (ham, pork and sausages cooked together with vegetables), or *pouchouse*, made from fresh fish from the Saône simmered in white wine (if red wine is substituted it becomes a *matelote*, and the colour of the accompanying wine changes accordingly).

Two dishes often found in the Mâconnais are refugees from the Ain, across the Saône. *Quenelles de brochet*, or flaked-pike moulds, should really only be eaten in restaurants of impeccable reputation, otherwise you might come up against a floury, *ersatz* version, while poached *poularde de Bresse* is a dish of great subtlety which is equally happy with either red or white burgundy.

At last people have realized that not all cheese has a miraculous effect on wine, and while the soft, creamy little goat cheeses of the Mâconnais and *fromage blanc* floating in cream are delicious with chilled Beaujolais, *Epoisses* and even *Cîteaux* often seem to be too strong and tangy for fine Côte d'Or wines. I prefer the Gruyère-related *Comté* or the savoyard *Beaufort*, one of the great, unsung cheeses of the world.

VINTAGES

As with any wine area, there is a general picture for each vintage, on which there is over-painting by individual growers. A poor winemaker will not suddenly produce tremendous wine in a fine year, and a skilled winemaker can make surprisingly attractive wine in conditions which are less than propitious. With older vintages, the assessments really only apply to Grands Crus and the top Premiers Crus.

1984: Cold weather in September prevented the spread of rot, but inevitably it also precluded real ripeness, and the wines were very low in natural alcohol. As a result, chaptalization came into its own, and there are undoubtedly unbalanced wines as a result. But it is also a pleasant surprise to see how successful some wines appear, with clean, fruity qualities. However, they do not have depth. In Beaujolais, the *crus* have made some really pleasant wines. The whites have good fruity projection which makes them tempting. The Chablis have typical *nervosité*, and the problem here is one of quantity, not quality.
1983: The best wines will confirm that this is an outstanding vintage, the finest since 1978. But there was rot, and hail in parts of the Côte de Nuits has stamped its imprint on a fair number of wines. Where these twin scourges were avoided, there are remarkable wines of power and concentration, with a good deal of tannin of a kind which is more penetrable than it was in 1976. This is a vintage to lay down, something for those who say that modern burgundy is "too light". The Côte Chalonnaise has produced some remarkable wines, and the Beaujolais wines are well structured. The white wines have great body and power, although a few seem to have too much (natural) alcohol on the nose. It would be a tragedy to drink the top wines too young.
1982: A record harvest, which had the unhappy side-effect of overcropping from the Pinot Noir. Consequently some red wines were mere shadows of their normal selves, and others were given too much of a helping hand or suffered from heating processes to extract colour. There are many fruity, gulpable wines for young drinking, and where a winemaker ran off a good deal of surplus juice during the vinification process, there is more structure. The whites are relatively forward, but delicious and easy.
1981: Hail made its presence felt in this vintage, and there are too many wines with this taint, while others just have a dry finish. A few, somewhat miraculously, taste good and concentrated, partly due to the small yield. Beaujolais was much more successful. The white wines have firm acidity and the grandest of them should still be kept for a few years.
1980: A controversial vintage, which unfortunately masked the reality of the situation. Where the grower treated wisely against rot, there are some very creditable wines, especially at reputed domains and particularly on the Côte de Nuits. There are reds of style and fine flavour, which should probably be drunk within the decade of their making. The whites do not have much character and in the main do not repay keeping.
1979: A large vintage, which inevitably brings an element of variability to the scene. Many wines have most attractive fruit and charm with an infinitely enticing taste. They are already drinking well, even near the top level. The whites share these qualities – some are rather forward, especially Chablis.
1978: An exceptional vintage, where both red and white wines have concentration, complexity and real interest. There is fruit on a sound structure, giving wines which are perfect candidates for long-term cellaring. It is the flavour and individuality of each *cru* and *climat* which really impresses.
1977: The wines are not marvellous, but could have been a lot worse – only the fine September weather saved the vintage from disaster. The reds tend to taste drier as they age – only the very best wines are not marked by this characteristic. The whites were better, everywhere, but they have no real pretensions to high quality.
1976: These wines are really atypical burgundy, overloaded

with tannin which sometimes succeeds in masking the fruit. Where the fruity character can break through, there are some exotic wines which will keep well. But many are slightly thick wines which remain dormant. The whites were rich and low in acidity, so many are flat or blowsy at ten years old. The top Chablis can be better balanced, although their fat character makes them lean more than usual towards the Côte de Beaune in style.

1975: A year all but ruined by rot, and the reds consequently have an unhealthy brown colour and a tainted taste. The whites on the Côte d'Or were slightly better, although now most have maderized. But Chablis produced wines of breed and balance, many of them gems.

1974: Fairly firm reds, with some body to them, but many were rather dull-tasting and lacked individuality. The whites had more interest, and some improved in the bottle.

1973: A very large vintage which produced lightish wines of charm and fruit. Some have not stayed the course, but nor have those which received too hefty a dose of sugar. The whites had low natural acidity, and were generally at their best when younger.

1972: The reds developed surprisingly well throughout the 1970s, and now many are firm and well structured, with good fruity character. Occasionally, they are a little green. The whites also suffered from lack of ripeness, but some have recovered well. However, this might be one of those rare years in Burgundy where the reds eventually turned out better than the whites.

1971: A very ripe vintage, in some instances overripe, with lovely richness and opulence. The best are a heady experience, while some are too full-blown. Patches of hail on the Côte d'Or affected a few wines. Some of the whites are a little blowsy now, although the best balanced, including Chablis, still stun with their beauty.

1970: A large vintage of soft, fruity wines. They were most attractive throughout the decade, but both red and white should now have been drunk, except in the case of certain Grands Crus.

1969: A superb vintage, stamped by the *breed* of the wines. The underlying acidity ensured that they lasted well, and they have that quality of great appellation character which is the hallmark of a fine vintage. All the whites, including Chablis, were exceptionally good.

1968: Not for the first, or the last, time the whites were better than the rotten reds.

1967: A year of mixed fortunes. When the reds were not over-chaptalized, there were some attractive bottles. The whites had breed.

1966: A highly successful year, with quantity and quality. Fruit and style in both the red and the white wines.

1965: A year to forget; there were too many in the 1960s.

1964: Very good, definite-tasting wine, equally successful for both white and red.

1963: Poor, and totally irrelevant now.

1962: Very good wines, with the fine balance giving them longevity. Extremely elegant whites.

1961: A small crop of excellent wines, with the concentration to taste magnificent at 25 years old.

Some older vintages of distinction:
1945, 1947, 1948, 1949, 1950, and 1952 for whites; 1953, 1955, 1957, 1959 for reds.

Wines & Villages

● ○ ◑ COTE D'OR

The Côte d'Or is the heart of Burgundy, golden in name and in reputation. Although historic Dijon is by far the largest town on the Côte, the pivotal centres for the wine trade are Beaune and Nuits-St-Georges. As with any wine area, there is a complex web of négociants, growers and brokers who make and sell the wines, each jealously guarding his position in the line of supply. But the Côte d'Or is the most democratic of wine regions, its vineyards divided up into hundreds of small plots which are either inherited or acquired by a diplomatic marriage. Some growers see their job as suppliers of grapes, leaving the négociant houses to do their own vinifications, while others like to control the whole process right up to the sale to the customer at the gate. There is a substantial number of growers who both make their wine, and sell a part of it to the négociants, via the brokers, to finance the proportion they wish to mature and bottle themselves. Somewhere in all this lurk magnificent winemakers who have made Burgundy the most show-stopping word in wine vocabulary. Others, who are less skilled or less caring, unfortunately have access to the same labels.

The greatest red and white burgundies are made on the Côte d'Or, particularly if you take a wine's ability to age as a criterion of quality. It is awesome to remember this if you drive from Dijon to Beaune, with the slope of the Côte on your right an imposing presence all along the way. Do this in autumn, when the leaves are changing colour, preferably with Vivaldi's Four Seasons playing to complete the scene, and let the vineyards create their magic. This is the Côte d'Or, and this is where some of the most intoxicating taste sensations in the world are created.

● ○ ◑ MARSANNAY

1983 production:	Red	*8,981 hectolitres*
	White	*1,669 hectolitres*
	Rosé	*1,420 hectolitres*

The choice of appellations lies between Bourgogne-Marsannay Rosé or Clairet, or Bourgogne-Marsannay for the red wine. Bourgogne Aligoté, Bourgogne Blanc and Bourgogne Passe-Tout-Grains are also produced on a small scale. Much less rosé wine is produced than in the past, with only about 15% now on offer, but this quantity does vary with the quality of the vintage – in good years, growers tend to opt for making red. The cooperative at Marsannay is less important than it was, responsible now for about 1,500hl of wine. On the better slopes, growers concentrate on making red wine, which has improved as the plantings have aged. The rosé should be drunk young, when it has a pleasant hint of strawberries, and is excellent in hot weather, when a red burgundy tastes flat and "soupy". Bourgogne Rouge from Marsannay is frank and gamey, slightly earthy in character, with good concentration if the year is good and the vines are old.

A Personal Selection of Marsannay Producers

Domaine Clair-Daü

They make all the appellations permitted in Marsannay and have a sound reputation for them.

Domaine Bruno Clair

The young team here is an example of the most encouraging aspect of Burgundy today – unblinkered, hard-working and conscientious. Perfumed rosé and Bourgogne Rouge with a bouquet of "wet dog" (which is very pleasant, I assure you) and a taste of redcurrants.

● ○ FIXIN

1983 production: Fixin *3,106 hectolitres*

It is interesting to see how a "marginal" appellation on the Côte de Nuits is divided between the appellations with regard to vineyard area:

Côte de Nuits-Villages and Fixin (the two are interchangeable)	*128.04 hectares*
Fixin Premiers Crus	*20.75 hectares*
Appellation Bourgogne	*56.84 hectares*
Bourgogne Grand Ordinaire	*37.91 hectares*

Premiers Crus: Les Meix-Bas (part), Le Clos du Chapitre (part), Aux Cheusots (part), La Perrière (part), Les Arvelets (part), Les Hervelets (part).

The Premiers Crus are on the upper part of the slope, which goes up to 350 metres (1,150 feet), on a base of Bajocian limestone. Le Clos du Chapitre is on a marked slope, with Bathonian brown soil very rich in pebbles. La Perrière is above it, on a 12–14% gradient, with its share of pebbles. Aux Cheusots, within which lies the Clos Napoléon, is virtually without a slope. Les Hervelets and Les Arvelets, once the same *climat*, lie between Fixin and Fixey on Bajocian limestone and, in spite of only a mild slope, there is in places barely 25cm (10in) of soil over the base. Where limestone is predominant, the wines have more finesse, but deeper soil with more clay content gives tougher, more tannic wines.

La Perrière and Clos du Chapitre fight for front ranking at Fixin. Both can be kept safely for a decade, from good years. In youth the taste is

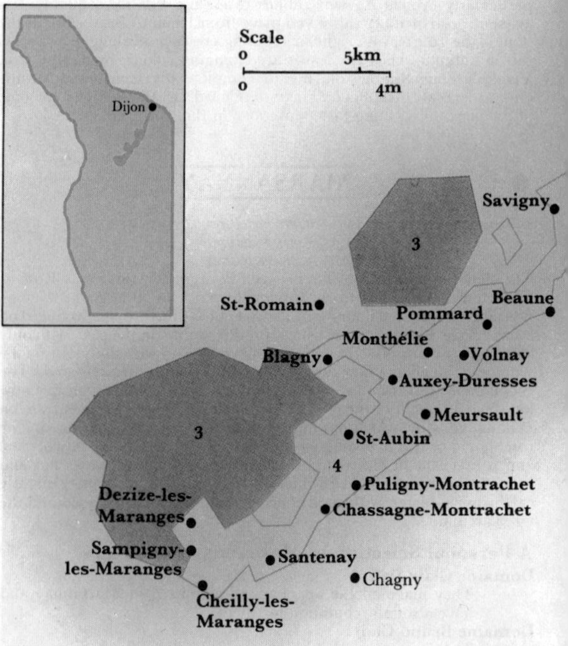

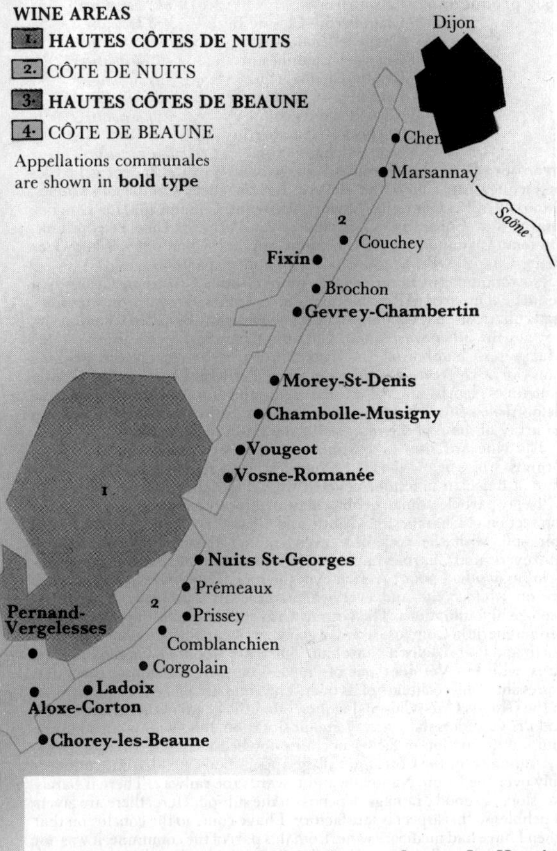

somewhat *sauvage* and gamey, with blackcurrant flavours. Les Hervelets and Les Arvelets are thought more "feminine", although in these days of *égalité* one should say that the fruit is softer. Aux Cheusots should have some finesse, although in the past I have been treated to some hefty Clos Napoléons which perplexed me somewhat. I think things are a little more *sain* nowadays.

A Personal Selection of Fixin Producers

Domaine Bruno Clair

White Fixin from the Pinot Blanc, vivacious when young, heavier after a few years in bottle – but I still wonder whether Chardonnay would not be better. Excellent Fixin Rouge, partly from 40-year-old vines so the yield is not big – pure raspberries.

Domaine Pierre Gelin

Fixin which has that *sauvage* character, even at five years old. Big, gutsy burgundy, without being "blackstrap", so the fruit holds its own against the weight, but often it could take a decade in bottle.

Domaine Philippe Joliet

Clos de la Perrière which has improved in recent years – the 1983 is certainly a *vin de garde*.

GEVREY-CHAMBERTIN

1983 production:	Chambertin	*688 hectolitres*
	Chambertin–Clos de Bèze	*478 hectolitres*
	Chapelle-Chambertin	*228 hectolitres*
	Charmes-Chambertin	*1,167 hectolitres*
	Griotte-Chambertin	*47 hectolitres*
	Latricières-Chambertin	*283 hectolitres*
	Mazis-Chambertin	*259 hectolitres*
	Ruchottes-Chambertin	*87 hectolitres*
	Gevrey-Chambertin	*15,894 hectolitres*

Premiers Crus: Les Véroilles, Village Saint-Jacques known as Le Clos St-Jacques, Aux Combottes, Bel-Air, Les Cazetiers, Combe aux Moines, Etournelles, Les Gémeaux, Lavaux, Poissenot, Champeaux, Les Goulots, Issarts, Les Corbeaux, Cherbaudes, La Perrière, Clos Prieur-Haut, Fonteny, Champonnet, Au Closeau, Craipillot, Champitenois known as Petite-Chapelle, En Ergot, Clos du Chapitre (part).

No commune in Burgundy has more Grands Crus than Gevrey – it could be compared to Pauillac boasting three First Growths, only more so. A peculiarity is that Chambertin Clos de Bèze may be called Chambertin, but not the other way round. Charmes-Chambertin can also be styled Mazoyères-Chambertin – the two names are interchangeable. Spelling runs riot at Gevrey – Les Véroilles alternates with Les Varoilles, Griotte sometimes sports an "s" at the end, and Etournelles can become Estournelles. But behind a certain disorganization in nomenclature, lies an array of some of the most seductive tastes in Burgundy.

The vineyard rises to 350 metres (1,150 feet), although the line of Grands Crus is below 300 metres (980 feet) on a gentle slope. They lie on a base of Bajocian limestone covered with thin debris, brown chalky soil with clay particles. Small pebbles play an important part, especially in the top section of Chambertin. Griotte and Chapelle-Chambertin have very thin soil, with the rock base even coming through in some places. Mazoyères and Charmes have gravelly soil of no more than 30–35cm [12–14in] in depth, a poor covering over the rock. Latricières and Ruchottes are on white oolite and everywhere there are outbreaks of the hard geological foundations. The Grands Crus shelter under the woods of the Montagne de la Combe Grisard, a good barrier against the winds from the north and it also helps against hail. There are woods above the Premiers Crus, with Les Véroilles, one of the very best, right amongst them and possessing a microclimate of its own. The vines are picked later here than in the Grands Crus. Clos St-Jacques, often the equal of the Grands Crus, and Les Cazetiers share a very similar situation, but Champonnet has the unusual distinction of facing north to northeast.

Unusually for the Côte, the Village appellation extends quite considerably over the Route Nationale and towards the railway. There is barely any slope, so good drainage depends on the subsoil. Here, there are layers of pebbles so this aspect is satisfactory. I have come to the conclusion that when I have had mediocre wines from this part of the commune, it was not because of the soil, but due to over-production or bad winemaking.

The whole palette of aromas and flavours can come into top Gevrey. When the wines are young there are strawberries and raspberries, violets, undergrowth, and game in the rich wines. As the wines mature, flavours of liquorice develop with some intensity. Amazingly enough, Griotte really can be marked by cherries! Chambertin combines finesse with power, needing years to develop – the best-bred Chambertin is never too generous with itself in youth. If there is a difference with Clos de Bèze, it is difficult to spot it, as often winemaking techniques or the respective age of the vines override any innate variation. Then, of course, there is the one-way interchangeability of the two names, so you have to be sure of what you are tasting – the best way to do this is when the wine is still in barrel and the winemaker himself describes the origin of each "lot". Latricières seems to have the most exquisite lacy quality, long and lingering but hardly ultra-powerful. Charmes-Chambertin can be less tannic and ready sooner than the other Grands Crus, while Chapelle-Chambertin can be too fruity.

Amongst the Premiers Crus, Clos St-Jacques has wonderful "animal" scents and sturdy attack when young, while Clos des Varoilles (for the whole 6ha of the Premier Cru is composed of this Clos) is tannic when young, mouth-filling when more mature. Liquorice is a feature of many of these wines, especially in years of overripeness. Straight Gevrey should be silkily soft and perfumed and easy to recognize.

A Personal Selection of Gevrey-Chambertin Producers

Domaine Bernard Bachelet
Denis Bachelet is doing splendid work here, right up to Charmes-Chambertin level. There is finesse, class and great perfume.

Domaine Lucien Boillot
Lovely bouquet of frank, fruity Gevrey-Chambertin – the 1982 clearly was affected by the high yield, but at least that is preferable to over-compensating by adding spurious "body".

Domaine Alain Burguet
Straight Gevrey-Chambertin, usually with a lovely bouquet, but sometimes a trifle too "big" on the palate for the seductive style of the appellation to dominate.

Domaines du Château de Beaune (*Bouchard Père & Fils*)
Chambertin of great finesse, all silky violets. They do not own in Clos de Bèze, but buy grapes – it sometimes seems more powerful and more backward than the Chambertin at the same time.

Domaine Clair-Daü
The whole *gamme* of Gevrey wines, from Fonteny, Cazetiers and Clos St-Jacques to Chapelle and Clos de Bèze. The domain is capable of making some of the finest wines on the Côte de Nuits, but family troubles have caused disruption. There is a good proportion of old vines, and the best wines keep magnificently.

Domaine Pierre Damoy
A domain owning untold riches – the biggest single share of Chambertin and Clos de Bèze plus Chapelle and Clos du Tamisot. Memorable old wines, also 1980, 1981 and 1983.

Domaine Drouhin
Griotte which is always very good indeed, a mixture of breed and balance . . . and those cherries.

Domaine Drouhin-Laroze
Latricières, Chapelle and Clos de Bèze which are very floral when young. They appear quite light, but some do age well, anyway for 8–10 years. However, I am sure the 1982s will not, and the prices are certainly too high.

Domaine Dujac
Les Combottes which shows that Jacques Seysses is as at home here as in Morey-St-Denis. Usually only a medium-keeper.

Domaine Faiveley
La Combe aux Moines 1er Cru, has a true Gevrey bouquet, violets and warm earth, and a taste of redcurrants, cherries and violets.

Labouré-Roi
This is not a domain wine, but their straight Gevrey is all juicy red fruit and the wines remain youthful in bottle – a good buy.

Domaine Philippe Leclerc
A good span of Gevrey wines, all kept in new oak – compare them with brother René's produce, which uses no new wood. These appear to be very good, although there is no long track record.

Domaine Pernot-Fourrier
Although the wines are not nearly as great as in the time of Fernand Pernot, the great-uncle of the current owner (whose 1969 Griotte and Clos St-Jacques are amongst the most amazing burgundies of my life), they do have breed and cherry-like qualities. But, at the moment, there is a hit-and-miss element.

Domaine Ponsot
Chambertin, Griotte and Latricières which tend to be big and rich, sometimes jammy – most last well.

Domaine Philippe Rossignol
Straight Gevrey-Chambertin which is exemplary, if you want to know what the appellation is about at a non-grandiose level.

Domaine G. Roumier
Ruchottes which can be quite splendid, amongst the stars of the Côte de Nuits.

Domaine Armand Rousseau
Apart from being one of the most engaging and generous characters in all Burgundy, Charles Rousseau is also a gifted

winemaker. The heritage of this estate is awe-inspiring, but present-day standards bow to no-one, and many are the tastings where, in my opinion, Rousseau wines come out top. The Clos St-Jacques always needs time, with its tight kernel of fruit – *une splendeur*! Also excellent Cazetiers, Ruchottes, Charmes, Mazis, Chambertin and Clos de Bèze. No serious Burgundy cellar should be without them.

Domaine Joseph Roty
A small domain, but where the Charmes usually lives up to expectations.

Domaine Jean Taupenot
Lovely Charmes, with breed and style. This grower resists the temptation to "bump up" in lighter years, like 1982, and consequently the wines are delicious and not artificially "big".

Domaine Gabriel Tortochot
Wines which are usually very big, sometimes impressive, sometimes a mite clumsy.

Domaine Louis Trapet
The colours are never dark here, and indeed can brown early, but the lingering flavours. . . . There have been ups-and-downs, but my greatest Latricières wines have come from this domain, sheer, lacy delicacy and breed.

Domaine des Varoilles
Co-owner and winemaker Jean-Pierre Naigeon makes a range of Gevrey wines; lasting, classy bottles. There is velvety fruit intermingled with the structure. Clos des Varoilles is superb and concentrated.

● ○

MOREY-ST-DENIS

1983 production:	Red	Clos de la Roche	*573 hectolitres*
		Clos de Tart	*253 hectolitres*
		Clos St-Denis	*206 hectolitres*
		Clos des Lambrays	*213 hectolitres*
		Bonnes Mares	*440 hectolitres*
		Morey-St-Denis	*3,030 hectolitres*
	White	Morey-St-Denis	*30 hectolitres*

Premiers Crus: Les Ruchots, Les Sorbés, Le Clos Sorbés, Les Millandes, Le Clos des Ormes (part), Meix-Rentiers, Monts-Luisants, Les Bouchots, Clos de la Bussière, Aux Charmes, Les Charrières, Côte-Rôtie, Calouères, Maison-Brûlée, Les Chabiots, Les Mauchamps, Les Froichots, Les Fremières, Les Genevrières, Les Chaffots, Les Chénevery (part), La Riotte, Le Clos Baulet, Les Gruenchers, Les Façonnières.

Morey-St-Denis considers that it is not sufficiently well known, sandwiched as it is between Gevrey and Chambolle – in 1985, a delegation of growers from the village even went to Japan to "spread the word". It is not very well publicized that there are two small cooperatives at Morey, which now vinify their grapes and sell the results to the négociants. But some of the greatest tastes in the whole of Burgundy can come from Morey-St-Denis, and luckily for us there is a handful of vineyard owners in the commune who are interested in achieving perfection, in spite of what the elements sometimes do to thwart them.

It is a considerable feat to have five Grands Crus in one commune, although only 1.84ha of Bonnes Mares lies in Morey – the remaining 13.70ha falls in the commune of Chambolle-Musigny. Clos des Lambrays was made a Grand Cru in 1981; in 1979 the estate had been sold to new owners after considerable time in the doldrums. Both Clos des Lambrays and Clos de Tart are in the hands of a single proprietor, which is a rare occurrence on the Côte d'Or. Clos de Tart and the Premier Cru Clos de la Bussière are typical abbey *clos* of the Middle Ages, completely surrounded by walls and with the buildings attached.

The slope of Morey-St-Denis lies next to that of Gevrey and shares the same geological makeup. The base is Bajocian limestone for the Grands Crus. The highest part of the Morey vineyard is Monts-Luisants at 350 metres (1,150 feet) on Bathonian limestone, with very poor, gravelly soil – the lack of clay and iron content makes it suitable for making the unusual white wine of the same name. The limestone rock is very evident, although Clos de la Roche probably refers to one rock which may have existed between Latricières-Chambertin and Clos St-Denis and which was used in Celtic or druidical rites. The calcareous vein comes from Bonnes Mares, crosses east-facing Clos de Tart and goes to the upper part of Clos des Lambrays, which is a little more sandy. Clos de Tart and Bonnes Mares have a very visible topsoil of calcareous debris, while Clos de la Roche and Clos St-Denis are on brown limestone soil with few pebbles, but benefiting from a good, sheltered microclimate.

These Grands Crus lead us into the realm of truffles, wild cherries and redcurrants. Clos de Tart may be the most tannic wine when young, but that derives as much from the winemaking techniques of no destalking and long vinification with the skins immersed as from anything else. Clos de la Roche has perfect structure and composition, the "bonework" covered by rich fruit, ideal for ageing.

The breed in this *cru* is again evident in Clos St-Denis, which combines finesse and charm with a certain chewy quality, *mâche*. It is difficult to place Clos des Lambrays at this precise moment, as about a third of the vineyard was replanted in 1980 and gradually a proper rotation of new plantations will have to be created – under the previous owners, nothing had been done for decades, and the average age of the vines was 70 years, a most unhealthy state of affairs. The wines are already fruity and attractive, but we know they will gain in depth in future years, depending also on what selections are made. Bonnes Mares from Morey is very limestone influenced, and can appear quite hard and taut when young, full of breed, and opening out with age.

Most of the Premiers Crus are on the northern side of Morey; they share characteristics with the Grands Crus, but lack their richness and staying power, while offering immense flavour and earthy scents. They say the taste is of almonds and cherrystones. The straight Morey appellation even tips over a little on to the eastern side of the Route Nationale – the wines can be delicious and redolent of red fruits.

A Personal Selection of Morey-St-Denis Producers

Domaine Pierre Amiot

Clos de la Roche with vibrant fruit, tastes of plums and lingering flavours.

Bouchard Père & Fils

Their Clos de la Roche is not a domain wine, but they are important buyers of grapes. The wine has finesse and structure, somewhat austere when young, which is how it should be.

Domaine Georges Bryczek

Morey-St-Denis from this domain is always highly seductive and full of smokiness and all the red fruits.

Domaine Clair-Daü

Their Bonnes Mares, which essentially lies in Morey, is always big and structured, needing time.

Domaine Dujac

A domain run with the greatest intelligence by Jacques Seysses who, not being born Burgundian, perhaps finds it easier to try new innovations in his quest for quality. The Morey-St-Denis Premier Cru is always splendid, strawberries and redcurrants, while the Clos de la Roche has glorious projection of fruit and complexity – farmyards and violets! Sometimes the colours are not deep, but the flavours will overwhelm and there is never excess alcohol. Also fine Clos St-Denis and Bonnes Mares.

Domaine Georges Lignier

This domain very often produces the "essence of the grape" taste – beautiful, clear, breedy wine. The Clos des Ormes is always a fine bottle, full of liquorice flavours, and there is also Clos St-Denis, Clos de la Roche and Bonnes Mares.

Domaine Ponsot

Clos de la Roche which always needs many years to develop, one-dimensional in youth, but a lovely scent and distinction when mature. Occasionally there has been oxidation, perhaps a bottling fault. The domain also makes white Monts-Luisants from the Chardonnay, but I have never seen a memorable bottle, perhaps because they have been too youthful.

Ropiteau

This house sells a Clos de la Roche, bottled for them at the property, which is all finesse and breed – delicious and classy.

Domaine G. Roumier
Clos de la Bussière which takes its time to develop as it is all raw fruit when young.

Domaine Armand Rousseau
Charles Rousseau's magic touch rarely deserts him – the wines are brimming with scent and class and luscious fruit. Clos de la Roche which is really superb, especially if given 5–10 years, even in good to moderate vintages, and then swirled in the glass.

Domaine Bernard Serveau
Les Sorbès which needs time in good years, but there is texture to match the framework.

Clos de Tart
Solely owned by the Mommessin family, this Clos produces remarkable wines. When young, they have a nose of violets, later a fascinating mixture of leather, humus and spices. The taste is redcurrants and vanilla when young (100% new barrels are used) and spicy concentration when mature. Only occasionally has there been a certain clumsiness and perhaps an excess of alcohol. These are burgundies to lay down.

● ○ CHAMBOLLE-MUSIGNY

1983 production:	Chambolle-Musigny (red)	*4,972 hectolitres*
	Musigny (red)	*299 hectolitres*
	Musigny (white)	*20 hectolitres*

Premiers Crus: Bonnes Mares (part), Les Amoureuses, Les Charmes, Les Cras (part), Les Borniques, Les Baudes, Les Plantes, Les Hauts-Doix, Les Châtelots, Les Gruenchers, Les Groseilles, Les Fuées, Les Lavrottes, Derrière-la-Grange, Les Noirots, Les Sentiers, Les Fousselottes, Aux Beaux-Bruns, Les Combottes, Aux Combottes, Les Chabiots, Les Carrières, Aux Echanges (part), La Combe d'Orveaux.

The Grands Crus are Musigny, of which there is a tiny amount of white wine, and Bonnes Mares, 13.7ha of which fall in this commune. The vineyards of Chambolle-Musigny lie at between 250–300 metres altitude (820–980 feet) on a variety of debris materials, from red alluvial soil to brown limestone. Musigny itself is on an important gradient, varying between 8–14%, necessitating frequent replacing of earth from the bottom to the top of the slope. The subsoil is white oolite on the upper parts and Comblanchien limestone farther down. There is up to 20% pebbles, permeable limestone (giving good drainage and finesse) and some red clay, which gives richness. Le Musigny is, of course, on the southern, Vougeot side of Chambolle, while Bonnes Mares borders Morey-St-Denis to the north. Les Amoureuses, which lies just below Musigny, has a subsoil which is full of geological faults, so that some of the roots go down to a depth of 10 metres (33 feet).

The top wines of Chambolle should have supreme scent and lacy delicacy. The light soil should lead to perfume, elegance and "femininity", rather than Nuits-type power and earthy splendour. The great complexity of the tastes should creep subtly up on you, not knock you for six with a sledgehammer. Of course, the fascinating comparisons are between Musigny and Bonnes Mares, or Musigny and Les Amoureuses, especially when they are made by the same man. Musigny combines a well-constructed framework, underlying body, with enormous subtlety and silky finesse. Bonnes Mares tends to have the more visible body and fat, while Les Amoureuses should be the epitome of elegance. Bonnes Mares has a bouquet which veers entrancingly from violets to the scent of undergrowth, a very Burgundian trait. Overall, in the wines of Chambolle-Musigny, raspberries and spices are often intermingled. The wines should never be robust (if they are, you have reason to be suspicious), but they should have projected scent and tenacity of flavour.

A Personal Selection of Chambolle-Musigny Producers

Domaine Bernard Amiot
Straight Chambolle with all the bouquet and charm which one should get from this appellation.

Domaine G. Barthod-Noëllat
Straight Chambolle and Les Charmes which are floral, spicy and well worth buying.

Domaine Clair-Daü
Fruity Les Amoureuses with a marvellous finish and classy Musigny, delightfully so with the 1980 vintage.

B. & J-M. Delaunay
Particularly delicate, refined selections in Les Chabiots.

Domaine Drouhin-Laroze
The wines are very light, especially in large yield years, but the Bonnes Mares 1983 just oozes delicacy and glorious bouquet.

Domaine Alain Hudelot-Noëllat
Straight Chambolle and Les Charmes which can be explosively good, with great breed and long finish. Just occasionally, there has been too rapid oxidation of the wine after opening, which could indicate a bottling problem (sulphur dioxide level). Everything else with these wines is absolutely lovely.

Domaine Georges Roumier & Fils
Straight Chambolle which is pure fruit and shows great style. There is also a particularly floral Musigny and Bonnes Mares as well as stylish Les Amoureuses.

Domaine Bernard Serveau
Really excellent Chabiots which are infinitely silky. Other producers might learn from this little-vaunted domain.

Domaine des Varoilles
Bonnes Mares which is rich, fat and glossy – exemplary wine which ages in grand style.

Domaine Comte Georges de Vogüé
Les Amoureuses which is floral and sometimes ethereal. On occasions the Musigny is not so very much better, which it should be for the price; at other times, it is magical. Bonnes Mares can combine voluptuousness with backbone. The Musigny Blanc, made from Chardonnay, is good, but the rarity justifies the price more than anything else. However, I do not agree with those who say you could think it was a red wine if blindfolded!

● ○

VOUGEOT

1983 production:	Clos de Vougeot	*1,611 hectolitres*
	Vougeot (red)	*374 hectolitres*
	Vougeot (white)	*53 hectolitres*

Premiers Crus: Les Petits Vougeots, Les Cras (part), Clos de la Perrière.

The Grand Cru is Clos de Vougeot, and this can only be red, whereas the modest quantity of Premiers Crus and Appellation Vougeot wine includes a small amount of white.

The Grand Cru dominates the commune, both by reputation and through its sheer size. It covers 50 hectares and accounts for more than four-fifths of the land under vines in Vougeot. Except for the fact that historically it is a *clos* surrounded by walls, all this land would almost certainly not be classed as Grand Cru, for the soil types and positions on the slope are amazingly disparate. The other drama is that if the Clos was in Bordeaux, it would almost certainly be in the hands of one owner, and not of just under 80. The single proprietor could then select the best *cuvées* of wine, from the *real* Grand Cru parts of the Clos, and make a genuine Grand Vin, perhaps with a second wine being created for the rest. However, this is not to be.

The Clos lies at an altitude of between 240 and 270 metres (785–885 feet), with a gentle 3–4% gradient. The vineyards go right down to the Route Nationale, which makes it the only Grand Cru to be so low on the Côte. It is this part that is especially worrying for those who *do* concern themselves about genuine Grand Cru status in Burgundy, because the soil here is deeper, on alluvial deposits, and not particularly well drained. It is impossible to make wines of intrinsic breed from soil of this composition, but it is just this quality which one seeks in a Grand Cru.

The top part of the Clos is on Bathonian oolitic limestone, with a covering of pebbles and little clay. In the middle of the slope it changes to Bajocian limestone with much more clay, but the pebbles help provide good drainage. There is no doubt that to have a hope of an element of real "class" in your Clos de Vougeot it would be as well to choose proprietors with vineyards in the upper part of the Grand Cru. Unfortunately, however, it is not as simple as that. The hand of man counts, as always, for a great deal, and much also depends on the size of the parcel owned, as vinifying a small amount of wine is always difficult and a certain "mass" is necessary for really satisfactory results. To this end, people with several plots in various parts of the Clos will put their grapes together to make one *cuvée*. This is sometimes beneficial when all the plots are well placed, but in other cases it "dilutes" the "real" Grand Cru plot by mixing it with grapes from a piece of land which would barely merit Premier Cru status in another commune.

There is no doubt that locally the difference between the upper and lower parts of the Clos has always been recognized; apparently, before World War II, there was even talk of taxing the two parts separately, but the idea was not followed through. Certainly, the most reputed *climats* (Musigny de Vougeot, Grand Maupertuis are examples) are in the higher part of the Grand Cru, although judicious blending between complementary plots of land can produce wines of great interest.

Clos de Vougeot should be rich, sometimes even chocolaty, with a powerful background. Some wines have violets on the nose and a liquorice finish, while the very ripe vintages can be redolent of roasted pecans. There should be good "flesh" and generosity, and a long, long finish. However, the wine should not be "massive" in the overwhelming sense – no burgundy should. The aim is to overpower with flavour and texture.

The Premiers Crus share some similarities with Chambolle-Musigny, with finesse and attraction, but without the body of the Clos. The Clos Blanc de Vougeot produces white wines and is in the hands of one owner – for this reason it is difficult to judge if its lack of excitement is due intrinsically to the plot or to the winemaking.

Straight Vougeot Village does not show style, but can be pleasant – many a beginner in wine has mistaken it for Clos de Vougeot.

A Personal Selection of Vougeot Producers

Domaine Robert Arnoux

Clos de Vougeot of a very high standard, and which does not betray its favoured position in the Clos. Rich, truffley and textured.

Domaine Bertagna

The vintages of the last ten years seem to be on the up – really lovely Vougeot Premier Cru, with wonderful bouquet and fruit, and good Clos de la Perrière, with cocoa and chocolate overtones. About half of this vineyard was replanted in the mid-1960s, so it has now "come of age".

Domaine Deroubaix-Indelli

Although not nearly as well placed as some, this is very reliable Clos de Vougeot, delivering the expected length and fruit.

Domaine Drouhin-Laroze

This estate owns plots in some of the best parts of the Clos, but the wines recently have been weak – overcropping?

Domaine Jean Grivot

Clos Vougeot of fine quality and real Grand Cru character. I have been unlucky with the 1980 though.

Domaine Jean Gros

Really superb Clos de Vougeot, classic and rich. Impressive.

Domaine Mongeard-Mugneret

Beautifully placed in the Clos, the wines are usually most honourable, although I did find the 1979 somewhat clumsy, a characteristic this vintage should not display.

Domaine Daniel Rion

Clos de Vougeot which can be really good, such as the 1980, but the 1981 was a disappointment. One to watch, as there is knowledgeable winemaking here.

Domaine G. Roumier

Beautiful, long-lasting wines worthy of the highest acclaim. I will always remember the 1976, which must be one of the best wines of this slightly neurotic vintage.

Domaine des Varoilles

These are classic Clos de Vougeot, big, rich, needing time to develop – a prime example of the improvement in the quality of the wine since the decision to vinify with another owner holding a complementary plot – the "mass" of wine became more important, and the wine immediately took on body, flesh and "gloss".

● FLAGEY-ECHEZEAUX

1983 production: Echézeaux *1,016 hectolitres*
Grands Echézeaux *265 hectolitres*

There are no Premiers Crus as such, although the two Grands Crus can be declassified, and the Village wine from Flagey is sold as Vosne-Romanée. But the glory is in the two Grands Crus. These are really *lieux-dits* which are above Clos de Vougeot and not near the village of Flagey at all. The upper part of Echézeaux, is certainly the best section of the vineyard, but the very size and disparity of this large area means that it sometimes does not reach the standard of the more homogeneous Grands Echézeaux.

The rock structure which underpins Echézeaux is immensely complicated, with lower Bathonian and upper Bajocian limestones in constant interplay. The vineyard of Echézeaux is placed very high for a Grand Cru, but the soil is deep enough, and has good pebbles, for the classification to be justified. However, there is great diversity, with excessive limestone in places, but rich clay and brown chalk in others. There is an enormous difference in gradient between the two Grands Crus, with the upper part of Echézeaux between 13–14% and Grands Echézeaux only 3–4%.

When one tastes a number of Echézeaux against Grands Echézeaux, one tends to think that the difference between the two is overstated. As always in Burgundy, the hand of man counts for so much, and I have had many Echézeaux which were better than their grander brother. In principle, Grands Echézeaux should live longer, with the power and structure to outlast the more elegant Echézeaux. But judicious new wood can give both wines body and, as for finesse, that really can be gained or destroyed forever in the fermenting vat. One should find a touch more complexity of bouquet in mature Grands Echézeaux.

A Personal Selection of Flagey-Echézeaux Producers

Domaine Drouhin
Grands Echézeaux and Echézeaux which have always impressed, earthy, spicy, superb and long-finishing.

Domaine Henri Jayer
Wonderful unfiltered Echézeaux, which is difficult to resist in comparative youth because of its glossy fruit and structured balance, but you know you should keep it!

Domaine Jacqueline Jayer
Echézeaux of glorious scent and lovely full fruit – chewiness even – but you probably would not keep them as long as the above estate. What an exercise in comparison to contemplate for the future!

Domaine Mongeard-Mugneret
Both the Grands Crus are found at this domain, and very fine they are too – not ultimate breed, but big wines.

Domaine de la Romanée-Conti
Here you usually do find that the Echézeaux matures faster than the Grands Echézeaux. 1980, in recent years, was an example, with the Echézeaux lacy and *fin* and seemingly ready very young. Grands Echézeaux often has a taste of raspberry pips. Maybe neither of them will last as their ancestors did – a question of a lack of balance? At their best – the epitome of spicy, gamey richness.

Domaine Robert Sirugue
Remarkable Grands Echézeaux – a small grower to watch.

● ○ VOSNE-ROMANEE

1983 production:

Romanée-Conti	*30 hectolitres*
Romanée	*15 hectolitres*
La Tâche	*100 hectolitres*
Romanée-St-Vivant	*130 hectolitres*
Richebourg	*125 hectolitres*
Vosne-Romanée	*4,012 hectolitres*

(It will immediately be seen that these were exceptionally low yields for 1983, but this commune was hit particularly badly by hail.)

Premiers Crus: Aux Malconsorts, Les Beaux Monts, Les Suchots, La Grand'Rue, Les Gaudichots, Aux Brûlées, Les Chaumes, Aux Raignots Le Clos des Réas.

There is an element of shared vineyards between Vosne and Flagey-Echézeaux, as the straight Appellation Vosne-Romanée comes from both communes. But the splendour of Vosne is its Grands Crus, a matchless yardstick by which to measure other great wines from the Côte de Nuits. However, it sets itself a rough task, since now that the potential of these great growths is known, they are also measured against the best that they themselves can do. If we find them lacking, we have every right to say so, just as the producers feel they have every right to charge very high prices.

The Grands Crus are on the middle part of the slope, where the limestone/clay/pebble mixture is at its most balanced. The ideal size of these pebbles, or small broken stones, is between 2mm and 1cm in diameter. Their presence facilitates good drainage, and the larger ones store heat during the day and help to stop the temperature descending too far at night. Romanée-Conti has brown chalky soil, with clay and irony content – finesse, depth and complexity. Romanée St-Vivant has far deeper soil, with clay but also rich in limestone. Aux Raignots, above La Romanée, has sandier soil, but the limestone rock is close to the surface, so much so that 20 years ago they used explosives to break it up and prevent chlorosis of the vines.

The degree of slope changes, with La Romanée having a gradient of about 16% and Aux Raignots and the top part of Aux Malconsorts between 14 and 15%. The lower part of La Tâche is not on such a marked slope, but the pebble/small stones content ensures perfect drainage. The Vosne vineyard goes up to about 350 metres (1,150 feet).

The tasting differences between the five Grands Crus are, naturally, studied at length – decision making of this sort is one of the least painful parts of the wine business even if it may hurt financially. Romanée-Conti and La Tâche seem to change positions according to the year – in one vintage Romanée-Conti runs away with the honours, in others it is La Tâche which sails straight to the top. What one finds in both, in good years, is an explosive array of sensations on the nose and great persistence on the palate. Truffles, undergrowth, wet earth, sheer voluptuous texture and flavour are all hallmarks of these two Grands Crus. There are also extraordinarily rich Richebourgs, velvet come to life, and astonishing La Romanée and Romanée St-Vivant, but they may not possess quite such a *brutal* amount of aromas and tastes. If you like your senses assailed, these are the wines for you – ascetics stay away. Rubens would have loved them.

La Grand'Rue lies between La Tâche and the Romanée wines, but does not display such depth and breed. As it is in the hands of one owner, it is difficult to say if it has the potential to rise higher – maybe it could. Aux Malconsorts can have great finesse, and Les Suchots and Les Beaux Monts hints of violets. Overall, the top wines of Vosne have an element of *spiciness* which is perhaps unique in Burgundy. It must be that irony, reddish soil. Straight Appellation Vosne is usually perfumed and elegant – it should not be clumsy and thick. There is often a smell of cocoa and chocolate.

A Personal Selection of Vosne-Romanée Producers

Domaine Robert Arnoux

Romanée-St-Vivant and Les Suchots which mix oak, red fruits and violets – much seems to be going right here, but the 1982s are not as good as the best.

Domaine Daniel Bissey

Absolutely perfect Les Beaumonts, with glorious scent, marked by that irony, minerally Vosne character, with a lovely violetty finish.

Bouchard Père & Fils

The family do not own in the Grand Cru Richebourg, but their selections are absolutely impeccable and I have had very great bottles of this wine.

Domaine Jean Grivot

My tasting notes are somewhat mixed on their Vosne wines – some of the weaker years seem a bit too alcoholic. But there are good wines here.

Domaine Jean Gros

Clos des Réas with a stunning bouquet, a real mouthful of flavour. I always seem to strike lucky with this estate.

Domaine Alain Hudelot-Noëllat

Some formidable wines emerge from this domain, including juicy, fat Les Suchots, Romanée-St-Vivant with a spicy, cocoa nose and a taste of toast – an exotic spice bazaar wine with great length – and incredible, rich, velvety Richebourg. *A ne pas manquer.*

Domaine Jacqueline Jayer

Now under the same winemaking "hat" as the Domaine Jean Grivot. Les Rouges always has a splendid bouquet – I like these wines when the violets come through the alcohol.

Domaine Lamarche

Sometimes these wines are too rustic for me – the best can be Malconsorts, but it needs time. Sole owners of La Grand' Rue.

Domaine Latour

Romanée-St-Vivant Les Quatre Journaux has always been a favourite, with some wonderful, flavour-packed wines.

Domaine Manière-Noirot

Les Suchots which is earthy and *sauvage* – lots of spicy appellation character.

Domaine Moillard

Malconsorts which has pleased me more than any of their wines, because it has that Vosne minerally taste and balance and is not just "big".

Domaine Mongeard-Mugneret

There is a rustic side to these wines, but Les Suchots has spiciness on the nose and definite quality on the palate.

Domaine Daniel Rion

Patrice Rion does make very good wines – just occasionally there have been traces of bitterness. I am slightly ambivalent about the 1981s, which have fruit and style nevertheless. But the 1978s! The charm is in comparing Les Chaumes with Les Beaux Monts.

Domaine de la Romanée-Conti

Superlatives abound here, and some of them are justified. When these wines are on form, they do have that "something" extra. Of recent vintages, "pick of the bunch" would be Romanée-St-Vivant Marey-Monge 1979 (violets and truffles), Richebourg 1980 (raspberries and spice on the nose, mouthfuls of truffles on the palate), and La Tâche 1979 (more spiciness, violets and truffles). I do not like it when the alcohol obliterates all that truffled fruit on the finish. The 1982s look good, although it is early days. Avoid the 1975s (which are no worse than anyone else's but the domain somehow thinks they were exempt from the troubles of this vintage!), the 1977s and the 1981s. La Tâche 1962 and 1952 are of those experiences made in heaven. The 1971s are opulence itself. Romanée-Conti was replanted in 1947 – previous vintages were on ungrafted vines – and 1952 was the first vintage after the replanting.

Domaine de la SCI du Château de Vosne-Romanée

This estate is owned by the Liger-Belair family, but the *élevage*, bottling and distribution is done by Bouchard Père & Fils. Les Raignots and La Romanée are the wines and they have the flavour and body to last beautifully.

● ○

NUITS-ST-GEORGES

1983 production: Red *10,747 hectolitres*
White *24 hectolitres*

Premiers Crus: (from the commune of Nuits) Les St-Georges, Les Vaucrains, Les Cailles, Les Poirets, Les Pruliers, Les Hauts Pruliers (part), Aux Murgers, La Richemone, Les Chaboeufs, Les Perrières, La Roncière, Les Procès, Rue de Chaux, Aux Boudots, Aux Cras, Aux Chaignots, Aux Thorey (part), Aux Vignes Rondes, Aux Bousselots, Les Poulettes, Les Crots (part), Les Vallerots (part), Aux Champs Perdrix (part), Perrière-Noblot (part), Les Damodes (part), Chaines-Carteaux (part), Aux Argillats. (From the commune of Prémeaux) Clos de la Maréchale, Clos Arlot, Les Argillières, Les Grandes Vignes, Aux Corvées, Les Forêts, Les Didiers, Aux Perdrix.

Nuits-St-Georges may be the most evocative name in Burgundy. It certainly is for me. A Nuits-St-Georges Les Argillats ensnared me for ever, led me to realize what wine and taste could be, and taught me to link the brain with the senses. It also made me love Burgundy, the whole blend of landscape and people and history. Perhaps most important of all, it helped me to reject wines which do the region no honour.

The top *crus* are on the southern side of Nuits towards Prémeaux, but that should not overshadow those other good vineyards on the northern side towards Vosne-Romanée.

The nuances of taste between the most exciting of the Premiers Crus (which some would class as Grands Crus should there ever be a "reshuffle") follow the subtle shifts in soil makeup. The overall picture is marl, intermingled with sand and pebbles which have come away from the hard calcareous summit of the slope. Mid-slope is where the silt and scree over marl formula works best, so here lie the best growths. In the Nuits-Prémeaux area, the subsoil is Bathonian limestone with outcrops of Bajocian limestone covered with clay. The two vineyards nearest the outskirts of Nuits, Rue de Chaux and Les Procès, have significant clay content and are also pebbly. La Roncière is on lighter, more gravelly soil, leading to earlier ripening (clay is a cold soil). The subsoil here is composed of a vein of Comblanchien hard limestone. Les Poirets and Les Cailles have deep clay soil with few pebbles, Les Perrières is higher with more pebbles. Les St-Georges has more sand in the mixture, less heavy soil than at Les Porets, while Les Vaucrains combines heavy, rich soil with considerable sand and pebbles for balance.

The northern Nuits vineyards veer more to Vosne in soil type. There are outcrops of Bajocian limestone with some alluvial soil. La Richemone has lighter, pebbly soil, while Aux Chaignots possesses more clay with the pebbles – this is further accentuated as one goes towards Nuits and the soil becomes heavier. Les Damodes looks towards Vosne in the type of wine it produces. Aux Argillats faces due south, while the general exposure of this area is southeast.

This, then, is the nursery of those great, rich, intoxicating Nuits wines. They have a severe backbone to them, an "irony" structure and a minerally gaminess which makes no compromises. That is why anodyne, soupy Nuits is a travesty – good Nuits is not merely meant to soothe, it is meant to challenge. Les Vaucrains is the slowest to mature, the most tannic and closed when young, but oh, so majestic when mature. Les St-Georges is the most complete wine, combining finesse with power, positively brambly and multidimensional in bouquet and taste. Les Poirets is known for its pure Nuits *goût de terroir*, earthy, irony, wild, but generous and all-enveloping underneath. Les Cailles is more elegant, balanced and rich in texture, while Les Pruliers has strong Nuits character, softening with bottle age. Les Perrières and La Roncière (the proof that blackberries are not just fanciful!) may not have the colour of their neighbours, but make up for that with a touch more delicacy. On the other side of Nuits, there is wonderful flavour, if less breed. Aux Chaignots and Aux Boudots give lovely bottles, wines of body and character. There is less flesh but plenty of olfactory interest in La Richemone and Les Damodes, more subtly Vosne, less sturdily Nuits.

A Personal Selection of Nuits-St-Georges Producers

Domaine Robert Chevillon

Les Vaucrains and Les Cailles which usually match up to one's expectations (if not one's dreams) of Nuits, with strong black cherries and structure.

Domaine Faiveley

It is sometimes quite difficult to spot the difference between a Faiveley domaine wine and one from their important négoce business, as the word "Domaine" does not actually appear on the label. But Clos de la Maréchale, ler cru, is solely owned by the Faiveley family and a cornerstone of their extensive estate. The wine is always powerful, occasionally a touch too alcoholic, but loaded with Nuits character and earthy flavour.

Château Gris

Owned by a shipper, Lupé-Cholet, Château Gris is not a Grand Cru, as it says on the label (there are none in Nuits), but an enclave in the Premier Cru Les Crots. There are impressive bottles – recent vintages are marked by new wood in youth and promise well.

Domaine Jean Grivot

Linked to Domaine Jacqueline Jayer inasmuch as Etienne Grivot, the son of Jean, has been doing the winemaking for both since the 1982 vintage. Marvellous Les Lavières (Vosne influenced) and Les Pruliers which is true Nuits, but I did find the 1982 a bit heavy and sweet (extra chaptalization?).

Domaine Henri Gouges

A visit to the Gouges cellars is a liquid lesson in how this appellation should taste. Rich and fruity Les Pruliers, earthy, enveloping Clos des Poirets, deep, tannic Les Vaucrains, and sublime Les St-Georges. There is also the strong and forceful white La Perrière, made from a white mutation of the Pinot Noir and not at all like Chardonnay.

Domaine Henri Jayer

Straight Nuits-St-Georges which is unfiltered, with a stunning colour, power and lots of raw fruit – these wines need years.

Domaine Jacqueline Jayer

Straight Nuits-St-Georges of extraordinary quality, where the complexity, concentration and heady bouquet come from a vineyard with a goodly proportion of old vines – they uproot a fiftieth each year, so they get perfect rotation.

Domaine Xavier Liger-Belair

Les St-Georges with body, but without the breed of this *cru*.

Domaine Machard de Gramont

The wines are always stylish, going for flavour and elegance rather than massive body. Les Hauts Pruliers is most successful.

Domaine Manière-Noirot

I have not seen enough of this domain to build up a picture of consistency, but their Les Damodes seems on the right track.

Domaine Alain Michelot

Les Chaignots which is good and earthy, although somewhat overawed by oak, even after five years.

Domaine Moillard

Clos de Thorey which has minerally Nuits character, vanillin and violets. The alcohol is fairly massive, but in the 1983s that is expected – the wines need time.

Hospices de Nuits

A charitable foundation with an auction which usually falls on the Sunday before Palm Sunday. As with its counterpart in Beaune, all depends on the *élevage*. The wines all come from Premiers Crus in Nuits. Dufouleur bottled a good Les Fleurières, Cuvée des Soeurs Hospitalières.

Domaine Henri Remoriquet

Les Allots which is full of Nuits scent and flavour. The 1982 was Tasteviné. It stressed the natural, easy fruit of this vintage and had not succumbed to any temptation to "put on weight".

Domaine Daniel Rion

This is a domain to watch as, within the confines of the weather (for instance, I found the 1981s dry and "mousy"), fine bottles are made, especially Les Vignes Rondes and Haut Pruliers.

Domaine Charles Viénot

Clos St-Marc – owned by the above firm, but the wine distributed by Bouchard Père & Fils – good bouquet and crunchy fruit.

● ○ PREMEAUX

The fate of Prémeaux is inextricably linked with that of Nuits-St-Georges, and the vineyard area is broken down into the following proportions:

Nuits-St-Georges Premiers Crus	*42.25 hectares*
Nuits-St-Georges	*11.79 hectares*
Côte de Nuits-Villages	*4.97 hectares*

There are a large number of *clos* among the Premiers Crus (listed under Nuits-St-Georges). Differences in taste exist between the Premiers Crus, but too often these are difficult to detect, as the style seems to be "solid négociant" rather than subtle and distinctive – these *clos* tend to be monopolies owned by the important négociant houses of Nuits. In principle, Clos des Argillières is often the most complete wine, combining structure with elegance – the vineyard is on rock with thin soil. This occurs again at the Clos Arlot, part of which is on a steep slope, whereas the Clos de la Maréchale is practically flat with deeper soil. Aux Corvées is on clay-limestone soil. There are many old vines in the area.

● ○ COTE DE NUITS-VILLAGES

1983 production: Red *5,997 hectolitres*
White *20 hectolitres*

The villages which make up this appellation are: Brochon, Comblanchien, Corgoloin, Fixin and Prémeaux (Prissey). Of these, only Fixin can choose to sell its wines either under the name of Fixin itself or Côte de Nuits-Villages. There has long been discussion and political manoeuvre as to whether Marsannay, Couchey and even Chenôve should have the right to the Côte de Nuits-Villages appellation, but so far promotion has been resisted. This is a pity, if only because this higher recognition would help to prevent the ever-spreading mushroom growth from Dijon of supermarkets, garages and all the other paraphernalia deemed necessary for comfortable modern living – Pessac in the Graves is under the same threat from the city of Bordeaux.

The wines can be quite blunt and tannic when young, but the graph of development is more rapid than with a better appellation, so at 3–5 years they are usually at their most appealing. The danger is that most Côte de Nuits-Villages is a blend of wines from varying sources, so one can end up with a very neutral brew.

For those interested in marble quarries, and their unsightly tips, they are spread out by the side of the road and up the Côte between Prémeaux and Ladoix. Comblanchien marble is a pink-beige colour, and it was used to build the Paris Opéra, the Palais de Justice in Brussels and, more recently, Orly Airport.

● ○ HAUTES COTES DE NUITS AND HAUTES COTES DE BEAUNE

1983 production: Hautes Côtes de Beaune *16,889 hectolitres*
Red *16,291hl*; White *598hl*
Hautes Côtes de Nuits *13,123 hectolitres*
Red *12,049hl*; White *1,074hl*

These are the villages which have the right to the Hautes Côtes de Beaune appellation: Baubigny, Bouze les Beaune, Cirey les Nolay, Cormot, Echevronne, Fussey, La Rochepot, Magny les Villers, Mavilly Mandelot, Meloisey, Nantoux, Nolay and Vauchignon. In Saône et Loire, the following villages are included: Change, Créot, Epertully, Paris l'Hôpital and part of Cheilly les Maranges, Dézize les Maranges and Sampigny les Maranges.

Much of this area is plateau. However, between Mavilly Mandelot and La Rochepot, the vineyards are on slopes at an altitude of 350–450 metres (1,170–1,470 feet). As a result, picking on the Hautes Côtes is about a week later than on the Côte d'Or. The geological debris favours vine growing and the slopes face east-south-east, which is very important at such heights. The plateau of Meloisey has brown limestone soil and is well sited for making wines of quality.

These are the villages which have the right to the Hautes Côtes de Nuits appellation: Arcénant, Bévy, Chaux, Chévannes, Collonges les Bévy, Curtil Vergy, L'Etang Vergy, Magny les Villers, Marey les Fussey, Messanges, Meuilley, Reule Vergy, Villars Fontaine, Villers la Faye.

Some of the best communes are on gentle slopes, sheltered from the west winds; examples are Villers la Faye, Magny les Villers. At Villers there is deep, brown limestone, which gives quality. It must be said that vineyards hovering round the 400 metre mark (1,300 feet) are at a disadvantage when it comes to consistent quality production, and they need the balancing benefit of the best possible site.

The wines from these two areas have the right to the basic Bourgogne appellation; only after tasting can the Hautes Côtes label be awarded.

A Personal Selection of Hautes Côtes producers

Domaine François Charles
Lovely raspberryish Hautes Côtes de Beaune from Nantoux.

Delaunay
Excellent wines from family and other vineyards in the Hautes Côtes de Nuits.

Domaine Guy Dufouleur
Vibrant, fruity Hautes Côtes de Nuits, reminiscent of loganberries.

Domaine Geisweiler
Large vineyards at Bévy produce fairly light Hautes Côtes de Nuits.

Les Caves des Hautes Côtes
The cooperative now vinifies about 25% of the total production, and the quality is very good. Recently I have been immensely impressed by their wines from the two Hautes Côtes, and consider them some of the best value in Burgundy.

Domaine Bernard Hudelot/Domaine de Montmain
Splendid Hautes Côtes de Nuits from Villars Fontaine, and good Chardonnay too.

Domaine Lucien Jacob
A leading figure in the Hautes Côtes, with much official clonal experimentation at his estate at Echevronne. He also finds time to make good Hautes Côtes de Beaune (and Savigny too).

Domaine Jean Joliot & Fils
Hautes Côtes de Beaune from Nantoux, with a scent of violets and the fruit and body to be delicious at 4–5 years old.

Château Mandelot
This is a most agreeable wine, vinified and distributed by Bouchard Père & Fils.

Domaine Naudin
Commendable Hautes Côtes de Nuits from Magny les Villers. Also very good Hautes Côtes de Beaune from Henri Naudin-Ferrand.

Domaine Michel Serveau
This grower in La Rochepot makes superb Hautes Côtes de Beaune, gloriously scented and fruity. Exemplary for the appellation.

Domaine Thevenot-le Brun & Fils
Hautes Côtes de Nuits Clos du Vignon which is attractive and very easy to drink.

● ○ LADOIX-SERRIGNY

1983 production: Red wine *1,855 hectolitres*
White wine *191 hectolitres*

Premiers Crus: La Micaude, La Corvée, Le Clou d'Orge, Les Joyeuses, Bois Roussot, Basses Mourettes and Hautes Mourettes.

The appellation name is really that of two villages, of which Ladoix is more important viticulturally. It marks the northern end of the Côte de Beaune. This is another of Burgundy's schizophrenic appellations, because much of its production can be classified as Grand and Premier Cru Aloxe-Corton, and it is rare to see Ladoix-Serrigny on a label. This wine is more often than not declassified into Côte de Beaune-Villages.

Brown limestone soils are suitable for the production of red wines, whereas white marl is better for the Chardonnay. Gréchons and Les Fautrieres, facing east-south-east and high up on the slope, produce good white wines.

The best-placed *climats* of Ladoix provide wines of body and character, derived from microclimate and a favourable position on the slope. Perhaps they are the bridge between the two Côtes. The names to trust are those that make good Aloxe, but there are some terrible "apologies" for fine burgundy in this area – overdoses of alcohol seem rampant. The Domaine Chevalier makes honourable Ladoix, with the bouquet perhaps even better than the taste.

● ○ ALOXE-CORTON

1983 production: Red wine *4,489 hectolitres*
White wine *26 hectolitres*

Premiers Crus in the commune of Ladoix-Serrigny: Les Maréchaudes, La Toppe au Vert, La Coutière, Les Grandes Lolières, Les Petites Lolières, Basses Mourettes. **Premiers Crus in the commune of**

Aloxe-Corton: Les Valozières (part), Les Chaillots (part), Les Fournières, Les Maréchaudes (part), Les Paulands (part), Les Vercots, Les Guérets.

The small village of Aloxe-Corton nestles beneath the Massif du Corton, with the vines so close to the houses that one would not be surprised to see them creeping through the doorways. The village has a share in the two glittering Grands Crus of Corton and Corton-Charlemagne, while the Premiers Crus and the straight Village wine spill over into Ladoix-Serrigny.

A further elaboration of the appellation edicts allows these vineyards to use the distinguished label Corton: in Ladoix-Serrigny – Les Vergennes (part), Le Rognet-Corton (part); in Aloxe-Corton – Le Corton, Le Clos du Roi, Les Renardes, Les Bressandes, Les Maréchaudes (part), Les Paulands (part), Les Chaumes, La Vigne au Saint, Les Meix Lallemand, Les Meix (part), Les Combes (part), Le Charlemagne (part), Les Pougets (part), Les Languettes (part), Les Chaumes et la Voierosse, Les Fiétres, Les Perrières, Les Grèves; in Pernand-Vergelesses – Le Charlemagne part) (red wines only).

The parts of this great bluff reserved for making red Corton are those where the soil is red and irony, while the white is made from more calcareous marl. As the base is rock and the soil is poor and thin, yields are not big. Corton-Bressandes is partly on an old quarry, always a feature of very hard limestone. Corton-Charlemagne is produced on the top of the hill, where the soil is whiter, with the Chardonnay planted right up to the Bois de Corton. Of course, the subsoil has an origin of lava, as can be seen in *crus* such as Clos du Roi or Les Perrières. In many of the Premiers Crus, such as Les Maréchaudes, Les Valozières, Les Chaillots, Les Fournières, and Les Vercots the soil is somewhat ferruginous and deeper. The straight Aloxe-Corton wines come from quite deep, red-brown soil, with more sand in the subsoil due to an alluvial influence.

These three famous appellations are spread over the three communes as the figures in the table below show:

	Hectares	Ares	Centiares
In Aloxe-Corton:			
Appellation Aloxe-Corton	111	82	
Appellation Aloxe-Corton ler Cru	29	17	
Appellation Corton	109	64	
Appellation Corton-Charlemagne	45	68	
In Pernand-Vergelesses:			
Appellation Pernand-Vergelesses	136	74	61
Appellation Pernand-Vergelesses ler Cru	56	51	09
AC Corton, Corton-Charlemagne & Charlemagne	17	25	89
In Ladoix-Serrigny:			
Appellation Ladoix-Serrigny	121		
Appellation Ladoix-Serrigny ler Cru	14	38	
Appellation Aloxe-Corton ler Cru	10	76	
Appellation Corton & Corton-Charlemagne	22	42	

Red Corton is the most powerful, often the most tannic of all the Côte de Beaune red wines. It needs time for its bouquet to develop and for a certain youthful hardness to soften. There is almost a thickness to it, a texture of mouth-coating body and richness. Corton-Clos du Roi is very structured in youth, even quite severe, but opens out majestically. Corton-Bressandes is rounder and fatter, with enormous flattering flavour on the palate. Corton-Renardes is meant to have a *côté animal*, which just might be autosuggestion, but there is a raw, gamey side to it, and always punchy flavour, which is a feature of these top growths. Truffles, too, can be detected in the top red wines from ripe years.

The Premiers Crus do not have this depth or richness, but some have finesse and elegance. It is a mistake to "make" them big when that quality is not intrinsically theirs, but there should be a pleasant fullness in good years. After all, a Premier Cru such as Les Valozières is just a path's distance away from Corton-Bressandes. Straight Aloxe-Corton will obviously have less style, but can be a good, generous bottle.

The sheer, flinty glory of Corton-Charlemagne is extolled under Pernand-Vergelesses, and nothing can replace that heady, honeyed bouquet and molten taste. Perhaps there is volcanic richness in it. White Aloxe-Corton is a rarity; the Domaine Senard makes it from the Pinot Beurot (Pinot Gris or Tokay d'Alsace). Planted here, the wine is round, powerful and alcoholic, not at all like Chardonnay.

A Personal Selection of Aloxe-Corton Producers

Domaine Adrien Belland
Corton Grèves, which seems to have a great future as the wines in extreme youth display such depth of fruit.

Domaine Bonneau du Martray
Often not very deep in colour, this Corton nevertheless shows lovely Pinot Noir character, if not always great depth.

Bouchard Père & Fils (Domaines du Château de Beaune)
Majestic Le Corton which can last and last.

Domaine Hubert Bouzereau-Gruère
Corton Bressandes with a smell of undergrowth and wet foxes. Oaky vanilla too, and good structure.

Domaine Chandon de Briailles
Corton Bressandes which can have glorious fruity depth, but there is something "hit and miss" with this domain, hence the oxidation detected on the Clos du Roi.

Domaine Chevalier
Corton Le Rognet and straight Aloxe-Corton which are really worthy of attention.

Domaine Dubreuil-Fontaine
Corton Bressandes and Clos du Roi which do not impose by their colour but most certainly do by their flavour.

Domaine Michel Gaunoux
Corton Renardes which is usually very big, strapping wine – some people think this is bliss, I think it is merely good.

Domaine Antonin Guyon
A fine span of Corton wines, all with true fruit style and very often with marked breed.

Domaine Louis Jadot
Corton Pougets displays good, juicy fruit, sometimes with a taste of strawberries. Corton Bressandes is just as reliable.

Domaine Louis Latour
Château Corton-Grancey is the jewel in the crown, and there are indeed some fine vintages – recently the 1981 was beautifully gamey and flavoursome. Sometimes the Corton Clos de la Vigne au Saint has more finesse and satiny sheen and there are some superb bottles. Aloxe-Corton Les Chaillots can taste of plums.

Domaine Moillard
The 1983s are massive and would seem to promise well. Have patience with the Clos du Roi. Corton-Charlemagne with a nose of mayblossom and cardamom and a texture of honey – it usually develops far more quickly than that of Louis Latour.

Domaine Parent
Corton Les Renardes with character and a kernel of flavour to it.

Domaine Rapet
Magnificent Corton, opulent and tannic in top years, less consistent when Nature is not so kind.

Domaine Daniel Senard
The Corton Clos des Meix is probably the best wine. Some successes here, but some disappointments.

Domaine Tollot-Beaut
Straight Aloxe-Corton which is a very good mouthful.

Domaine Tollot-Voarick
Fine Corton Languettes and Aloxe-Corton Les Brunettes, where the plums fight for dominance with the cherries.

Domaine Michel Voarick
Corton Bressandes and Clos du Roi which can be somewhat pedestrian, but can also rise to something altogether better.

● ○ PERNAND-VERGELESSES

1983 production:	Corton (red)	*3,177 hectolitres*
	(white)	*59 hectolitres*
	Corton-Charlemagne	*1,651 hectolitres*
	Pernand-Vergelesses (red)	*2,876 hectolitres*
	(white)	*776 hectolitres*

Premiers Crus: Ile des Hautes Vergelesses, Les Basses Vergelesses, Creux de la Net (part), Les Fichots, Caradeux (part).

This pretty village, in the shadow of the *montagne* of Corton, has rather a schizophrenic existence, sharing as it does the red Grand Cru Corton and the white Grand Cru Corton-Charlemagne with the villages of Aloxe-Corton and Ladoix-Serrigny. Pernand also shares with Aloxe-Corton the currently unused white Grand Cru appellation of Charlemagne. The Pernand-Vergelesses side of the great hill of Corton is better suited to producing great white wines than red. The soil here is less ferruginous, with a higher limestone content in the marl, and a fair idea of what should be planted where on the Corton hill can be obtained by the naked eye – where the soil is redder, it should be Pinot Noir, where it is more chalky white, the Chardonnay is unsurpassed. The "nervy" character of Corton-Charlemagne is undoubtedly due to vine roots going down into the rock to a depth of 2 metres (7 feet) or more, with slight differences in the ultimate taste according to whether the soil is blue or white marl, the former a touch richer and more perfumed, the latter more dry and flinty. The best site is farther away from the village, facing south-south-west. Les Vergelesses comes from soil with about one-third clay in its content, leading to firmer red wines than lesser *crus*.

Corton-Charlemagne is probably the slowest to mature of all Burgundian white wines, and it is nearly always drunk too young. With bottle-age, its great bouquet, often slightly peppery in youth, turns to grilled almonds and cinnamon. There is a tautness about top Corton-Charlemagne which is not found in the richer, more unctuous Montrachet. White Pernand-Vergelesses is, naturally, much softer and should be drunk relatively young. Red Corton is, of course, a *vin de garde* to rival the Grands Crus of the Côte de Nuits, but red Pernand-Vergelesses at Premier Cru level is much softer, more seductive, with its bouquet of raspberries and violets, sometimes with a taste of quince jelly on the palate. Together with Savigny-lès-Beaune, these are the *prettiest* wines of the Côte de Beaune. Straight Villages Pernand is more earthy and less charming, even harsh in some years, but usually good value. Pernand has long made a speciality of its Aligoté, planted on marly, well-sited slopes which gives it a round, full taste.

A Personal Selection of Pernand-Vergelesses Producers

Domaine Besancenot-Mathouillet
Picked later than his Beaune wines of the domain (vines on the slopes need longer to attain ripeness), there is sometimes an earthiness in the taste, but a good deal of fruit too.

Domaine Bonneau du Martray
Lying at the very heart of Pernand-Vergelesses and Aloxe-Corton, and probably the original estate of the Emperor Charlemagne, this is a remarkable domain with fabulous Corton-Charlemagne. They even make stunning wine in medium-quality years such as 1974. Warm, fruity Corton, not of a massive style.

Domaine Chandon de Briailles
Somehow their Ile des Vergelesses should be better. In recent vintages, the fruit seems to be masked (caskiness?) and the whole rather "unmarried".

Domaine Chanson
Excellent Les (Basses) Vergelesses, floral and redolent of violets.

Domaine Chapuis
Delicious Corton-Charlemagne, not as long-lived as some.

Delaunay
Make particularly good selections from Les Basses Vergelesses.

Domaine Dubreuil-Fontaine
The Clos Berthet red is perfumed and tempting at 4–5 years; the white is absolutely lovely at 2–4 years. A delicious pair.

Domaine Jacques Germain
François Germain makes superb white Pernand, all rich cinnamon and honey. Utterly delicious.

Domaine Antonin Guyon (Domaine de la Guyonnière)
Red and white wines of finesse.

Domaine Laleure-Piot
This is really a white-wine specialist, including very good Aligoté; but this should not denigrate the reds.

Domaine Louis Latour
Consistently fine Ile des Vergelesses, often violets and strawberries. Exemplary Corton-Charlemagne, built to last.

Domaine Rapet Père & Fils
Very good wines, with the test of time behind them.

Domaine Maurice Rollin & Fils
Their Ile des Vergelesses can be fairly raw and rustic, but the fruit and natural flavour carry it through. The domain also produces good Aligoté.

Domaine Michel Voarick
Quite big for Pernand-Vergelesses, with the taste often better than the bouquet – nice texture and flavour of cherries.

● ○ SAVIGNY-LES-BEAUNE

1983 production: Savigny red *10,728 hectolitres*
Savigny white *544 hectolitres*

Premiers Crus: Aux Vergelesses, Bas Marconnets, Les Jarrons (formerly Les Hauts Jarrons and La Dominode), Basses Vergelesses, Les Lavières, Aux Gravains, Les Peuillets (part), Aux Guettes (part), Les Talmettes, Les Charnières, Aux Fourneaux (part), Aux Clous (part), Aux Serpentières (part), Les Narbantons, Les Hauts Marconnets, Les Hauts Jarrons, Redrescut (part), Les Rouvrettes (part), Petits Godeaux (part).

Technically, it should always be Savigny-lès-Beaune, with the accent, as *lès* comes from the Latin *latus*, presumably "at the side" of Beaune. Savigny is a beautiful Burgundian village, to be glimpsed from the autoroute, but only to be savoured if visited at leisure. After Beaune and Pommard, Savigny produces more red wine than anywhere else on the Côte de Beaune, and although the wines do not have the staying power of the best examples of its rivals in size, there are some exquisite bottles of Savigny.

The village itself is at the entrance of the lovely valley of Fontaine-Froide. The vineyards can be neatly divided into two parts – those on the Pernand-Vergelesses side and those on the Beaune side. The former group forms a broad sweep under the charmingly named wooded summit of the Bois de Noël, facing due south, and including Aux Vergelesses, Les Lavières, Aux Gravains, Aux Serpentières and Aux Guettes. Here the soil is rough and gravelly, with irony oolite above. Below Les Lavières, it is straight appellation territory, with reddish brown limestone, some clay and few pebbles – the drainage is thus less good, the wines a little blunter. On the opposite hillside, on the slopes of Mont Battois, there are vineyards such as Les Narbantons, Les Jarrons, Les Marconnets and Les Peuillets, facing east-north-east. Here the soil is more sandy and less pebbly, with deeper debris at the foot of the slopes.

The great mark of good Savigny is a heady perfume, a searing scent of violets, raspberries, flowers and red fruits. There is sometimes an enchanting lightness of touch in Savigny, an enticing quality that is particularly seductive when the wines are quite youthful. The wines of the Pernand side, Premiers Crus such as Les Lavières and Aux Guettes, should often be drunk young to see this unforgettable charm, while the Premiers Crus on the Beaune side, Les Narbantons, Bas Marconnets, Les Peuillets and la Dominode are more solid, they have a bit more "stuffing" and that bouquet might take a few more years to reach its apogee. A great deal depends, as always, on the age of the vineyard. I remember drinking remarkable 20-year-old La Dominode from venerable vines. The rare whites can be charming and floral when drunk young – there is some Pinot Blanc here as well as Chardonnay. It must be nostalgia which causes some producers to retain the Pinot Blanc, as in Burgundy the Chardonnay certainly makes more interesting wine. The Pinot Blanc seems to be at its best in Alsace.

A Personal Selection of Savigny-lès-Beaune Producers

Domaine Simon Bize
Copybook wines which could provide a valuable lesson to some other producers. The son of the house, Patrick Bize, makes Les Vergelesses, Les Marconnets and Aux Guettes – the latter redolent of violets. These are true, frank, fruity wines – delicious at 4 to 5 years old.

Domaine Henri Boillot
Ile des Vergelesses which stays very young in bottle, frank, even raw fruit – very natural and a good glassful.

Domaine Capron-Manieux
White and red Savigny, which have promise but are sometimes a bit rustic – perhaps the red could spend less time in cask?

B. and J-M. Delaunay
These reputed *commissionnaires en vins* make superb selections in Peuillets and Aux Guettes.

Domaine G. Girard-Vollot
Straight Savigny and Les Peuillets which both have good fruit projection on the nose and satisfying taste.

Domaine Pierre Guillemot
Outstanding examples of Savigny, including a white which is immensely flowery and enchantingly full of fresh fruit.

Domaine Jean-Marc Pavelot
Straight Savigny and Aux Guettes with real potential for quality.

Domaine Parent
Les Lavières reminiscent of raspberries.

Domaine Tollot-Beaut
Champ-Chevry with a rich, sweet, old-style Pinot nose, and lovely depth and length on the palate.

● ○ BEAUNE

1983 production:	Beaune red	*13,701 hectolitres*
	Beaune white	*419 hectolitres*

Premiers Crus: Les Marconnets, Les Fèves, Les Bressandes, Les Grèves, Les Teurons, Le Clos des Mouches, Champs Pimont, Clos du Roi (part), Au Coucherias (part), En l'Orme, En Genêt, Les Perrières, A l'Ecu, Les Cent Vignes, Les Toussaints, Sur les Grèves, Aux Cras, Le Clos de la Mousse, Les Chouacheux, Les Boucherottes, Les Vignes Franches, Les Aigrots, Pertuisots, Tiélandry or Clos Landry, Les Sizies, Les Avaux, Les Reversées, Le Bas des Teurons, Les Seurey, La Mignotte, Montée-Rouge (part), Les Montrevenots (part), Blanche Fleur (part), Les Epenottes (part).

To many, Beaune is the hub of Burgundy, and certainly it must feel so to the bevy of historic firms which make up *le négoce beaunois*. It is everything a provincial town should be – a historic and artistic centre, a vibrant market town and an active business community. Wine has made it international and even those who will never visit it utter its name with awe. And yet the remarkable ramparts seem to keep its essential spirit to itself. The summer streets may be crowded with cars bearing foreign numberplates, and for three days each November the Hospices de Beaune Auction is a magnet for both the wine trade and amateur wine lovers; but for the rest of the year, Beaune is quiet, even sleepy, with everyone battened down in their homes by nightfall. People work hard in Beaune, and wine is a serious business. The Hospices Sale engenders a heady atmosphere of pushing and bustling, lights over the cobbled streets and cafés brimming, but a more typical Beaune scene is to see that same Auction Hall transformed into the Saturday morning market, full of fruit, vegetables, cheese and charcuterie.

After having visited the magnificent Hôtel-Dieu, and seen tapestries, flamboyantly tiled roofs and beautiful woodwork, just wander through the streets looking at the fine town houses and the handsome churches. By day you will see the intricate stonework, by night the most lovely buildings and churches are suffused with soft light. This is when Beaune is magic, with the air smoky and cold and your heels on the cobbles the loudest sound in the air. These cobbles hide endless arched cellars, where the liquid wealth of Beaune matures and breathes and the walls blacken with age and humidity.

When stones and architecture hold no more fascination, go out into the vineyards, which come right down to the perimeter of Beaune.

The slope of the Beaune vineyards is divided in two by the Route Nationale 470 (the Route de Bouze, which is amusing for English speakers). On the northern side of Beaune, near the border with Savigny, the Autoroute slashes through the top vineyard Les Marconnets, but apparently the original plan was to route it through Le Montrachet so perhaps we should heave a sigh of relief. The vineyards go up to about 330 metres (1,080 feet) and the soil is basically limestone debris. There are the usual nuances between the *climats*, and even within the *climats* themselves: Le Clos des Mouches, for example, is planted with Chardonnay on the upper part, and Pinot Noir below where the soil is browner and heavier. There is clay and less gravel in Les Boucherottes and Les Chouacheux, while Les Grèves, naturally, has gravel and faces southeast. Les Bressandes and Les Fèves are on marked slopes, while the thin soil of Les Marconnets, Les Fèves and Clos du Roi, and the fact that the roots have to dig deep, contribute to their longevity.

As a generalization, the Premiers Crus on the northern side of the Montagne de Beaune are the wines which take the longest to mature, while the vineyards to the south of the Route de Bouze are more delicate and show their beauty a little sooner. For instance, in a series of Beaune wines, one might begin with a Clos de la Mousse, go on to Beaune Teurons, then Marconnets, and finally Grèves, which combines finesse with depth. Clos du Roi is usually more robust than Cent Vignes.

Finally, it is often said in a somewhat derogatory manner that the Beaune vineyards are nearly all owned by the Beaune négociants, who combine that exacting role with being very important domain proprietors. Personally, the exact social and commercial status of a vineyard owner has never concerned me overmuch; it is the quality of the wine in the bottle that counts, and there are many superb Beaune Premiers Crus from these historic owners that have stood the test of time and given much pleasure. Unadorned Villages Beaune is usually straightforward and without complication, produced on deeper soil with more clay, more often susceptible to frost than the Premiers Crus. The whites have an earthy touch and seem best when quite young, when their fruit and flavour are at their apogee, and the reds, too, are sturdy and almost crunchy in youth – drink them at about five years old, and then go on to the Premiers Crus.

A Personal Selection of Beaune Producers

Domaine Robert & Michel Ampeau

Clos du Roi of structure and character.

Domaine Besancenot-Mathouillet

An amazing array of Premiers Crus, including Grèves of finesse, rich Cent Vignes, robust Teurons, mouth-filling Clos du Roi.

Bouchard Père & Fils (Domaines du Château de Beaune)

The largest owner of Beaune Premier Cru vineyards, there is a magnificent range of wines, culminating in their splendid Grèves, Vigne de l'Enfant Jésus, a satiny beauty of power and longevity. An excellent introduction to Beaune would be their Beaune du Château, a non-vintage Premier Cru blend in both red and white.

Domaine Chanson Père & Fils

Recently I have liked young vintages of Bressandes, Clos du Roi and Grèves, which have all had style and fruit, but my experience of mature bottles has been a little less favourable.

Domaine Bernard Delagrange

Straight Beaune which is delicious and fruity when quite young – perfumed and tempting. What I like about it is that the temptation is resisted to "bump up" a frank Villages wine with over-chaptalization.

Domaine Joseph Drouhin

Red and white Clos des Mouches of high quality. I have a particular weakness for the white, which is rich and musky, with flesh and a taste of hazelnuts – a wonderful mouthful. There is often more than a hint of cherries in the red wines of Drouhin.

Domaine Jacques Germain

François Germain makes wine of enormous finesse and perfume, from the Château de Chorey, Chorey-les-Beaune, through to Cent Vignes, Vignes Franches and Les Teurons – highly recommended. Look out for the Premier Cru Domaine de Saux.

Domaine Louis Jadot
Their Clos des Ursules, an enclave within Les Vignes Franches, is usually a very good, sturdy bottle of Beaune, but I have often found their Theurons and Boucherottes even better.
Domaine Michel Lafarge
Grèves which takes time to develop, but which is worth the wait.
Domaine Louis Latour
Vignes Franches which is robust and straightforward when young, developing more complexity and texture with bottle-age.
Domaine Chantal Lescure
Well-made Chouacheux, with character and impact.
Domaine Machard de Gramont
Truly beauteous Les Chouacheux, all raspberries and flavour and impeccable balance.
Domaine Moillard
Beaune-Grèves 1983 is still at an elemental stage, a huge wine with a bouquet of liquorice and a taste of cocoa – leave for 10 years.
Domaine Albert Morey
Really top-class Grèves of robust nature and concentration.
Domaine Mussy
Les Epenottes which promises well but needs considerable time.
Domaine Parent
Les Epenottes, sometimes "jammy", but always honourable.
Domaine Jacques Prieur
Beaune Aux Cras Clos de la Féguine which is big and solid, needing time.
Domaine Tollot-Beaut
Grèves with a wonderful bouquet, the kind that revives memories of past great bottles. There is always body and concentration in these wines, sometimes a dash too much alcohol for sheer perfection, but the standard is consistently high.

HOSPICES DE BEAUNE

The Sale of the Hospices' wines is held on the third Sunday of November. It is far too early to give really definite pronouncements on taste, especially in the case of the white wines, which are always shown with a considerable amount of residual sugar, but the date remains immutable. Since the wines are sold for the benefit of the Hospices, in a welter of publicity, and the Burgundians do genuinely feel they are supporting their local charity, prices are artificially high and do not always reflect the real market situation. The Hospices Sale prices tend to increase regardless of the quality of a particular vintage; it therefore follows that it is better value to buy at the Hospices in a good year rather than in a mediocre one.

The *cuvées* produced by the Hospices are named after its benefactors and are nearly all blends of several vineyards in one village. We show the current list below with the composition of each *cuvée*; the Mazis-Chambertin Madeleine Collignon is the only wine from the Côte de Nuits and the most recent donation, auctioned for the first time in 1977.

The Sale itself is interminably long – unlike the snappy pace at which business is done at Christie's and Sotheby's in London. Many of the Beaune négociants are faithful buyers and often out of *politesse*, one feels, their foreign agents are mentioned as co-buyers.

Monsieur André Porcheret took over the direction of the Hospices wine in 1977, and since then there has been immense improvement in all aspects of the winemaking. Twenty-three fulltime *vignerons* are employed in the vineyards, and both vine treatments and the amount of fertilizer put in the ground (dehydrated manure) are strictly controlled. No weedkillers are used and pruning is not over-generous. Wine made from vines under eight years of age is not sold at the Sale but labelled differently under the Centre Hospitalier name. Fermentation is in open wood *cuves*, with men treading to keep the skins in contact with the juice, and the wine is subsequently put into 100% new wood. Usually, a third of the stems are kept, but in 1983 the grapes were entirely destemmed as there was rot and the must was already tannic. The press wine is added in entirety, and the machines are changing to the Willmes pneumatic type.

So, at the level of the Hospices itself, everything that can possibly be done to achieve quality is set in motion. But, as always the quality of your Hospices de Beaune wine will depend to a very large extent on the people responsible for its *élevage* or maturing. They can make or mar a wine. The rule seems to be *always* to find out, in shop or restaurant, who did the *élevage*. Then follow the names you trust: if you do not normally like Maison X's style of wine, do not buy an Hospices wine matured by the same house, because it most certainly will have left its mark on it.

Red wines

Charlotte Dumay: Corton Renardes 2ha, Les Bressandes 1ha, Clos du Roi 0.5ha.
Docteur Peste: Corton Bressandes 1ha, Chaumes & Voirosses 1ha, Clos du Roi 0.5ha, Fiètre 0.4ha, Les Grèves 0.1ha.
Rameau-Lamarosse: Pernand-Vergelesses Les Basses Vergelesses 0.6ha.
Forneret: Savigny Les Vergelesses 1ha, Aux Gravains 0.66ha.
Fouquerand: Savigny Basses Vergelesses 1ha, Les Talmettes 0.66ha, Aux Gravains 0.33ha, Aux Serpentières 0.14ha.
Arthur Girard: Savigny Les Peuillets 1ha, Les Marconnets 0.8ha.
Nicolas Rolin: Beaune Les Cents Vignes 1.5ha, Les Grèves 0.8ha, En Genêt 0.4ha.
Guigone de Salins: Beaune Les Bressandes 1ha, En Senrey 0.8ha, Champs Pimont 0.6ha.
Clos des Avaux; Beaune Les Avaux 2ha.
Brunet: Beaune Les Teurons 0.88ha, Les Bressandes 0.66ha, La Mignotte 0.5ha, Les Cents Vignes 0.33ha.
Maurice Drouhin: Beaune Les Avaux 0.8ha, Les Boucherottes 0.4ha, Champs Pimont 0.6ha, Les Grèves 0.4ha.
Hugues et Louis Bétault: Beaune Les Grèves 0.88ha, La Mignotte 0.5ha, Les Aigrots 0.4ha, Les Sizies 0.33ha, Les Vignes Franches 0.2ha.
Rousseau-Deslandes: Beaune Les Cent Vignes 1ha, Les Montrevenots 0.66ha, La Mignotte 0.4ha, Les Avaux 0.33ha.
Dames Hospitalières: Beaune Les Bressandes 1ha, La Mignotte 0.66ha, Les Teurons 0.5ha, Les Grèves 0.33ha.
Dames de la Charité: Pommard Les Epenots 0.4ha, Les Rugiens 0.33ha, Les Noizons 0.33ha, La Refène 0.33ha, Les Combes Dessus 0.2ha.
Billardet: Pommard Petits-Epenots 0.66ha, Les Noizons 0.5ha, Les Arvelets 0.4ha, Les Rugiens 0.33ha.
Blondeau: Volnay Champans 0.6ha, Taille Pieds 0.6ha, Ronceret 0.33ha, En l'Ormeau 0.2ha.
General Muteau: Volnay le Village 0.8ha, Carelle sous la Chapelle 0.33ha, Cailleret Dessus 0.2ha, Fremiet 0.2ha, Taille Pieds 0.2ha.
Jehan de Massol: Volnay-Santenots Les Santenots 1.5ha.
Gauvain: Volnay-Santenots Les Santenots 1.5ha, Les Pitures 0.33ha.
Lebelin: Monthélie Les Duresses 0.88ha.
Boillot: Auxey-Duresses Les Duresses 0.75ha.
Madeleine Collignon: Mazis-Chambertin 1.5ha.

White wines

Françoise & de Salins: Corton-Charlemagne 0.25ha.
Baudot: Meursault-Genevrières Les Genevrières Dessus 0.66ha, Les Genevrières Dessous 0.75ha.
Philippe le Bon: Meursault-Genevrières Les Genevrières Dessus 0.2ha, Les Genevrières Dessous 0.4ha.
de Bahèzre de Lanlay: Meursault-Charmes Les Charmes Dessus 0.5ha, Les Charmes Dessous 0.4ha.
Albert-Grivault: Meursault-Charmes Les Charmes Dessus 0.5ha.
Jehan Humblot: Meursault Le Poruzot 0.6ha, Grands Charrons 0.1ha.
Loppin: Meursault Les Criots 0.6ha.
Goureau: Meursault Le Poruzot 0.33ha, Les Pitures 0.33ha, Les Cras 0.2ha.
Paul Chanson: Corton-Vergennes 0.25ha.

● ○ CHOREY-LES-BEAUNE

1983 production: Red wine *4,662 hectolitres*
White wine *12 hectolitres*

The vineyards of Chorey-lès-Beaune lie on each side of the Route Nationale, but more to the east on a plain of geological debris – the height is only 230 metres (755 feet) and the soil is predominantly alluvial. There are no Premiers Crus, but a few *climats* are recognized. Les Champs-Longs and Pièce du Chapitre are among the best, on sandy alluvial topsoil, strong in iron content and more pebbly on the slope. Les Beaumonts, Les Ratosses, Les Crais and Poirier-Malchaussée are also good sites. Logically, it would seem that Les Beaumonts and Les Ratosses are more Savigny in type, while Les Champs-Longs resembles an Aloxe-Corton from the plain, and Poirier-Malchaussée and Les Crais, on marl, have good structure. All should be drunk relatively young, in order to enjoy their fruity charm.

The three domains which do honour to Chorey are: **Jacques Germain of the Château de Chorey**, **Tollot-Beaut** and **Tollot-Voarick**. The two brothers at the **Domaine Gay** also make good wine from old vines; less refined and more rustic than the more noted domains, but well worth buying. In fact, the overall value at Chorey is not to be denied. Much of the wine made at Chorey is sold as Côte de Beaune-Villages.

● ○ COTE DE BEAUNE

1983 production: Red wine *354 hectolitres*
White wine *153 hectolitres*

This is really a redundant appellation. It covers the area of Beaune itself, as well as the *lieux-dits*: Les Topes-Bizot, Les Pierres Blanches, Les Mondes Rondes, Les Monnières, and La Grande Châtelaine, which is owned by the négociant Louis Max.

Two wines worth finding are the red Clos des Pierres Blanches from **Rossignol Frères** in **Volnay** and a white Côte de Beaune from the **Lycée Agricole et Viticole de Beaune**, which owns 4.58ha of vineyards and rents another 19.10ha, covering a range of appellations.

● POMMARD

1983 production: Pommard (red) *10,564 hectolitres*
Premiers Crus: Les Rugiens Bas, Les Rugiens Hauts (part), Les Grands Epenots, Les Petits Epenots (part), Clos de la Commaraine, Clos Blanc, Les Arvelets, Les Charmots, En Largillière, Les Pézerolles, Les Boucherottes, Les Saussilles, Les Croix Noires, Les Chaponnières, Les Fremiers, Les Bertins, Les Jarolières, Les Poutures, Clos Micot, La Refène, Clos de Verger, La Platière (part), Les Chanlins Bas (part), Les Combes Dessus (part), La Chanière (part).

Pommard can be over-priced and over-alcoholic, but when the best *crus* are made by the most gifted winemakers, they are probably the most exciting wines of the Côte de Beaune. Unfortunately, an easily pronounceable name has given the appellation added impetus on the transatlantic market and many less scrupulous producers and négociants have taken advantage of this fact.

Leaving Beaune to the south, the seeker after Pommard practically falls into its vines. Many of them are somewhat hidden behind strong vineyard walls and there are a number of important *clos* (current law on the use of the word *clos* insists that the named vineyard must be completely surrounded by a wall, unless the *clos* has been known as such for more than one hundred years). With the exception of the Premiers Crus, Clos Micot and Les Combes Dessus, all the vineyard between the two roads N.74 and N.73 is straight Appellation Pommard. The greatest Premiers Crus, Les Epenots and Les Rugiens, are on either side of the village of Pommard, Les Epenots nearest Beaune and Les Rugiens nearest Volnay. Within Les Epenots, which faces south-south-east, there is the Clos des Epeneaux; also the Clos des Epenots and Le Clos de Citeaux. Les Arvelets, Les Petits Noizons (a village wine) and Les Charmots face south, while Les Rugiens Bas are beautifully sited facing south-south-east. The Premiers Crus are mostly mid-slope and the clay-limestone (about 30% limestone) is red in colour, becoming very pebbly and white at the top of the appellation. Les Rugiens Hauts slopes more and is on a rocky subsoil, while Les Rugiens Bas is on a subsoil of Argovian limestone covered with a thick layer of fine marly-calcareous debris. All this leads to good drainage and wines of excellent colour and structure, more tannic than most wines of the Côte de Beaune. The straight Appellation Pommard between the two roads has far more clay and is less stony, except for Les Perrières and La Levrière, which are on pebbly debris.

If one had the joyous task of awarding two new Grands Crus to the Côte de Beaune, they would have to be Les Grands Epenots and Les Rugiens Bas. Both have the capacity to age with true grandeur, which is one of the prerequisites for Grand Cru status. Les Rugiens Bas benefits from a superb microclimate which often enables the grapes to attain great ripeness. Here you can feel the power and richness in the wine, with concentration and intense perfume of liquorice and violets, and a colour reminiscent of the glowing red of the earth. Les Epenots also has fine character and construction, often more fruity and less hard in youth than Les Rugiens.

A Personal Selection of Pommard Producers

Domaine Robert & Michel Ampeau

Straight Pommard of character and flavour.

Domaine Comte Armand

The Clos des Epeneaux, owned in entirety by Comte Armand, is for those who say that present burgundy is too light. This wine always takes years to open out, with power, structure and great flavour.

Domaine Henri Boillot

Les Jarollières with an excellent scent and, in good years, powerful structure – wine with the ability to age.

Domaine de Courcel

Madame de Courcel makes exemplary Epenots, with depth of bouquet and taste, real class, and a flavour of pure red fruits.

Domaine Bernard Delagrange

Very honourable Chanlins, always carefully made.

Domaine Michel Gaunoux

Grands Epenots which is rich and spicy – the wines always seem to have the body to last, and there are many old bottles to prove it.

Domaine Louis Glantenay

Even the straight Pommard at this domain is built to last.

Domaine Guillemard-Dupont & ses Fils

Based at Meloisey, in the Hautes Côtes de Beaune, these vignerons make strawberry-scented Pommard, balanced and unfettered with excess alcohol. It has a raw flavour when young and a lovely aftertaste.

Louis Latour

Their Epenots is not a domain wine, but must come from an impeccable source, as it is always excellent.

Domaine Lejeune

Les Argillières with a deep bouquet of strawberries – the 1983 has a tarry, tannic background which needs time to soften. Rugiens of good colour, power, always an excellent mouthful.

Domaine Machard de Gramont

Stylish, elegant, totally frank wines – Le Clos Blanc and Les Batins.

Domaine de Montille

Stupendous Rugiens, immensely long on the palate, and Pézerolles which is rich in glycerol and fruit. Both are made for keeping – if you can.

Domaine Mussy

Straight Pommard and Epenots, both big wines, solid (even thick) and designed for cellaring.

Domaine Parent

Elegant, fruity wines, with delicious Pinot Noir character and the flavour of the appellation, without perhaps the sheer richness of the very best.

Domaine Pothier-Rieusset

Excellent Epenots, Rugiens and Clos de Verger. The style is luscious fruit backed by firm tannin.

VOLNAY

1983 production: Volnay (all red) *6,837 hectolitres*
Premiers Crus: Les Caillerets, Cailleret Dessus, En Champans, En Chevret, Frémiets, Bousse d'Or, La Barre or Clos de la Barre, Clos des Chênes (part), Les Angles, Pointes d'Angles, Les Mitans, En l'Ormeau, Taille Pied, En Verseuil, Carelle sous la Chapelle, Le Ronceret, Carelles Dessous (part), Robardelle (part), Les Lurets (part), Les Aussy (part), Les Brouillards (part), Clos des Ducs, Pitures Dessus, Chanlins (part), Les Santenots (red), Le Village (part).

Volnay has some of the most beautiful old Burgundian houses on the Côte, reassuringly solid with their deep roofs and sense of permanence. However, only about 400 people live here, and most of them seem to be called Rossignol! The village sits proudly above its vineyards which face east and south, with the Premiers Crus situated over a wide variety of soils. Les Santenots, of course, lies in the commune of Meursault, but the Pinot Noir does splendidly on the Bathonian limestone covered with reddish earth and a fair amount of pebbles. Les Caillerets also straddles the two communes, again with reddish soil, pebbly and beautifully sited, with the top part of both En Champans and Cailleret Dessus sitting firmly on a rocky base.

Above them, the Clos des Chènes is on Bathonian limestone, with poor, pebbly soil having difficulty clinging to the marked slope, but benefiting from a beautiful east-south-east position. Taille Pied, Bousse d'Or and the Clos des Ducs are right up against the village, but here the soils are white Argovian limestone.

Les Caillerets is probably the grandest of all Volnays, the most likely to reach a superb old age in ripe years. Although one is never looking for power in Volnay, but rather fragrance and elegance, there can be fine structure in a Caillerets. Clos des Chênes is sometimes more lean than Caillerets, with finesse and a certain tautness when young but, with Champans, ageing well. All can have the Volnay scent of violets and sometimes redcurrants. Taille Pied will not have the flesh of Caillerets but will be delicate, while flowery Frémiets, in spite of being near Pommard, has the Volnay fragrance. The Clos de la Bousse d'Or has potential for ageing, as does the Clos des Ducs. Santenots can last in bottle exceptionally well, especially from Les Santenots du Milieu.

A Personal Selection of Volnay Producers

Domaine Marquis d'Angerville
These wines rarely have much colour or power in evidence, but Clos des Ducs and Champans from good years can age with elegance. In smaller years, the wines are sometimes swamped by oak. At their best, d'Angerville wines are the essence of elegant Volnay.

Domaine Bitouzet Prieur
Taillepieds which repays cellaring.

Domaine Bouchard Père & Fils (Château de Beaune)
Superb Volnay-Caillerets Ancienne Cuvée Carnot, with structure and fruit, and scented Frémiets, Clos de la Rougeotte, with breed rather than power – just as it should be.

Domaine Bernard Delagrange
Very typical Volnays, displaying attractive appellation character.

Domaine Louis Glantenay
Beautifully structured wines, anyway from ripe years – they need time.

Domaine Michel Lafarge
Clos des Chênes which is all satin and silk, showing the *charm* of Volnay, but with good depth of fruit.

Domaine des Comtes Lafon
Volnay-Santenots (du Milieu) of concentration and breed, which develops outstandingly in bottle.

Domaine de Montille
Maître Hubert de Montille is almost a sorcerer among winemakers – the tastes he conjures out of the vine! Floral Taillepieds, Les Mitans (young vines) tasting of cloves and chocolate, and brilliant, complex, long-lasting Champans with

its bouquet of roses. The wines of Maître de Montille are the living, breathing example that excessive alcohol is not necessary to make superlative burgundy – he prefers 12.1% or 12.2% to 13%.

Domaine de la Pousse d'Or

Gérard Potel makes satiny wines, full of fruit and flavour, especially the Caillerets Dessus Clos des 60 Ouvrées and Clos de la Bousse d'Or. He even makes a success of less propitious years, with only the 1982s perhaps not quite of the same high standard.

MONTHELIE

1983 production: Monthélie red *3,434 hectolitres*
Monthélie white *77 hectolitres*

Premiers Crus: Sur La Velle, Les Vignes Rondes, Le Meix Bataille, Les Riottes, La Taupine, Le Clos Gauthey, Le Château-Gaillard, Les Champs Fulliot, Le Cas Rougeot, Les Duresses (part).

Monthélie is really the forgotten little sister of Volnay, sharing many of this appellation's characteristics but in more muted form. The span of life is shorter, and Monthélies are generally at their most delectable when relatively young. Sandwiched between Volnay and Meursault, Monthélie is another lovely Burgundian village, with old stone houses flanking the sloping streets. The vines, too, are on the slopes above Meursault, and it is only comparatively recently that the wines of Monthélie have had an identity completely their own. The appellation is virtually all red wines – white wines can be made, but they have a tendency to maderize easily and the growers feel that this is best left to Meursault next door.

There are, in fact, two distinct viticultural areas at Monthélie: the Coteau de Volnay, above the village, where the Premiers Crus are found – the vineyards face south or southeast, on Bathonian limestone, with reddish earth and marl on the summit; and the Vallée d'Auxey-Duresses, at the foot of the village along the north-south valley, with the vines thus facing west and east, and white Argovian limestone soil.

Good Monthélie, like Volnay, can have a tempting, scented bouquet and a sheen on the texture. It should never be heavyweight, but the best sites produce wines of good structure. It is generally considered that the wines from the Coteau de Volnay have more finesse than those from the Coteau de la Vallée d'Auxey, where the wines can be broader. The Premiers Crus certainly have character, and when they have the balance, they can age well too.

A Personal Selection of Monthélie Producers

Château de Monthélie

M. Robert de Suremain sells his red Monthélie under the Château name and over the years it has proved to be the best of the appellation.

Domaine A. Ropiteau-Mignon

There have been good Les Champs Fulliot from this domain and a Duresses had a delicate nose, but too much apparent alcohol on the palate.

MEURSAULT

1983 production: Meursault white *14,748 hectolitres*
Meursault red *800 hectolitres*

Premiers Crus: (For red and white wines) Les Cras (part), Les Caillerets (part), Les Charmes-Dessus, Les Charmes-Dessous, Les Perrières Dessus (part), Aux Perrières, Les Perrières Dessous (part), Les Chaumes des Perrières (part), Les Genevrières Dessus, Les Chaumes de Narvaux (part), Le Poruzot Dessus, Les Poruzots Dessous, Les Genevrières Dessous, Les Bouchères (part), Les Gouttes d'Or, Le Poruzot (part). (For white wines only) Les Santenots Blancs, Les Plures (part), Les Santenots du Milieu, La Jeunelotte, La Pièce sous le Bois (part), Sous le Dos d'Ane (part), Sous Blagny (the last four in the commune of Blagny).

When the Santenots are planted with Pinot Noir, the wines are called

Volnay-Santenots, but the 2ha which are planted to Chardonnay are called Meursault-Santenots.

Many people's image of the perfect white burgundy is based on their tasting impressions of Meursault. It usually has an imposing bouquet, slightly nutty with overtones of cinnamon, and strong, persistent flavour. The best wines are also rich and fat with a long finish, all of which adds up to happy memories. The "village" itself is large and prosperous, a real county town, dominated by a tall and elegant church spire. Many of the Premiers Crus have the right to produce both red and white wines, but the vast majority have opted for white.

The first slope of Meursault at the Combe de St-Aubin is of Bathonian limestone, while calcareous marl and pure marl dominate the middle part of the vineyard area, and there is a good deal of debris on the upper part of the slope. On the Blagny-Meursault side, there is brown calcareous soil over Callovian limestone, as well as white Argovian marly limestone. The vineyard rises to 300 metres (984 feet), with its southeast facing position giving a microclimate which is very favourable to quality. There is no doubt that the worldwide demand for white wine has led to some planting of the Chardonnay on parcels which are better suited to making red wines, and these are probably the heavy Meursaults without finesse.

Les Perrières could be considered as the Meursault which has the most class and refinement, particularly from Les Perrières Dessus, where the vines frequently attain great ripeness, giving power, but the rock base of the site gives the distinguished nose. A tiny path separates Les Perrières from Les Genevrières, which also has its partisans. Elegant, scented, with the real bouquet of hazelnuts, Genevrières produces immensely pretty and seductive wines. Les Poruzots is solid with a flinty nose, with excellent keeping potential, while Les Gouttes d'Or, as the name suggests, has a lovely golden colour and great capacity for ageing – robust rather than delicate. The steep slope compensates for the less well-exposed site. Les Charmes is at its best from Les Charmes-Dessus (which includes the middle part of the slope), while Les Charmes-Dessous is on deeper soil, with lovely round, fruity qualities.

A Personal Selection of Meursault Producers

Domaine Robert & Michel Ampeau
Superb Les Perrières and Les Charmes, which last beautifully in bottle. Also good Blagny La Pièce sous le Bois.

Domaine Michelot Buisson
Big, rich Charmes and Genevrières – everybody's idea of fine Meursault.

Domaine Jean-François Coche Dury
Good Charmes, and Perrières with more structure and a long finish. There is no filtering at this domain, so maximum flavour is preserved.

Domaine Bernard Delagrange
A large domain and a welcoming man; the Meursaults are pretty, for young drinking.

Sélection Jean Germain
Extremely reliable wines, made by an experienced and careful winemaker. Very good Les Poruzots, and Les Cras Clos Richemont from Domaine Darnat now comes under this Sélection.

Domaine des Comtes Lafon
Superb Meursault, from Les Perrières to Clos de la Barre, beautifully constructed and ageing in bottle to perfection. No filtering here.

Louis Latour
The firm makes splendid selections in straight Meursault, Meursault Château de Blagny and Genevrières.

Domaine du Duc de Magenta
Usually very good and stylish, but Les Meix Chavaux 1982 certainly suffered from over-cropping. Some producers got round this by judicious use of new oak, but this wine was too self-effacing.

Domaine Maroslavac-Tremeau
Elegant Meursault-Blagny Premier Cru, with evidence of new wood.

Domaine Joseph Matrot & Pierre Matrot
Oaky and structured wines, which can age.

Château de Meursault
Patriarche own this beautiful property and the wines are excellent.

Domaine G. Michelot
Slightly more rustic style than some, but strong wines.

Domaine Jean Monnier
Wines of elegance and finesse, including delightful Genevrières.

Domaine Pierre Morey
Pierre Morey is, in fact, the vigneron of Comte Lafon; his Charmes combines fruit and oak in a lovely mouthful.

Domaine Guy Roulot
Excellent wines continue to be made by the nephew of Guy Roulot, with velvety Charmes and fat Les Perrières. Les Tessons makes the bridge between a straight Villages wine and the Premiers Crus. Meursaults usually have a nose of hazelnuts – the 1983 Roulot wines are all walnuts!

● ○ BLAGNY

1983 production: Blagny Rouge *210 hectolitres*

This little village, squeezed in between Puligny-Montrachet and Meursault, has always posed a problem for the legislators, but the essential fact is that the appellation is for red wine only, although wine of both colours is made. White wine from the *climats* of La Pièce sous le Bois, La Jeunelotte and Sous le Dos d'Ane can be called Meursault Premier Cru, but red wine would be Blagny Premier Cru. White wine made from the *climats* of Sous le Puits, La Garenne, Hameau de Blagny and Le Trézin can be called Puligny-Montrachet, but the red must be Blagny.

Red Blagny has a very distinctive taste, slightly earthy, slightly gamey. It can really "attack" the palate when young, but it is this very lack of neutrality which is so alluring. White wine from Blagny is usually very fruity, very accessible – good value in restaurants, as it shows that someone has had the courage to leave the better-known *climats* of Meursault and Puligny, and you thus pay for a delicious taste rather than an overworked name. As for recommended producers, they are those who make their wine well in the neighbouring two appellations.

● ○ PULIGNY-MONTRACHET

Virtually all white wine.

1983 production:		
	Montrachet	*377 hectolitres*
	Bâtard-Montrachet	*557 hectolitres*
	Bienvenues Bâtard-Montrachet	*189 hectolitres*
	Chevalier Montrachet	*144 hectolitres*
	Puligny-Montrachet (white)	*9,435 hectolitres*
	Puligny-Montrachet (red)	*364 hectolitres*

Premiers Crus: Le Cailleret, Les Combettes, Les Pucelles, Les Folatières (part), Clavoillon, Le Champ Canet, Les Chalumeaux (part), Les Referts, Sous le Puits, La Garenne, Hameau de Blagny.

An innocent visitor to Puligny-Montrachet would never believe that it is the centre of what many would call the greatest dry white wines of the world. There are days when even the proverbial dog does not bark to break the silence. It is another of those slightly schizophrenic communes in Burgundy, rivalling Aloxe-Corton and Pernand-Vergelesses, because some of its most famous Grands Crus are shared with the neighbouring village of Chassagne-Montrachet. Chevalier Montrachet and Bienvenues Bâtard-Montrachet are entirely within the boundaries of Puligny-Montrachet, but Le Montrachet and Bâtard-Montrachet share their favours with Chassagne-Montrachet, whereas Les Criots lies entirely within Chassagne-Montrachet.

These fabled Grands Crus are the result of perfect microclimates, so sheltered and positioned on the slopes that they frequently give very ripe grapes, whereas elsewhere the sugar levels might be only adequate. Le Montrachet lies on a base of hard Bathonian limestone covered by debris, with an iron-oxide content. Chevalier Montrachet is on Bajocian marly limestone, and Bâtard-Montrachet is composed of brown limestone rich in gravel. Bienvenues Bâtard-Montrachet is virtually an enclave within

Bâtard-Montrachet, with the same soil and facing east-south-east. Chevalier Montrachet has a more marked slope, situated above Le Montrachet. The lower part of Le Montrachet has slightly deeper soil.

The sheer imposing glamour of the Grands Crus should not cause us to forget the Premiers Crus, which are of remarkable beauty at Puligny-Montrachet. Les Combettes is on pure rock with very thin soil, except where there are faults in the rock which allow the depth of the soil to jump from a matter of centimetres to metres. Les Referts and Clavoillon have very similar soil, while Les Folatières is on a more marked slope, with white limestone debris near the top; there is always the risk of erosion here. Le Cailleret shares many characteristics with Le Montrachet, but it is more pebbly and the orientation is not quite as good as for the Grand Cru. The Premiers Crus are divided from the Village wines by the Sentier de Couches, which continues into Chassagne and Santenay.

In Puligny, the cellars cannot be underground, as is usual in Burgundy, because of the relatively high water table.

So, what is all the fuss about? Why are Le Montrachet and its satellites "the best"? Without doubt, if you drink any of these wines too young, particularly Le Montrachet, you will ask yourself this very question. The bouquet, particularly, takes time to develop, and it is really a vinous crime to drink Le Montrachet at under ten years of age. The colour begins as greenish yellow and deepens to a splendid gold in bottle, while with the years the taste gains in depth and complexity. Honey, almonds, hawthorn and great textured richness are all found in Le Montrachet, provided the wine is served at no less than 13°C (about 55°F), which is perfect cellar temperature, and not refrigerator frozen.

There are those who would put Chevalier Montachet next in the hierarchy, followed by Bâtard, Bienvenues and Criots. Certainly I have had stupendous Chevalier, sometimes even surpassing Le Montrachet, for the hand of the winemaker counts just as much in this hallowed ground as anywhere else in Burgundy. The first two wines, particularly, need nearly as long to develop as Le Montrachet, and all are rich and mouth-filling. White burgundy of this rank is almost a food as well as a wine, it is so multidimensional and nutritious, powerful and fleshy.

Among the Premiers Crus, Les Pucelles usually develops more slowly than Les Combettes, which can be soft in some years, less *nervoux* than other Premiers Crus. It has a certain hazelnuts quality which makes one think of neighbouring Meursault and is broader in taste than Clavoillon and Les Folatières, which both show great finesse. Le Cailleret has a good deal of body, but Le Champ Canet and Les Chalumeaux are lighter and ready for drinking earlier.

A Personal Selection of Puligny-Montrachet Producers

Domaine Robert & Michel Ampeau
Les Combettes of great beauty and ability to age.

Bouchard Père & Fils
Important owners in Le Montrachet (domain wines are always sold under the Domaines du Château de Beaune label), they make long-lasting, rich wine, uninfluenced by oak but full of subtle flavour. There is also fine Chevalier Montrachet within the domain, with the 1983 astoundingly good, the nearest thing to liquid honey that I have ever seen.

Domaine Gérard Chavy
Good straight Puligny-Montrachet.

Domaine Henri Clerc
Very pleasant Puligny, well-made and thoroughly enjoyable.

Domaine Madame François Colin
Les Demoiselles which is amazingly seductive and expansive of bouquet and taste.

Joseph Drouhin
This Folatières is not a domain wine, but it is always delicate and acacia soft.

Domaine Louis Jadot
Chevalier Montrachet Les Demoiselles is shared with Louis Latour, and I always like the non-domain Les Referts.

Domaine Marquis de Laguiche (*Joseph Drouhin*)
The must is sent into Beaune for Drouhin to do the vinifying, *élevage*, bottling and eventual selling. This is Le Montrachet of enormous charm and fruit, balanced and luscious.

Domaine Louis Latour
Chevalier Montrachet Les Demoiselles is positively exotic, rich, oaky and a great keeper. Non-domain Les Folatières and Les Referts are splendid wines, all almonds and mayblossom.

Domaine Leflaive
Quite simply, this domain makes some of the best white wines in the whole of Burgundy, ergo, the whole of the world. They own no Montrachet (if it was in my gift, I would love to give them a few plots I could name, and watch the improved results!) but have a magnificent spread of the other wines. There are few things more pleasant in life than trying to decide with M. Vincent Leflaive if his Bienvenues, his Bâtard or his unbelievable Chevalier is reminiscent of hawthorn, blackthorn or mayblossom. At the last attempt, I detected lavender honey in the Chevalier. Then there is floral Pucelles, rich Combettes, greengages on young Clavoillon and limetree blossom on the straight Puligny. There is always undeniable quality and breed.

Domaine Joseph Matrot
Les Chalumeaux with lovely fruit marrying with the oak, sometimes needing bottle-age to "fatten".

Domaine Monnot
Les Folatières with a smoky, mayblossom nose and smooth breed.

Domaine de la Romanée-Conti
Montrachet of great style, simply crying out for bottle-age in order to show its voluptuous paces.

Domaine Etienne Sauzet
Glorious Combettes, with a bouquet of woodsmoke and greengages, backed up by oak.

Domaine du Baron Thénard
Le Montrachet from this domain is marketed by the firm of Remoissenet and the wine is usually very fine and stylish.

Henri de Villamont
This négociant is responsible for some lovely stylish Pucelles, with a smoky nose and oak on the palate.

● ○ CHASSAGNE-MONTRACHET

1983 production:	Criots Bâtard Montrachet	*41 hectolitres*
	Chassagne-Montrachet (red)	*6,482 hectolitres*
	Chassagne-Montrachet (white)	*6,015 hectolitres*

Premiers Crus: *Red wines* – Clos St-Jean (part), Morgeot (part), Morgeot known as Abbaye de Morgeot (part), La Boudriotte (part), La Maltroie (part), Les Chenevottes, Les Champs Gain (part), Les Grandes Ruchottes, La Romanée, Les Brussonnes (part), Les Vergers, Les Macherelles, En Cailleret (part). *White wines* – Morgeot (part), Morgeot known as Abbaye de Morgeot (part), La Boudriotte, La Maltroie, Clos St-Jean, Les Chenevottes, Les Champs Gain, Grandes Ruchottes, La Romanée, Les Brussonnes, Les Vergers, Les Macherelles, Chassagne or En Cailleret.

Many of the best wines of Chassagne are made by members of three families – the Gagnards, the Delagranges and the Moreys. It is the second-but-last important village on the Côte de Beaune, with only Santenay to follow. Naturally, the white wines are world famous, but the reds represent very good value and are frequently forgotten in the rush to get a more fashionable name. If the Grands Crus are white, the finest Premier Cru wines are red. The Clos St-Jean, surrounded by walls, possesses very gravelly soil, while Les Vergers, Les Macherelles and Les Chenevottes have red soil, clay with little gravel. Morgeot, the lower part of La Boudriotte, Les Champs Gain and Les Petits Clos are on white marl above and red gravelly earth lower down. The basic subsoil is oolitic limestone, grey, beige and pink and, when it is polished, it looks like marble and makes beautiful flagstones and fireplaces in the local houses. There is still a quarry above Clos St-Jean. Truffles apparently grow on a base of Bathonian limestone debris, on the edge of the vineyards and on uncultivated land, although I have not seen (or eaten) any evidence of this.

There are those who make the distinction between the Puligny part of Montrachet, facing southeast, and the Chassagne part which faces more due south, following the turn of the slope. The Puligny section is meant to have the edge in terms of finesse and sheer distinction, but to my knowledge this has never been proved at some meticulously organized tasting. As always, it is probably the hand of man which makes the difference between fine and divine.

The one Grand Cru lying entirely in Chassagne, tiny Les Criots, has all the body and structure of its fellows. Among the white Premiers Crus, Les Ruchottes, Morgeot, Caillerets, Vignes Blanches and Les Champs Gain tend to have more body, while Les Vergers, Les Macherelles, Les Chenevottes and Les Chaumées are very fragrant and floral. La Boudriotte and Le Morgeot are the two most powerful reds, built for lasting in ripe years, reputed to have a taste of kirsch, and certainly the analogy with cherries is very detectable. Clos St-Jean often has softer fruit and matures a little earlier – prunes, peaches and violets can all be seen in these wines, while some are earthy in youth.

A Personal Selection of Chassagne-Montrachet Producers

Domaine Adrien Belland

Red Morgeot Clos Charreau with a raw, fruity nose redolent of strawberries – young wines only seen, but they should develop prettily.

Domaine Blain-Gagnard

Connected with Delagrange-Bachelet, this is a grandson making honeyed Bâtard, needing time for its full potential to emerge, and white Morgeot of full, robust flavour – both show oak when young.

Domaine Madame François Colin

White Les Vergers of great style, balance and flavour.

Domaine Michel Colin-Deléger

White Les Chaumées (classed as Premier Cru, but one of the *lieux-dits* which usually disappears inside a better-known name) with a heady smell of apricots – marked alcohol in 1983, but then, many wines show this trait in this vintage.

Domaine Delagrange-Bachelet

Biscuity white Les Caillerets, with a full taste much better than the bouquet.

Domaine Georges Deléger

White Morgeot which is worth finding and, usually, drinking relatively early.

Domaine Jean-Noël Gagnard

The Bâtard-Montrachet of this brilliant winemaker opened my senses to white burgundy, many years ago, and for that I shall always be grateful. He is still making stunning wine, rich, explosive of taste and beautiful enough to silence conversation. There is also white Les Caillerets, Morgeot and straight Chassagne, as well as a range of reds – I recommend that you try his Morgeot.

Domaine Gagnard-Delagrange/Domaine Fontaine-Gagnard

A renowned estate, where standards remain high. Even the straight white Chassagne-Montrachet is impressive, oaky, with a bouquet of acacia, mayblossom and woodsmoke leading to a smooth, firm taste. The young red is a mixture of loganberries and wood which promises well.

Château Génot-Boulanger

Charles Génot makes whites which need a few years to look their best – Les Vergers is floral and smoky, becoming plumper on contact with the air. I have been less impressed with the reds under this banner.

Domaine Jacques Girardin

Red Morgeot which has a lovely fresh fruit nose and is most pleasant, if not of marked distinction.

Château de la Maltroye

Rather a disturbing property as the potential is there but many of the wines are spoilt by careless handling, such as a dirty red Clos du Château de la Maltroye 1979, and the white 1982 was faulty. But a white Morgeot Vigne Blanche 1981 was excellent. If everyone exercises care in buying, the owners will surely see that it is in their interests to make fine, clean wine.

E. & D. Moingeon
This négociant-éleveur (in Beaune) produces straight red Chassagne with a deep Pinot nose and a good fruity taste.

Domaine Albert/Bernard Morey
Red Chassagne which has a lovely frank taste of crunchy strawberries. White Les Caillerets often takes a few years to open out, while Les Baudines softens sooner. There is also white Les Embrazées at this domain.

Domaine Pierre Morey
Incredibly good Bâtard-Montrachet, tight at first, then full, rich and toasty.

Domaine Michel Niellon
An exemplary array of wines, from Bâtard and Chevalier down to straight Chassagne, all full, fat and strong on aromas and flavour.

Domaine Jean & Fernand Pillot
Very honourable straight white Chassagne, with oak giving structure, and lovely tastes of vanilla, cinnamon and acacia.

Domaine Paul Pillot
Morgeot which gives generously at quite a young age, lovely lush white wine.

Domaine Ramonet-Prudhon
Some patchiness in the quality, but a Bienvenues, bottled by Delaunay, had great potential for ageing.

● ○ AUXEY-DURESSES

1983 production: Auxey-Duresses red *3,311 hectolitres*
Auxey-Duresses white *1,143 hectolitres*

Premiers Crus: Les Duresses, Bas des Duresses, Reugne, Les Grands-Champs , Climat du Val known as Clos du Val (part), Les Ecusseaux (part), Les Bréterins.

Auxey-Duresses is tucked in behind Monthélie, in a fertile valley at the foot of Mont Melian, and surrounded by slopes covered with vines. The appellation produces about one-third white wine to two-thirds red, but the areas of their production are quite well divided, with the white coming from the Coteaux du Mont Melian, an extension of Meursault and Puligny, and the red from the Montagne du Bourdon, an extension of Monthélie and Volnay. Les Duresses, on the Montagne du Bourdon, sits on a very pebbly marly-calcareous base, with more soil at the foot of the slope than on the top. It faces east and southeast. La Chapelle is very similar to Duresses, with a little more marl than calcareous matter. The Clos du Val is magnificently situated facing due south, very calcareous, with more marl and pebbles than Les Duresses and La Chapelle and very little soil on the upper slopes. The soil on the Montagne du Mont Melian is even thinner, far better suited to making white wine than red.

Les Duresses produces fruity wine with some finesse, with notes of raspberry and good colour. La Chapelle can have more body and take longer to develop, with Clos du Val more powerful still, both leaning towards cassis. White Auxey has a lovely biscuity flavour, but should be drunk relatively young – its development is quicker than a Meursault.

A Personal Selection of Auxey-Duresses Producers

Domaine Robert & Michel Ampeau
Soft, warmly earthy red wine, fruitily charming when young.

Bouchard Pére & Fils
White Auxey of pedigree – gloriously biscuity when young.

Domaine Jean-Pierre Diconne
Wood is very evident in both red and white wines, with Les Duresses therefore needing some time to emerge from the ageing. The white Auxey is lanolin smooth and very rich – drink young when the pleasure is at its optimum.

Domaine Alain Gras
Very reliable red. He also vinifies for René Gras, and there is a good, mild white Auxey under this label.

Domaine Charles Jobard
Les Ecusseaux was certainly very tannic and alcoholic, but this could be the 1983 style rather than the appellation. Bouquet of minty earth and redcurrants.

Domaine Leroy
The headquarters of the Leroy empire, but they also own vineyards in Auxey. The wines are always big and long-lasting.
Domaine du Duc de Magenta
Fine white wine, and usually good red.
Domaine Michel Prunier
Good white which is full of character.
Domaine Bernard Roy
Le Val which is a real keeper, worthy of the *cru*.

● ○ ST-ROMAIN

1983 production: St-Romain red *1,594 hectolitres*
St-Romain white *1,380 hectolitres*

There are no Premiers Crus.

This is really a forgotten little village, on a steep slope, and formerly belonging to the Hautes Côtes rather than to the Côte de Beaune. With cliffs and rocks all around, little of the area is planted with vines. The basic soil is calcareous clay with some pebbles. Slightly more red than white wine is produced, although the white has a wider reputation. Certain sites are better suited to the Chardonnay, such as the marly Sous Roches and the chalky Les Jarrons, facing from southeast to west. La Combe Bazin has rather irony red soil at the foot of the slope (above it is always more limestone-marl), Les Poillanges on the opposite slope has roughly the same soil makeup, facing east like the pebbly Sous le Château. The best sites have good sun exposure, protection from wind and lack of humidity.

The red wines have a strong cherry flavour and a certain *goût de terroir*. The whites are fresh and fruity, developing quite quickly, best when they have a sprightly taste and attack.

A Personal Selection of St-Romain Producers

Domaine du Château de Puligny-Montrachet
This is the wine of Roland Thévenin, who has done so much for the appellation. Both red and white are more than respectable.
Domaine Alain Gras
Elegant white and good non-filtered, strong red.
Domaine René Gras Boisson
Delicious red St-Romain, with a nose of crushed violets and a taste of violet creams and redcurrants.
Domaine René Thévenin-Monthélie
Very commendable white wine, with some style.

● ○ ST-AUBIN

1983 production: St-Aubin red *2,482 hectolitres*
St-Aubin white *1,233 hectolitres*

Premiers Crus: The situation is extremely complicated, with 16 *climats* encompassing 29 *lieux-dits*. In practice, several *lieux-dits* are grouped together under the same Premier Cru, the most frequently used being: La Chatenière, En Remilly, Les Murgers des Dents de Chien, Les Champlots, Le Charmois, Le Village, Les Castets, Sur le Sentier du Clou, Les Cortons, Les Frionnes, Sous Roche Dumay, Les Perrières.

Perhaps this is one of the "undiscovered" gems of Burgundy, since the growers here seem to be particularly conscientious and the wines uniformly good. Recent tastings have produced extremely few disappointments and many delectable bottles, at prices which are not as exorbitant as other parts of the Côte d'Or. St-Aubin is a tiny village behind Puligny-Montrachet and Meursault, near the hamlet of Gamay, with the vineyards facing in all directions from southeast to southwest. The soils vary, as there are really two distinct parts of St-Aubin: the vineyards below Gamay on the Roche du May, which is the end of the Côte d'Or slope; and those on the Montagne du Ban which runs westwards. Here, the steep slopes contain much limestone, affecting Premiers Crus such as Frionnes, Sentier du Clou and Castets, while the Roche du May, Champlots, La Chatenière, Sous Roche Dumay and Dents de Chien (where but Burgundy would one find such names?) are on marl covered by calcareous debris and brown clay and chalk.

It is not deleterious to St-Aubin to say that its wines are slightly lighter, fresher versions of grander appellations. The reds can resemble Chassagne-Montrachet, with less body, and the whites veer more towards Puligny than Meursault, with less intense perfume and fat. I have found that many of the reds have a taste of strawberries, and there are inevitable nuances between the Premiers Crus – Sous Roche Dumay tends to have more body and tannin in youth, while the limestone of Les Castets gives finesse. The best whites often come from La Chatenière and Les Murgers des Dents de Chien. Here, the hazelnuts bouquet is very marked.

A Personal Selection of St-Aubin Producers

Domaine Madame Jean Bachelet
Delicate whites, redolent of hazelnuts and mayblossom.

Domaine Clerget
This is the big name in St-Aubin and the Clerget family have done much for the appellation. The domain makes wonderful Frionnes Blanc, with fruit, balance and breed, while the white wines of Raoul Clerget, négociant-éleveur, are consistently fine. Their white Domaine du Pimont le Charmois is good, floral and oaky. The red wines tend to have lengthy barrel-ageing.

Domaine Marc Colin
White La Chatenière, aromatic, and with a taste of rose petals.

Louis Jadot
Has good, white St-Aubin.

Domaine Michel Lamanthe
I have liked the full, nutty white wine, but have been more dubious about a bitter taste in a red.

Domaine Lamy
Hubert Lamy makes excellent red Castets, built to last, while the white Frionnes mixes acacia with oak in a very stylish way.

Domaine Aimé Langoureau
Gilles Bouton, the grandson, makes white En Remilly which is rich and oaky, in a rather broad style.

Domaine André Moingeon
Pretty red wine, for relatively young drinking.

Domaine Henri Prudhon & Fils
Intensely strawberryish, light reds, and delicious white wine, marked by vanillin and clean oak and with a honeyed finish.

Domaine Roux Père & Fils
Meticulous winemaking produces lovely whites of finesse, especially La Chatenière, and cherryish reds.

● ○ SANTENAY

1983 production: Santenay red *12,016 hectolitres*
Santenay white *241 hectolitres*

Premiers Crus: Les Gravières, Le Clos de Tavannes, La Comme, Beauregard, Passetemps, Beaurepaire, La Maladière, Le Petit Clos Rousseau (part), Le Clos des Mouches, Le Clos Faubard, Le Grand Clos Rousseau.

Coming from the south, this is where the Côte de Beaune begins. Wits say that this is where water and wine meet, since Santenay is also a thermal resort. It is certainly a suitable port of call for those with digestive, liver or gout problems. And where there is a *Station Thermale*, there is always a Casino. . . . The soil is somewhat varied, with the Premiers Crus of La Comme and Les Gravières, on the northern slope of Santenay, having a topsoil of gravel over marly-limestone. Whereas Les Gravières is nearly flat, La Comme and the very pebbly Beauregard are on the side of the slope. The appellation is essentially red, but within Les Gravières there is a plot producing white wine, including the very good Clos des Gravières. On the south side of Santenay, the soils are either brown limestone or deep in character, and the wines are inevitably more earthy here.

The red wines of Santenay are often marked by a *goût de terroir* and can be quite tannic and hard in youth with a marked earthy quality. Les Gravières has the greatest finesse, while La Comme is more robust. La Maladière can be elegant and supple and ready for drinking sooner. Violets, chestnuts, strawberries and almonds have all been found on the nose, while the whites can have a youthful bouquet of hazelnuts and ferns.

A Personal Selection of Santenay Producers

Domaine de l'Abbaye de Santenay, Louis Clair
Their Premier Cru Les Gravières has very good appellation character and the domain maintains a high standard.

Domaine Adrien Belland
Good Santenay and even better, robust Santenay-Comme.

Domaine Hubert Bouzereau
Exemplary Santenay – gamey, "wet dogs", crushed strawberries.

Domaine Guy Dufouleur
The Clos Genêts of this domain has very good, earthy Santenay character, full but fruity and frank, not over-alcoholic and soupy.

Domaine Fleurot-Larose
A large domain also linked with Maufoux.

Domaine Jean Giradin – Château de la Charrière, Gravières
This is the top Girardin wine, with very good keeping potential. Straight Santenay too, and from Jacques Girardin.

Domaine des Hautes-Cornières, Philippe Chapelle & Fils
Straight Santenay which is vibrant, gamey, rustic and frank, plus Les Gravières.

Domaine Hervé Olivier
Good, straight Santenay, with some finesse in the 1981.

Domaine Lequin-Roussot
A sizeable domain, with a good spread of Premiers Crus. The wines are made to last and are full of character. There is also a Santenay Blanc. René and Louis Lequin run the domain.

Mestre-Père & Fils – Santenay Clos Faubard
Earthy and fruity. A large domain, important in the Premiers Crus. Less than half the wine made is domain-bottled.

Prosper Maufoux
The most important négociant for the appellation, and their Santenay Blanc Clos des Gravières is particularly impressive, with a fresh, nutty nose, a scent of hedgerows and rich fullness.

Domaine Bernard Morey
Superb Grand Clos Rousseau, with new wood and sheer finesse.

Domaine de la Pousse d'Or – Clos de Tavannes and Les Gravières
Very often the best wines of the appellation. The only vintage which seemed not quite up to standard was the 1982.

Domaine Prieur-Brunet – Santenay-Maladière
The wines are reliable, with good appellation character.

Domaine Roux – Santenay Premier Cru
Santenay made with a St-Aubin hand, and very fruity too!

Domaine St-Michel
A very important domain in the village, with Pierre Maufoux and Michel Gutrin running it jointly, but with the house of Maufoux doing the selling. Maufoux wines are marked with wood, strong in alcohol and meant for ageing.

● COTE DE BEAUNE-VILLAGES

1983 production: Red *7,147 hectolitres*

This is an appellation which covers the following sixteen villages: Auxey-Duresses, Blagny, Chassagne-Montrachet, Cheilly les Maranges, Chorey lès Beaune, Dézize les Maranges, Ladoix, Meursault, Monthélie, Pernand-Vergelesses, Puligny-Montrachet, St-Aubin, St-Romain, Sampigny les Maranges, Santenay, Savigny lès Beaune.

All these villages can sell their wine under their own name but, especially in the case of the lesser-known villages or in communes where the white wines are paramount, it is more advantageous to use the Côte de Beaune-Villages label. This is, in fact, an appellation mostly sold by the négociants, who can make a more satisfactory wine by inter-village blending. There is another option, rarely seen, when the producer puts on the label the name of the village appellation followed by the term Côte de Beaune in letters of the same size. The wines can be quite structured and tannic, needing a few years in bottle to soften. Cheilly, Dézize and Sampigny are not in the *département* of the Côte d'Or, but are just over the border in the Saône-et-Loire. They share the Premier Cru of Maranges, which faces due south, and the soil has much more clay than elsewhere. Hence the wines are quite tough and powerful.

A–Z of BURGUNDY PRODUCERS

The directory that follows lists in alphabetical order a selection of wine producers (whether growers, négociants, or négociants-éleveurs) in Burgundy. Each entry gives the name and address of the producer, and then (where available) the total area under vines in hectares (ha), whether the land is owned or worked directly, or whether some other form of tenure is practised, for example *métayage* or *fermage* (forms of shareholding). Then follow details of individual vineyard holdings and production figures, again where available, in bottles per annum or hectolitres per hectare (hl/ha). These production figures are approximate averages as supplied by each property. The author's personal comment concludes most entries.

As a rule, the general density of planting of vines in the Côte d'Or is 10,000 vines per ha, whereas in Chablis it is 6,000 per ha.

Pierre Amiot

21000 Morey-St-Denis. Clos de la Roche, Morey-St-Denis 1er Cru Les Millandes, Gevrey-Chambertin Aux Combottes. Remarkably good wines with a bouquet of undergrowth and truffles. The 1984 Combottes is astonishing for the vintage.

Robert Ampeau & Fils

6 rue du Cromin, 21190 Meursault. 10ha (owned). Puligny-Montrachet Combettes; Meursault Perrières, Charmes and La Pièce sous le Bois, Meursault (all white wine). Pommard, Volnay-Santenots, Beaune Clos du Roi, Blagny La Pièce sous le Bois, Savigny-lès-Beaune Lavières, Savigny-lès-Beaune, Auxey-Duresses Ecusseaux (all red wine).

Robert Ampeau and his son Michel work immensely hard and produce some astonishing wines. At first, it was the whites which were renowned, but now the reds are excellent too. The whites last beautifully, with explosive flavours, heady bouquets and vanillin textures – they are frequently in full flight while other wines of the same appellation are tiring. The reds ooze gamey fruit – I like the Blagny and Auxey, and even the Savignys, while they are still quite young and precocious, but obviously the Pommard, Beaune Clos du Roi and Volnay Santenots last longer. An Ampeau bottle is always a treat, but they are not seen as much as they should be – M. Ampeau does not much like selling his wines!

Pierre André

Château de Corton-André, Aloxe-Corton, 21420 Savigny-lès-Beaune. 22.43ha. Bourgogne 6ha, 30,000 bottles; Ladoix Clos des Chagnots 2ha, 8,500 bottles; Savigny-lès-Beaune: Les Godeaux 2.50ha, 10,000 bottles; Clos des Guettes 2.50ha, 10,000 bottles; Aloxe-Corton 2ha, 8,000 bottles; Aloxe-Corton 1er Cru 1.50ha, 6,000 bottles; Corton Clos du Roi 1ha, 4,000 bottles; Corton Château de Corton-André .33ha, 12,000 bottles; Pernand-Vergelesses 1ha, 4,500 bottles; Ladoix Blanc 1ha, 4,000 bottles; Corton-Charlemagne 2ha, 6,800 bottles; Savigny-Vergelesses .60ha, 2,800 bottles.

Pierre André is both a négociant and an important proprietor of vineyards. The labels depict the beautiful, flamboyantly tiled roofs of Burgundy. M. André founded and owns the firm of La Reine Pédauque. I am afraid that I do not get on at all with the wines, which I find sweet, alcoholic and jammy. But the sales in France are big – exports are much smaller.

Domaine B. Bachelet (M. Denis Bachelet)

21000 Gevrey-Chambertin.

Domaine Bachelet-Ramonet Père & Fils

Chassagne-Montrachet, 21190 Meursault. 10ha, including parcels of Bâtard-Montrachet, Chassagne Les Caillerets, Ruchottes, La Romanée, La Grande Montagne, Morgeot, Clos St-Jean, Clos de la Boudriotte.

André Bart
24 rue de Mazy, 21160 Marsannay-la-Côte. 9.6ha, 5.4ha in Bourgogne Rouge, Blanc and Rosé at Marsannay and Couchey, 1.8ha at Fixin, 1.6ha at Santenay, .8ha in the Grands Crus Bonnes Mares and Clos de Bèze.

Thomas Bassot
5 quai Dumorey, 21700 Nuits-St-Georges. Négociants.

Jules Belin
Prémeaux-Prissey, 21700 Nuits-St-Georges. 12ha in Prémeaux (Nuits 1er Crus Clos Arlots, red and white wines), and Comblanchien.

Adrien Belland
Place du Jet d'Eau, 21590 Santenay. 11ha. In Santenay: Clos Genet 1.49ha, Charmes .52ha, Hâtes 1.09ha, Commes Dessus .44ha, various 1.57ha, 1er Cru Clos des Gravières 1.21ha, 1er Cru La Comme .85ha. In Chassagne-Montrachet: 1er Cru Morgeot Clos Charreau .48ha. In Puligny-Montrachet: .45ha. In Aloxe-Corton: Les Bouthières .58ha. Grands Crus: Corton-Grèves .55ha, Corton-Perrières .69ha, Corton Clos de la Vigne au Saint .49ha, Chambertin .41ha. Production: Santenay, Chassagne, Puligny, Aloxe-Corton all 40hl/ha; Grands Crus 32–35hl/ha.

An archetypal, fragmented Burgundian domain, but this one is well run – always a feat when the vineyards are so scattered, from southern Santenay right up to Chambertin. M. Adrien Belland is now helped by one of his sons and they follow a policy of destalking, long vatting, fermentation with *chapeau flottant* and *pigeage* twice a day, ageing in oak casks and bottling after 20–22 months. Recent vintages have impressed me and I will watch their progress with interest. M. Belland sells to just about everyone, which could be called a safe policy – private clients, restaurants, négociants in France, and to all the usual markets abroad.

Domaine Bertagna
21640 Vougeot. 11ha. Nuits 1er Cru Murgers 1ha; Vosne 1er Cru Beauxmonts 1ha; Vougeot 1er Cru: Clos de la Perrière 2ha, Petits Vougeots 2.50ha, Cras 1ha, Clos Bertagna .30ha; Vougeot Grand Cru: Clos Vougeot .30ha; Chambolle 1er Cru Plantes .20ha; Chambolle-Musigny .40ha; Clos-St-Denis Grand Cru .50ha; Chambertin Grand Cru .20ha. 40,000–45,000 bottles.

A fine "clutch" of Vougeot vineyards. The vinification is traditional, with manual *pigeage* (using poles, instead of feet!), and *élevage*, or maturing, in new oak barrels. Sales are divided 50% direct at the domain and 50% export. I have been impressed in recent tastings, especially in the vintages of the late 1970s, but 1982 and 1983 are also fine.

Domaine Besancenot-Mathouillet
19 rue de Chorey, 21200 Beaune. 7.6ha, 6.4ha in Beaune 1ers Crus (Bressandes, Clos du Roi, Toussaints). Also rents some Aloxe-Corton 1er Cru and 1ha Pernand-Vergelesses. An important, well run domain with some classic Beaune.

Maison Albert Bichot
6 bis boulevard Jacques Copeau, 21200 Beaune. 64.80ha. Vosne-Romanée Domaine du Clos Frantin 17ha in Gevrey-Chambertin, Richebourg, Clos Vougeot, Grands-Echézeaux, Echézeaux, Vosne-Romanée Les Malconsorts, Nuits-St-Georges and Corton; Long-Depaquit: Vaudésir Grand Cru 2.59ha, Moutonne 2.43ha; Lupé-Cholet: Nuits 1er Cru Les Crots 4.04ha, Clos de Lupé 3.23ha.

A huge firm, concentrating on exports. They have a multitude of *sous-noms*, including Paul Bouchard and Jean Bouchard, not to be confused with other Beaune Bouchards. I am happiest with their Chablis wines, the splendid La Moutonne and also the wines of Long-Depaquit.

GAEC Simon Bize & Fils
21420 Savigny-lès-Beaune. 14ha (6ha *en fermage*). Savigny 1er Cru Les Vergelesses 3ha, 15,000 bottles, Les Guettes .50ha, Savigny-lès-Beaune 6ha, 25,000 bottles, Bourgogne Les Perrières 3ha, 15,000 bottles.

An extremely serious family estate, passed from father to son for 150 years. Patrick Bize is now making the wine, with great respect for the *fruit* and no excess weight or camouflage. He seems to have the right formula for this weight of wine – 10-day fermentations, about 18 months in oak before bottling, with a third new wood. Bravo. Snap up the Savigny-Vergelesses if you can.

Domaine Henri Boillot

Volnay, 21190 Meursault. 21.6ha. 4ha Volnay, 4ha Puligny-Montrachet, 2.2ha Pommard 1er Cru.

Jean-Claude Boisset

2 rue des Frères Montgolfier, 21700 Nuits-St-Georges. Includes a 10.93ha domain in Nuits 1er Cru Les Damodes, Gevrey-Chambertin, Côte de Nuits-Villages.

This is a négociant with only 25 years behind it but large sales. They buy both wines and grapes. I am afraid these burgundies give me absolutely no "lift" at all.

Domaine Bonneau du Martray

Pernand Vergelesses, 21420 Savigny-lès-Beaune. 11ha. Pernand-Vergelesses 4.50ha, Aloxe-Corton 4.50ha. Produces two Grands Crus exclusively: Corton-Charlemagne (white) 41,000 bottles, Corton (red) 9,000 bottles.

A very well-run domain, with vineyards mid-slope on the Montagne de Corton. The owner, the Comte Jean le Bault de la Morinière, comes down from Paris every weekend. For their great Corton-Charlemagne, stainless steel vats are used for the first, tumultuous stage of the fermentation, thereby keeping the temperature below 20°C (particularly useful with the 1985 vintage), and then the wines finish fermenting in new oak barrels. The Corton-Charlemagne is a rich, nutty experience – all the expected years are superb, but even more modest vintages, like 1974, are intense, wonderful drinking over a decade after their birth. The Corton is vinified in open oak vats and the *élevage* is in a mixture of new, 2nd- and 3rd-year oak *pièces*. There is elegance in these wines, and weight too in years like 1971, 76 and 78. 92% of production is exported to 19 different countries, but in France the only sales are to restaurants which have been awarded Michelin stars.

M. Roland Bouchacourt

Au Pavillon, 69840 Juliénas. 20ha (four *métayers*). Juliénas: Domaine de la Bottière Pavillon 4.42ha, 32,800 bottles; Chénas: Domaine du Fief 1.96ha, 15,000 bottles; Beaujolais-Villages: Domaine de la Chize 12.92ha, 101,200 bottles.

Traditionally made Beaujolais and Chénas, but for the Juliénas longer vatting *à la bourguignonne* to make a wine that lasts. Apart from private clients, the wine is sold through the négociants Pellerin.

Bouchard Aîné & Fils

36 rue Ste-Marguerite, 21203 Beaune. 23ha. AOC Mercurey Rouge 19ha, AOC Mercurey Blanc 1.75ha (La Vigne du Chapitre, Le Clos la Marche, Les Couchois, La Rochelle); 1984 vintage: 506hl (which is less than 25hl/ha).

Of course, Bouchard Aîné are first and foremost very important Beaune négociants, so it may come as something of a surprise to discover that their main vineyard holdings are on the Côte Chalonnaise. They stress the importance of limited yields, and follow a vinification policy of long maceration in open wood *cuves* and maturing in barrels made from Allier oak, with a third new each year. The wines usually keep well and are often *tastevinés*, but they are seen more frequently in the region than on the export markets. Bouchard Aîné also buy the grapes and make the wine of the Domaine Marion, which includes Chambertin Clos de Bèze. The négociant wines puzzle me somewhat, as sometimes they are rather good, and on other occasions best avoided. This is a pity, as the better wines certainly win friends for them.

Bouchard Père & Fils (Domaines du Château de Beaune)
Au Château, 21200 Beaune. 93.26ha. La Romanée (red) .85ha, 3,960 bottles; Beaune du Château (red) 28.64ha, 150,000 bottles, Beaune Clos de la Mousse (red) 3.36ha, 18,000 bottles; Beaune Grèves (red) Vigne de l'Enfant Jésus 3.91ha, 21,000 bottles; Beaune Marconnets (red) 2.32ha, 13,000 bottles; Beaune Teurons (red) 2.30ha, 13,000 bottles; Le Corton (red) 3.94ha, 17,000 bottles; Savigny-lès-Beaune Les Lavières (red) 3.20ha, 21,000 bottles; Volnay Caillerets (red) 3.72ha, 20,000 bottles; Volnay Fremiets (red) Clos de la Rougeotte 1.52ha, 9,000 bottles; Volnay Taillepieds (red) 1.10ha, 5,400 bottles; Brouilly (red) Domaine de Saburin 28ha, 150,000 bottles; Montrachet (white) 1ha, 6,000 bottles; Meursault Les Genevrières (white) 1.40ha, 8,500 bottles; Corton-Charlemagne (white) 3ha, 17,000 bottles; Chevalier-Montrachet (white) 2ha, 11,000 bottles; Beaune du Château (white) 5.87ha, 30,000 bottles; Beaune Clos Saint Landry 12,000 bottles; Pommard 1er Cru 6,000 bottles; Ladoix Clos Royer 4,500 bottles; Aloxe-Corton 2,500 bottles; Chambolle-Musigny 4,000 bottles; Bourgogne Aligoté Bouzeron 34,000 bottles; Chambertin 800 bottles.

A considerable family firm, selling their burgundies around the world. In the négociant business, they manage to combine quantity with quality, within the bounds of the possible, for when one is in the market for 1,000 cases of an appellation, you cannot expect the individuality of a small, specialist estate. But the domain wines of BPF, known as the Domaines du Château de Beaune, are very good indeed, and it is only a pity that on some export markets they do not have the distribution or reputation that they should. BPF have always been in the vanguard of technical advance, and they have a splendid new computer-controlled vinification plant, necessary for the huge amount of grapes they now buy in. But the traditional side is well preserved, with the domain wines being kept in beautiful convent cellars, and enormous investment in new wood barrels.

Pierre Bourée
21220 Gevrey-Chambertin.

This is a small négociant, with wines from both Côtes. People seem to "discover" the wines every few years, but they are not really to my taste, seemingly too alcoholic and top-heavy, although others like the style. The firm is sole owner of Gevrey-Chambertin Clos de la Justice.

Lionel J. Bruck
6 quai Dumorey, 21700 Nuits-St-Georges. Négociant – deals with 44ha in the Côte d'Or, incl. the 6ha Domaine of the Château de Vosne-Romanée, a parcel of Corton Clos du Roi, and 6.8ha of Savigny 1er Cru Les Guettes.

Domaine Georges Bryczek
Morey-St-Denis, 21220 Gevrey-Chambertin. 3.2ha 1er Cru Clos-Sorbés and a parcel of Morey-Village.

Calvet
21200 Beaune.

This is a large négociant, much in evidence on the boulevard around Beaune. I have to say that they produce some of the most disappointing burgundies I have ever encountered.

Domaine Camus Père & Fils
21220 Gevrey-Chambertin. 14.8ha, incl. 1.6ha of Chambertin and 6.4ha of Charmes Chambertin, with parcels of Latricières and Mazis.

Château des Capitans (R. Sarrau)
69840 Juliénas. 11ha. Juliénas 7ha, 45,000 bottles; Fleurie 4ha, 20,000 bottles.

Robert Sarrau owns the property and the wine is exclusively sold by the firm of Sarrau at St-Jean d'Ardières. 65% of the production is exported, 35% sold in France. Traditional vinification, with *grillage*, or a meshed lid, keeping the *chapeau* of skins submerged in the must, giving powerful wines which keep. Domain bottling.

Louis Carillon & Fils

21190 Puligny-Montrachet. 12ha. White wines: Bienvenues-Bâtard-Montrachet (the Carillon own a small patch), 800 bottles; Puligny-Montrachet 1er Cru 2.50ha, 10,000–12,000 bottles; Puligny-Montrachet 5ha, 12,000–15,000 bottles; Chassagne-Montrachet .25ha, 1,500 bottles; Bourgogne Aligoté .25ha. Red wines: Chassagne-Montrachet 1ha, 4,500 bottles; Mercurey 1ha, 2,500 bottles; Côte de Beaune-Villages 1ha, 3,000 bottles; Bourgogne 1ha, 3,000 bottles.

Carillons have been making wine since 1632, and know their métier very well. They sell direct, export and deal with négociants. Their white wines are matured in oak barrels for a year, then spend 3–6 months in stainless steel or enamel-lined containers before bottling. The red grapes are entirely or partially destalked, according to the character of the year, vatting/fermentation takes 8–10 days, and the *élevage* is the same as for the whites. The Pulignys have elegance and style.

Cave Coopérative La Chablisienne

89800 Chablis. Handles grapes from 496ha, including 334.8ha Chablis, 96ha 1ers Crus, 50ha Petit Chablis, 14.8ha Grands Crus.

Cave Coopérative des Grands Vins de Fleurie

69820 Fleurie. 388ha. Fleurie 277ha, Moulin-à-Vent 16ha, Morgon 22ha, Chiroubles 2ha, Beaujolais-Villages 61ha, Beaujolais 10ha. Fleurie 150,000 bottles, Beaujolais-Villages 10,000 bottles.

A very well-run cooperative, with good, true Fleurie. Their two top *cuvées* are the Cuvée Presidente Marguerite (named after a wonderful lady, Mlle Marguerite Chabert, who presides over the Cave), a perfumed "feminine" Fleurie, and the Cuvée du Cardinal Bienfaiteur, which is more powerful and can take some bottle age.

Caves Coopératives des Grands Vins de Juliénas
(Château du Bois de la Salle)

69840 Juliénas. 164ha in AC Juliénas, covering the communes of Juliénas, Jullié and Pruzilly; production 9,000hl, approx. 1,200,000 bottles.

A very "serious" cooperative, founded in 1961 with 83 members and 94ha. In 1985, there were 306 members and 341ha (including other appellations). The Cave sells to négociants, direct, and on the export markets – and they do a very good job of work. This is an example of a successful cooperative in the Beaujolais which is also playing a valuable role in today's market.

Cave Coopérative des Grands Vins Rosés

21 rue de Mazy, 21160 Marsannay-la-Côte. Includes 19 members whose properties vary between .8ha and 14ha.

Cave Coopérative de Liergues

69400 Villefranche. 480ha: Gamay 478ha, Chardonnay 2ha. Beaujolais Blanc 7,000 bottles, Beaujolais Rosé 3,000 bottles, Beaujolais Rouge 20,000 bottles.

Founded in 1929, this is the oldest cooperative in the region. They are great Beaujolais Primeur specialists, concentrating on producing this fast-turnover, charming wine. It may be fashionable to knock the stuff, but it is still a lovely shot in the arm every November! Fairly light wines and delicious roses-and-strawberries Rosé.

Les Caves des Hautes Côtes Groupement de Producteurs

Route de Pommard, 21200 Beaune. 300ha. Bourgogne Hautes Côtes de Beaune (red and white) 100ha, Bourgogne Hautes Côtes de Nuits (red and white) 90ha, Bourgogne (red) 30ha, Bourgogne Aligoté (white) 40ha, Gamay 20ha, Pommard 1ha, Nuits St-Georges 1ers Crus (Pruliers, Thory, Gravières, Vignes Rondes) 1ha, Nuits-St-Georges 1.20ha, Savigny-lès-Beaune .50ha, St-Romain (red and white) .80ha, Crémant de Bourgogne 6ha, Chorey-lès-Beaune .30ha, Pernand-Vergelesses 1ha. 800,000 bottles. Remainder is sold in bulk.

This is a group of 120 producers who sell to négociants, the export markets and directly to the public. Their vinification has improved greatly in recent years, and the *élevage* now includes 1,200 oak *pièces*. The wines are fruity, fresh and charming, and good value. This is a very good source of supply for Burgundy's generic wines.

Yves Chaley (Vignobles du Val de Vergy)
Curtil-Vergy, 21220 Gevrey-Chambertin. 10ha. Bourgogne Hautes Côtes de Nuits red 32,000 bottles, white 3,000 bottles; Bourgogne Aligoté 8,000 bottles.

A well-situated domain, vital in the Hautes Côtes. Traditional methods, with the reds kept 16 months in oak *foudres*. The white wines are in stainless steel tanks, and are slowly fermented at 18°C both in order to obtain the maximum perfume and freshness. M. Chaley both exports and sells his wines direct.

Domaine Louis Champagnon
Les Brureaux, Chénas 69840 Juliénas. 7.50ha (1.50ha *en métayage*). Chénas 3.50ha, 18,000 bottles; Fleurie .70ha, 3,000 bottles; Moulin-à-Vent 3.30ha, 15,000 bottles.

Take no notice of the rather sombre black labels – these are remarkable wines, with astounding Moulin-à-Vent and Chénas (I have never tasted the much smaller production of Fleurie). The recipe seems to be fermentations of 8–10 days in wood *cuves*, with controlled maceration and vatting to obtain wines which will have body and keeping potential. Sales are to private customers and restaurants in France, and on the usual export markets (Belgium, Switzerland, Holland, America, England and Germany). The quality is really all that one would wish in one's wildest dreams, and the only question is, why cannot other people do the same? I also found that the wines remain impeccable on ullage, not that that happens very often with Champagnon bottles.

Champy Père & Cie
5 rue du Grenier à Sel, 21200 Beaune. 7.30ha. Clos Vougeot 2.42ha, Savigny 1er Cru La Dominode 2.02ha, Beaune 1ers Crus Les Avaux 2.83ha, and a little Clos des Mouches.

A small, old-established négociant and proprietor (founded in 1720, they might be the oldest négociant of all, but there is always someone to dispute this). Rather thick, heavy wines.

Domaine de la Chanaise (Pierre Piron)
69910 Villié-Morgon. 10.05ha (owned) in Morgon; 60,000 bottles.

Vinification is with semi-carbonic maceration at constant temperature to avoid too-rapid fermentation. According to M. Piron the wines keep for 5–10 years, depending on the type of vintage, but I have no experience of his bottles at such an age. A very wide range of customers in France, plus exports to Common Market countries and the USA.

Emile Chandesais
Château St Nicolas, BPI Fontaines, 71150 Chagny. 7.50ha (owned). 4.50ha Pinot Noir AC Bourgogne, 35,000–40,000 bottles; 3ha Chardonnay AC Bourgogne, 15,000–20,000 bottles.

An important négociant, based in the Côte Chalonnaise. They always buy at the Hospices de Beaune and I have been impressed by some of their *élevages*, which are usually silky and evidence new wood. I have also liked their Passe-Tout-Grains but not their Rully wines. The domain wines receive careful vinification, the reds in stainless steel vats, with total destalking and maturing in oak barrels, some of which are new. The whites are fermented in new oak barrels. Domains they distribute include Château de Néty (Beaujolais-Villages), Domaine Hermitage (Rully Rouge and Blanc, Mercurey and Bourgogne), and Domaine Gouffier (Bourgogne, Mercurey and Aligoté). 70% of sales is on the French market and the rest is exported to the UK, Switzerland, Belgium, Japan, Germany and the Netherlands.

Domaine Chandon de Briailles

21420 Savigny-lès-Beaune. 12.80ha in the three communes of Savigny-lès-Beaune, Pernand-Vergelesses and Corton; 54,000 bottles. All the grapes grown are Pinot Noir, except for 1% Chardonnay vines, producing Corton Blanc.

Owned by Comte Aymard-Claude de Nicolay and his children, who are related to the Chandons of Champagne fame, this is an estate with excellent vineyards (and a magnificent French garden). Winemaking methods are traditional, and sometimes one finds a very good bottle, but there is a feeling that with a little tighter control or technical help, things could be even better. More than half of the Domaine sales are on the export markets.

Chanson Père & Fils

10 rue Paul Chanson, 21200 Beaune. 44.55ha. Beaune Clos des Fèves 3.76ha, Teurons 6.07ha, Bressandes 2.10ha and parts of all the best Beaune *climats*.

Chanson is one of those Beaune houses combining an important *négoce* business with being owners of some very fine vineyards. Recent vintages of the domain wines have seemed excellent, although some of the négociant wines are dull.

Domaine de la Chapelle de Vatre

Jullié, 69840 Juliénas. 8ha. Beaujolais-Villages 8ha, producing 63,000 bottles per annum.

Traditional Beaujolais vinification produces wines which are not Primeurs, but which are ready for drinking from February after the vintage. The wine is distributed exclusively by the firm of Sarrau in St-Jean d'Ardières after bottling in their cellars – 65% goes to the export markets, 35% stays in France.

Domaine Maurice Chapuis (formerly *Louis*)

21420 Aloxe-Corton. 10ha (9 currently in production). Grands Crus and AC. Corton-Charlemagne 2,000 bottles; Corton-Perrières 3,000 bottles; Corton-Languettes 3,000 bottles; Corton 1,500 bottles; Aloxe-Corton 1er Cru 3,000 bottles; Aloxe-Corton 3,000 bottles.

Louis Chapuis, who has been such a mine of information on Burgundy over the years, retired at the end of 1985, and his son Maurice (who has been working with his father since 1974) has now taken full charge. A highly respected domain, which combines selling to négociants with direct selling locally and on the export markets. There has been recent modernization and construction of new cellars. Total destalking for Pinot Noir, with 10-day fermentations on average, and *élevage* in barrels (15% new each year) for 18 months to two years. Obviously, there is a rush to buy their excellent Corton-Charlemagne, but the reds are very honourable, exemplified by their Corton-Perrières 1983.

M. François Charles

Nantoux, 21000 Hautes Côtes de Beaune.

Domaine du Château de la Chaize

Odenas, 69460 St-Etienne-des-Oullières. 260ha. 96ha are planted with vines, 48ha are *en métayage*. All vineyards within the parish of Brouilly-Brouilly Château de la Chaize. Production: 58hl/ha. Average annual production: 500,000 bottles.

The Marquise de Roussy de Sales reigns over the largest integrated private wine estate in Beaujolais and Burgundy, which supports 24 families – the property includes extensive woods. The Château, built in 1676 following the plans of Mansart and Le Nôtre, is of great classical symmetry. Enormous attention to detail goes into making this fine Brouilly, which has the body and fruit in good vintages to last three to five years. Length of vatting is from five to seven days, and the wine is stocked in wooden *foudres* and then in stainless steel in order to ensure optimum freshness.

Domaine du Château de Chamirey (Antonin Rodet)
71640 Mercurey. 25ha. Pinot Noir 19ha (Clos du Roi 1er Cru, Clos l'Evêque, La Maladière); Chardonnay 6ha (La Mission, Les Sazenay).

The domain wines of Mercurey Château de Chamirey are distributed by négociant Antonin Rodet. I have mixed views about the *négoce* wines, although recently the standard seems to be improving. The domain wines are vinified in the very latest stainless steel *cuves*, but all the wine is aged in new oak barrels. The white Château de Chamirey is particularly successful and has given me much pleasure. The Marquis de Jouennes d'Herville, son-in-law of Antonin Rodet, owns the domain and is head of the négociant firm. Their wines are seen widely around the world, and on aeroplanes and ships.

F. Chauvenet
6 route de Chaux, 21700 Nuits-St-Georges. 44.55ha. Domaine de Pérignon 43.74ha, Nuits-St-Georges .80ha.

A large négociant, linked with the table-wine firm of Margnat – the Corsican Connection! Other names include Louis Max and Marc Chevillot. They have important holdings in the Yonne, the Domaine de Pérignon, known for its Passe-Tout-Grains.

Robert Chevillon
68 rue Felix Tisserand, 21700 Nuits-St-Georges. 8.70ha, 6.65ha *en métayage/fermage*. Nuits-St-Georges 1ers Crus, Les Roncières, Les Cailles, Les Perrières, Les Vaucrains, Les St-Georges. Produced 239hls in 1983, 215hls in 1984.

A comparatively recent (in Burgundian terms) estate which is growing in reputation. Traditional vinification, with quite long fermentations depending on vintage, followed by a maceration of the wine and skins for several days. Open *cuves* and *pigeage* and *remontage* every day. 80% of the total production is bottled at the domain, the rest sold to local négociants. Exports to a spread of countries. Successful 1980s here, as so often in this area. A winemaker to watch.

M. Bruno Clair
3 rue de la Maladière, 21160 Chassagne-Montrachet. 9ha. Savigny-lès-Beaune, Morey-St-Denis, Fixin, Marsannay-la-Côte.

Domaines Clair-Daü
21160 Marsannay-la-Côte. 51.23ha. Marsannay 27.10ha, Gevrey-Chambertin 1er Cru Clos St-Jacques 2.40ha, Clos du Fonteny .80ha, Grand Cru Clos de Bèze 2ha, Bonnes Mares 1.66ha; also parts of Chapelle-Chambertin. Les Amoureuses and "Village" land; Vosne-Romanée Grands Crus of Romanée Champs-Perdrix 1.01ha; Côte de Beaune Savigny 1er Cru La Dominode 2.02ha.

A very important domain, with some top *crus*, especially in Gevrey-Chambertin, Morey-St-Denis and Chambolle-Musigny. Unfortunately, family troubles caused occasional lapses in winemaking management, and real technical competence was sometimes missing. In the latter part of 1985, the Domaine was bought by the American wine importers Kobrand, who had already acquired the négociant business of Louis Jadot. Let us hope that this heralds a more stable era.

Georges Clerget
21640 Vougeot. 3ha owned and 1ha farmed. Equal plots in Chambolle-Musigny 1er Cru Charmes, Chambolle Village, Vougeot 1er Cru, Morey-St-Denis and Vosne-Romanée. Rents 1ha in Echézeaux and a very small parcel in Bonnes Mares.

Maison Raoul Clerget
St-Aubin, 21190 Meursault. 17ha. Domaine du Pimont 12ha (Chassagne Montrachet Rouge Les Chaumeés 3,000 bottles, Chassagne-Montrachet Blanc 15,000 bottles, St-Aubin Le Charmois (white) 30,000 bottles, (red) 15,000 bottles. Clerget 5ha St-Aubin Frionnes (white) 6,000 bottles, (red) 10,000 bottles.

A serious family domain; at the same time the Clergets are négociants. They regard lengthy wood ageing as important for the red wines, and the whites, too, often show oak influence when they are young.

Domaine Y. Clerget

Volnay, 21190 Meursault. 5.20ha. Bourgogne .35ha, Volnay 1.08ha, Volnay 1er Cru (L'Ormeau, Carelles, Champans) .47ha, Volnay Carelle Sous la Chapelle .31ha, Volnay Caillerets .31ha, Volnay Santenots .68ha, Volnay Clos du Verseuil .68ha, Pommard Rugiens .85ha, Meursault .37ha. 16,000 bottles.

This must be the family of growers with the oldest history in Burgundy – passed down from father to son in Volnay since 1270. Clergets abound, but this branch goes right back to the source. 1978 and 1983 are real *vins de garde*.

Domaine J-F. Coche Dury

21000 Meursault.

Paul Collonge

Domaine de Ruyère, 69910 Villié-Morgon. 11.50ha. Morgon 9ha, Beaujolais-Villages 2.5ha. 35,000 bottles.

The vineyards are well placed, facing south and southeast. The wines are robust, generous and keep well – M. Collonge calls the bouquet "kirsch and framboise" which is "typically Morgon". Direct selling in France and exports.

François Condemine

Château de Juliénas, 69840 Juliénas. 20ha in Juliénas producing 50hl/ha.

Semi-carbonic fermentations with whole uncrushed grapes *à la beaujolaise*. Temperature control possibilities, both for heating and cooling. The vinifications are relatively long for the region, as the intention is to make wines which can last up to five years or even more. The results are absolutely splendid, although I have never waited as long as this.

Coron Père & Fils

21200 Beaune. 4ha in 5 Beaune 1ers Crus.

Domaine de Courcel

21630 Pommard. 8.20ha. Grand Clos des Epenots 1er Cru 5ha, 15,000–20,000 bottles; Rugiens 1er Cru 1ha, 3,000–4,000 bottles; Croix Noires 1er Cru .60ha, 2,000 bottles; Fremiers 1er Cru .70ha, 2,500 bottles; Vaumuriens .20ha; Bourgogne .70ha, 3,000 bottles. Also two to three casks of Pommard sold in bulk.

Another old-established family domain to make the *parvenus* shudder; more than four centuries lie behind this estate. Extraordinary wine, deeply coloured and intensely concentrated, the result of long vatting and several *pigeages* each day to obtain the maximum extraction. No destalking, or only partial destalking, according to the year, and two years in new wood before bottling. These are wines to keep – and I wish I had more Rugiens 1978 in my cellar.

Cruse & Fils Frères

21700 Nuits-St-Georges.

Domaine Damoy

20 rue des Forges, 21190 Meursault. 5.7ha in Chambertin and Clos de Bèze. Also makes Chapelle-Chambertin and Gevrey-Chambertin *Monopole* Clos du Tamisot.

Domaine Darnat (Vincent L. Darnat)

20 rue des Forges, 21190 Meursault. 2.50ha, of which 2ha are currently in production. "Clos Richemont" Meursault Premier Cru Les Cras (sole owner of Clos Richemont) .60ha, 4,000–5,000 bottles. Meursault AOC Climats: Les Pelles, Les Charrons, Le Meix Tavaux 1.20ha, 8,000 bottles. Bourgogne AOC Blanc .20ha, 1,000–1,500 bottles.

The Domaine Darnat has belonged to the same family for more than a century and Clos Richemont has enjoyed an excellent reputation for a long time. The wine is exported to the USA and UK, and in France there are private clients – I have also seen the Clos Richemont sold under the Sélection Jean Germain label. Vinification owes nothng to "new" methods, Vincent Darnat being convinced that fermentation and ageing must be carried out in oak barrels for the wines to preserve all their character. And they most certainly do, even after years in bottle. There is always great flavour, and it would be a pity to drink the Clos Richemont too young. Unfortunately, there is very little of it.

R. Darroze, Clos des Quatre Vents

69820 Fleurie. 15ha *en métayage*, Fleurie mid-slope, south facing, 850hl/ha.

This is copybook Fleurie, sold only through two négociants: two-thirds is taken by Les Caves Bujard at Lutry in Switzerland, the rest by Georges Duboeuf, part of this going to the USA. The Fleurie for Switzerland is under the Clos des Quatre Vents label, the Duboeuf share is sold as the Domaine des Quatre Vents. It is interesting that the Swiss *cuvées* are made especially to bring out the aromatic character of the wine, whereas a longer vatting is given to the wines going to the USA via Duboeuf in order to give them more structure.

Domaine Darviot

21200 Beaune. 16ha (owned), 4.4ha Beaune 1ers Crus, 1.6ha Meursault, also land in Monthélie and Savigny-lès-Beaune.

GAEC Dauvissat (René & Vincent)

8 rue Emile Zola, 89800 Chablis. 9.27ha (.27ha *en métayage*). Chablis Grand Cru: Les Preuses 1ha, Les Clos 1.75ha, 16,000 bottles; Chablis 1er Cru: La Forest, Vaillons 6.50ha, 40,000 bottles.

Here is a gifted winemaker! These Chablis are really exemplary, combining the fruit and "nerviness" we should find in this appellation, and the kind of flavour which just makes one go "mmmm". This is how M. Dauvissat does it: pressing, *débourbage* or clarifying, of the must, slow fermentation at low temperature (achieved by cooling) in vat, where the wine stays until after the malolactic fermentation. However, 10% of the must is fermented in oak barrels. The wine is aged in oak casks from April to November, and then bottled from December to March after refrigeration and light filtration. The wines keep beautifully. M. Dauvissat thinks 1981, 1975 and 1983 were his very best wines. The wines go to Parisian and provincial restaurants, private customers and all around the world. Since 1950, the property has quadrupled in size, and there have been modern innovations alongside the traditional. One only wishes the Dauvissats could expand even further, and then there would be more wine for us devotees!

David & Foillard

69830 St-Georges-de-Reneins. Probably the largest négociants in the Rhône.

Domaine Delachanal (Jean-Pierre Charmette)

69460 Odenas. 5ha, half of which are in Brouilly, half in Côte de Brouilly. Three-quarters are old vines on the southern side of the hill of Brouilly. 15,000 bottles per annum, 2,000 magnums (in Côte de Brouilly).

Traditional vinification in wooden vats and bottling in March of the following year. Vatting is usually 6–7 days here, so this is not ephemeral Côte de Brouilly. Sells to négociants, as well as to private clients, and exports to Switzerland. Speciality of amusing labels, "personalized" presents designed for customers, such as the Cuvée des Pompistes, Cuvée des Douaniers, and even the Cuvée des Bordelais!

Domaine Delagrange-Bachelet

Chassagne-Montrachet, 21190 Meursault. 10ha. .5ha each of Bâtard-Montrachet and Criots-Bâtard-Montrachet. 1ha of 1er Cru Caillerets, 2ha of Morgeot (red and white) and small plots of Volnay and Pommard 1er Cru.

B. & J-M. Delaunay

Château de Charmont, L'Etang-Vergy, 21220 Gevrey-Chambertin.

This is a family firm of *commissionaires en vins*, who work entirely on the export markets. Their strength is in their tasting and selecting ability, so any burgundy bought from them really tastes of its appellation. They cover the whole of the region, from Dijon down to the Beaujolais.

André Delorme (Les Caves Delorme-Meulien, Domaine de la Renarde)

Rully, 71150 Chagny. 60ha, two-thirds of which are owned by J-F. Delorme, the rest by members of his family. Bouzeron (Bourgogne Aligoté de Bouzeron) 2ha; Rully (Varot 18ha) 50ha (Monthelon, Montmorin, Les Cloux, La Chaume, La Fosse, Marissou, Grésigny, Chaponnière, Moulène, La Martelle, La Bergerie); Mercurey 4ha (Le Clos, Les Murgers, Les Lamberots, Les Monthelons, Ropiton, Les Crêts, Les Velles, Les Chenaults); Givry 4ha (Clos du Cellier aux Moines); La Rochepot. (Pinot Noir and Chardonnay for making Crémant de Bourgogne).

Jean-François Delorme has done much for the renaissance of the Côte Chalonnaise and has greatly extended his vineyard holdings of the Domaine de la Renarde. As the vines age, the quality visibly improves. The white grapes are pressed very slowly, to avoid any bitterness, and then go through a *débourbage* at low temperature to concentrate aromas. The reds are partially destalked, with the aim of achieving finesse and fruit. Rully Varot, principally planted to Chardonnay, is an 18ha parcel and the wines have a seductive cinnamon quality. The négociant business of Delorme-Meulien/André Delorme makes very good selections, especially a Bourgogne Rouge La Croix-Lieux, and the house is renowned for its Crémant sparkling wines.

Michel Derain

Saint Désert, 71390 Buxy. 5.60ha. Appellation Bourgogne Pinot Noir 4.50ha, 8,000–10,000 bottles. Gamay .50ha. Appellation Givry Blanc Chardonnay .30ha, 1,500–2,000 bottles. Aligoté .30ha, Passe-Tout-Grains and Aligoté sold in bulk to négociants.

Michel Derain adheres faithfully to the old methods of winemaking with the harvest from his clay-limestone slopes. The grapes are not destalked, treading is practised and the vattings are long, with reference to the character of the year, in order to make red wines with body and the ability to age. The Chardonnay wines are aged on their lees, aiming for a touch of acidity to give the wines longer life in bottle. Their Bourgogne Rouge Clos St-Pierre and their Givry Blanc, with its taste of hazelnuts, are both good buys.

GFA Domaine Desvignes (Château des Jean Loron)

71570 La Chapelle-de-Guinchay. 17.50ha, of which 13ha are planted to Gamay: 8ha north-to-south-facing Moulin à Vent; 3ha west to east; 2ha south-to-north-facing St-Amour. Total production 800,000 bottles.

The Château des Jean Loron has belonged to the Desvignes family since 1816. Jean Loron was manager of the domain in the 15th century. Normal Beaujolais methods are used, with a slightly longer vatting to obtain wines which can age. The Desvignes are keen on preserving aromas so that the wine also has fruity charm and slips down easily. Two-thirds of production is bottled by négociants for export, the rest is sold by the Desvignes to French clients.

Louis Claude Desvignes

La Voûte-au-Bourg, 69910 Villié-Morgon. 13.55ha, ownership and *métayage* combined, of which 8.75ha are worked. Vines are scattered over the commune: 4.50ha are in the best *climats* of Morgon Côte du Py and Morgon Javernières. Only a part – 25,000–30,000 bottles – of the annual production is sold direct in bottle. The rest is sold in bulk.

A family domain, worked *de père en fils* for seven generations (since 1712!). They follow traditional methods and aim for keeping wines typical of Morgon. They bottle after 6–12 months.

Maison Doudet-Naudin (Marcel Doudet-Naudin)
21420 Savigny-lès-Beaune. 2.58ha (owned). Savigny-lès-Beaune Les Guettes (red) .79ha, 4,000 bottles; Redrescut (white) .59ha, 3,500 bottles, Petits Liards .48ha, 1,800 bottles; Bourgogne Le Village (white) .20ha, 1,200 bottles; Corton – Le Corton (red) .46ha, 2,500 bottles; Aloxe-Corton Les Maréchaudes (red) .71ha, 5,000 bottles, Les Boutières (red) .46ha, 3,000 bottles; Beaune Clos du Roy (red) .41ha, 2,500 bottles; Ladoix La Maréchaude (red) .11ha, 800 bottles; Pernand-Vergelesses Les Fichots (red) .59ha, 3,000 bottles.

This house is known above all for its négociant wines, which tend to divide opinions. The style is big, rich, dark and jammy, with alcoholic backbone – consequently, the wines last, but I find it easier to recognize a Doudet-Naudin wine than to identify which commune it might come from. For their own wines, they practise long vinifications in oak *cuves*, with partial destalking according to the character of the year.

Paul Droin
3 rue Montmain, 89800 Chablis. Grands Crus 3.6ha: Vaudésir, Les Clos, Valmur, Grenouilles. 1ers Crus 6.8ha: Mostly Vaillons. 1ers Crus wines are kept in barrel for 6 months, Grands Crus for 12.

Maison Joseph Drouhin
7 rue d'Enfer, 21200 Beaune. 61ha. Côte d'Or 25ha, Chablis 36ha.

Joseph Drouhin, now run by Robert Drouhin, is a highly reputed Beaune négociant, but is also an important domain proprietor – many people forget how much they own in Chablis. They combine tradition with new developments and are always willing to try new techniques if they are improvements. The red wines are fermented in open *cuves* with floating *chapeau*, and they go through long macerations at controlled temperatures. The white grapes are pressed slowly and the last pressings are not used, and fermentation takes place in 228-litre casks. The white and red Beaune Clos des Mouches are flagships, but all the wines are highly recommended. The Chablis is influenced by oak and delicious. The *négoce* business buys in grapes and turns them into wine with the same care as those of their own domain. The business only sells AC Bourgogne wines and has never created a *vin de marque*.

Georges Duboeuf
71570 Romanèche-Thorins. 5ha. Pouilly-Fuissé (commune of Chaintré) 4ha, 25,000 bottles, Beaujolais Blanc (commune of Chaintré) 1ha, 8,000 bottles.

The domain, good as it is, must inevitably be dwarfed by the vast Duboeuf négociant empire, one of the great wine trade success stories of this century. Georges Duboeuf, through sheer hard work, a deep knowledge of his region and a sure touch for the genuine, has done more than anyone else for the spread of the true taste of Beaujolais and Mâconnais wines. Stocks now run to 4–5 million bottles. Some of the wines he chooses are bottled at the individual domains, the rest go to his ultra-modern plant. What are the secrets? He buys all his requirements very early, and so tends to get top quality. He also practises no *acténisation*, or flash pasteurization, and relies on Kieselguhr membrane filters and cold sterile bottling. As a result, Duboeuf wines are always fresh and fruity.

Robert Dubois & Fils (GAEC)
Prémeaux, 21700 Nuits St-Georges. 15ha (9.80ha owned, 5.20ha *en fermage* and *en métayage*). Aligoté .50ha, Pinot 12.01ha, Gamay 1.15ha. Prémeaux-Prissey: Bourgogne Aligoté .50ha, 4,700 bottles, Bourgogne Rosé .56ha, 5,200 bottles, Bourgogne Passe-Tout-Grains 1.72ha, 15,000 bottles, Nuits 1er Cru Clos des Argillières .43ha, 2,280 bottles, Bourgogne Rouge 2.45ha, 35,000 bottles. Prémeaux and Nuits St-Georges: Nuits St-Georges 3.20ha, 16,700 bottles, Nuits 1er Cru Les Pôrets St-Georges .58ha, 3,000 bottles. Beaune: Beaune Les Blanches Fleurs .30ha, 1,000 bottles. Comblanchien & Corgolain: Côte de Nuits-Villages 2.78ha, 13,800 bottles, Bourgogne Rouge 2ha. Chambolle: Chambolle Musigny Les Combottes .25ha, 1,000 bottles. Flagey-Echezeaux: Vosne-Romanée Les Chalandrins .25ha, 800 bottles.

A family domain, with Régis Dubois now in charge – they would like to widen their range of appellations even further. They follow the practice of heating the must to 40°C for 4 hours before fermentation in order to extract colour and aromas, then cooling to 28°C for a traditional Burgundian vinification. The wines are certainly keepers, but I have not appreciated them as much as some, always finding something slightly "tainted" about them – I am not sure whether it is the heating or the tastes from some barrels which causes this. Exports account for 60% of sales, but there is also an important private clientele in France.

Domaine P. Dubreuil-Fontaine Père & Fils

Pernand-Vergelesses, 21420 Savigny-lès-Beaune. 17.75ha. Pernand 1er Cru Ile des Vergelesses .79ha; Corton Clos du Roi .98ha, Les Bressandes .77ha, Les Perrières .60ha, Corton-Charlemagne .77ha; Aloxe-Corton 1.04ha; Savigny-Vergelesses 1er Cru 3.71ha, Pernand (red) 2.81ha, (white) 1.52ha, Clos Berthet (red) .50ha, (white) 1ha; also Bourgogne Rouge, Aligoté and Passe-Tout-Grains. All wines 60,000 bottles in total. Grands Crus – 25hl/ha, Premiers Crus and Villages – 30hl/ha.

Bernard Dubreuil now manages this excellent domain, which sells half its wines on the export markets, and half in France. Vinification is traditional in wood *cuves*, with a floating *chapeau* of skins which is pushed down into the fermenting must (*pigeage*) twice each day. They aim for wines which will keep, in those years where this is possible. His family know all there is to know about Pernand, and are especially proud of their Clos Berthet (which they own in entirety) and of their Corton-Bressandes.

Dufouleur Frères

1 rue de Dijon, 21701 Nuits-St-Georges. 7ha (owned). Mercurey, Mercurey Clos l'Evêque, Mercurey Champs Martin, Côte de Nuits-Villages Les Vaucrains, Clos Vougeot les Grands Maupertuis, Musigny; 2,000,000 bottles produced by the *négoce* business.

Dufouleur is a name that is certainly *du métier* because a *fouleur* is the man who treads the grapes to crush them. This is a large négociant business, exporting all over Europe, with the domain activity somewhat dwarfed by the négociant side. Vinification is traditional in oak vats, with long vatting and floating *chapeau* of skins. Destalking only takes place in certain, well-defined cases. Some of the wines are kept in *fûts* – the firm selects and buys the oak two years beforehand so that it can be aged. They are particularly proud of their Clos Vougeot.

Domaine Dujac

7 rue de la Bussière, Morey-St-Denis, 21220 Gevrey-Chambertin. 11ha. Bonnes Mares .40ha, 1,200 bottles, Clos de la Roche 1.80ha, 7,500 bottles, Echézeaux .65ha, 1,500 bottles, Clos St-Denis 1.50ha, 6,000 bottles, Charmes-Chambertin .70ha, 3,000 bottles, Chambolle-Musigny 1er Cru Les Gruenchers .32ha, Morey-St-Denis 1er Cru .42ha, 1,800 bottles, Gevrey-Chambertin 1er Cru Aux Combottes, 1.15ha, 4,000 bottles, Morey-St-Denis-Village 3ha, 11,000 bottles, Chambolle-Musigny Village .45ha, 1,500 bottles, Bourgogne Chardonnay .12ha, Aligoté .15ha. (Chambolle-Musigny 1er Cru being replanted; next vintage in 1986.)

Jacques Seysses bought this domain in 1968 and has since built it up to be one of the most notable on the Côte de Nuits through a combination of hard work and intelligent winemaking. He took the trouble to qualify as an oenologist at the University of Dijon and is always willing to experiment, although conserving everything that is good in traditional techniques. Here, there is no destalking, a rarity nowadays. The Grands and Premiers Crus are matured in new barrels, the Villages wines are in *fûts* that have only been used once. The wines are fined with whites of egg and bottled after 15 months, without filtration. Great character is therefore preserved in all the appellations. 90% of production is exported.

Jean Durup

Domaine de l'Eglantière, Maligny, 89800 Chablis. 100ha. Vines in communes of: Maligny, Villy, Beines, Fyé, Chablis. Petit Chablis (2ha) Chablis, Chablis 1er Cru Fourchaume, Chablis 1er Cru Montée de Tonnerre, Montmain, Vaudevey. 500,000 bottles.

A highly efficient domain, which is just as well, given its size. M. Durup has been at the forefront of the Chablis policy of expansion, although his family has been in Maligny for five centuries. There is no oak in the cellars here, but the vinification is "*le plus proche possible de la nature*". There are pneumatic presses, which are very gentle on the grapes, and the vats are concrete lined with fibreglass or enamel. The result is wines which are pretty and floral, rarely deep in flavour but always elegant.

Domaine René Engel

Vosne-Romanée, 21700 Nuits-St-Georges.

This is a domain with some precious land in a very good part of the Clos Vougeot, as well as in Grands-Echézeaux, Echézeaux and Vosne-Romanée. There have been some great old bottles of Engel wines, but perhaps at the moment the reputation is not at its strongest.

Domaine du Clos des Epeneaux

Place de l'Eglise, 21630 Pommard. Excellent new winemaking.

Maison J. Faiveley

8 rue du Tribourg, 21700 Nuits-St-Georges. 105.27ha owned, 103.62ha cultivated, 9.69ha *en fermage* (Nuits-St-Georges 1er Cru Clos de la Maréchale) Gevrey 8.47ha. Chambolle .48ha, Clos de Vougeot 1.29ha, Echézeaux .87ha, Nuits-St-Georges 20.32ha, Corton 3.44ha, Mercurey 65.45ha, Rully 4.95ha. 636,000 bottles per annum.

The domain wines of this important négociant have seemed to me to take a grand leap forward in recent years. In the past, I often found them to be clumsy. The policy revolves around very long vinifications (three weeks, even a month in some years), avoiding high temperatures in order to preserve aroma. Fermentation takes place in enamel-lined metal *cuves* which are equipped with a cooling system by means of running water down the sides of the *cuves* (seen more often in Bordeaux than in Burgundy). The wines are aged in oak *pièces* for 18 months, with Grands and Premiers Crus in new oak. There is light fining with egg white, and the wines are kept for a minimum of six months after bottling before being sold. The aim is to make aromatic wines which keep – the 1983s certainly fulfil this desire. They are very large owners in Mercurey, including the Clos des Myglands. Faiveley also buy in grapes and vinify themselves – notably in Morey-St-Denis. France takes just over half the wines and the family business has existed since 1825. François Faiveley now directs the domain.

Pierre Ferraud & Fils

31 rue Maréchale Foch, 69823 Belleville. 8ha (owned): Morgon Les Charmes 2ha, 12,000 bottles; Beaujolais-Villages Le Chavel 6ha (*en métayage*), 60,000 bottles. Have exclusive rights over the following properties: Pouilly-Fuissé Domaine de l'Arillière 40,000 bottles, Fleurie Clos des Garands 4,000 bottles, Beaujolais Eloi 50,000 bottles, Moulin-à-Vent Des Marquisats 8,000 bottles, Fleurie Château de Grand Pré 40,000 bottles, Morgon Domaine de l'Evêque 50,000 bottles, Côte de Brouilly Le Grand Cuvage 15,000 bottles, Brouilly Domaine Rolland 8,000 bottles.

This is an extremely "serious" négociant-éleveur, which manages a number of domains while doing the *élevage* and bottling of others. Sometimes they buy the proportion of the wine belonging to the owner (while his *métayer* keeps his share), and sometimes the whole crop, except for some sold direct by the grower. Where they do the vinifications, they are semi-carbonic maceration with vattings lasting from 4–7 days according to the age of the vines and the type of wine desired (Primeurs, carafe wines or keeping wines). They look for perfume, finesse and AC character, rather than too-powerful wines which lack individuality. In my view, they succeed admirably, and a Ferraud wine inspires complete confidence.

Domaine Fleurot-Larose

21590 Santenay. 6.8ha Chassagne-Montrachet 1er Cru Abbaye de Morgeot (red and white) and 5ha Santenay 1er Cru. Some Le Montrachet and Bâtard-Montrachet.

Domaine de la Folie (Messieurs E. and X. Noël-Bouton)
71150 Chagny. 19.87ha owned, 5.01ha *en fermage/métayage*. Rully Clos de Bellecroix (white) 1.05ha (red) 4.25ha; Rully Clos Roch (white) 3.5ha; Rully Les St-Jacques 1.89ha; Rully Clos St-Jacques 4.95ha, Bourgogne Aligoté Bouzeron 1.05ha, Clos de Bellecroix .72ha; Rully (white) 2.05ha, En Chaponnière 1ha. 100,000–150,000 bottles.

A well-run domain, with both red and white wines. Xavier Noël-Bouton believes in long vattings at low temperature in order to make wines which will keep. But I have always found these wines extremely pleasant when comparatively young. Sales are to French restaurants, direct to private clients and to the export markets.

Domaine Gagnard-Delagrange
Chassagne-Montrachet, 21190 Meursault. 5.2ha. .8ha Le Montrachet, 1.8ha Chassagne 1er Cru (Morgeot and Boudriotte), .2ha Bâtard-Montrachet, 2ha red Chassagne, .4ha Volnay Champans.

Abel Garnier
21190 Meursault. Small négociant specialising in Meursault, where he also has 4ha of vines.

Domaine F. Gaunoux
21190 Meursault. Brother of Michel Gaunoux of Pommard. 11.2ha. 4.4ha Meursault (2ha in 1ers Crus Perrières and Goutte d'Or), 1.2ha Volnay Clos des Chênes, .8ha 1ers Crus Beaune Clos des Mouches and Pommard (Rugiens and Epenots), 2.8ha Pommard Village.

Domaine Michel Gaunoux
Rue Notre Dame, 21630 Pommard. 10ha. Pommard Grands Epenots 3ha, Corton-Renardes 1.50ha, Beaune 3ha, Rugiens .69ha, Pommard 1er Cru .70ha.

Those wishing to try the wines of Michel Gaunoux will probably have to go to France, as very little is exported – top French restaurants and a following of private customers have got there first. The owner finds it difficult to assess how many bottles he makes each year: it depends, he says, on the weather sent by "*le grand maître*". Methods are more than traditional, with treading carried out by a *pigeur* in each wooden *cuve*. Many growers say they wish to produce *vins de garde*, but M. Gaunoux really achieves it, especially with the very good Pommard Grands Epenots.

Geisweiler
1 rue de la Berchère, 21700 Nuits-St-Georges. 86ha in Côte d'Or – biggest growers in the Hautes Côtes de Nuits. Domaine de Bévy 69.2ha, Domaine des Dames Hautes 16.8ha. Red and white wine.

Domaine Pierre Gelin
62 route des Grands Crus, 21220 Gevrey-Chambertin. 24ha approx. Gevrey-Chambertin 3ha (incl. Mazis and Clos de Bèze), Fixin 14ha (incl. Premiers Crus), Clos du Chapitre 4.8ha, Clos Napoléon 3ha, Les Hervelets .6ha.

Domaine Alain Geoffroy
4 rue de l'Equerre, Beines, 89800 Chablis. 25ha. Chablis 15ha, 105,000 bottles; Chablis 1er Cru Fourchaume 1.50ha, 10,000 bottles; Chablis 1er Cru (Beauroy & Troesmes) 8.50ha, 59,000 bottles.

Alain Geoffroy is a great supporter of the expansion of the vineyard area at Beines, and he himself certainly proves that fine Chablis can be made there. The winemaking is quite orthodox for Chablis, but includes no wood. The wines are sold young, but keep well in bottle for those who have the foresight to lay some down. I like the stylish, fresh character, which is instantly recognizable Chablis. Judges at competitions must like them too, as they scoop up medals with great regularity. I am not always in accord with the verdicts of these august juries, who often see wines when they are very young and miss the faults that develop later in the bottle, but in this case, I approve! If I did not, it probably would not worry them greatly.

Domaine Jacques Germain

Château Chorey-lès-Beaune, 21200 Beaune. 15.59ha (.31ha *en métayage*). Beaune 1er Cru 5.94ha; Cent-Vignes .58ha, 2,000 bottles; Teurons 2.03ha, 7,000 bottles; Cras 1.42ha, 5,000 bottles; Vignes-Franches .96ha, 3,000 bottles; Boucherottes .96ha, 3,000 bottles; Chorey-lès-Beaune 4.25ha, 10,000 bottles; Pernand-Vergelesses (white) 2.77ha, 4,000 bottles; Bourgogne (red) 2.63ha, 10,000 bottles.

François Germain now makes the wines at this domain founded 100 years ago by his great-grandfather. The wines are uniformly excellent, whether they be simple Chorey-lès-Beaune or grand Beaune les Teurons. The emphasis is on finesse and perfume, making every vintage a pleasure to drink. Vinification is in wood *cuves* with quite long vattings of 10–15 days. There is no destalking, except in years where the grapes are either rather unripe or affected by rot. The *élevage* is partly in new wood – the amount varies with the *cru*, with the Beaune Premiers Crus being matured in 50% new barrels, the Chorey-lès-Beaune 25% and the Pernand-Vergelesses Blanc 20%. Exports account for 75% of sales, with Switzerland and the UK the best customers.

Jean Germain

9 rue de la Barre, 21190 Meursault. 2ha (1ha owned, 1ha *en fermage*). Meursault Meix Chavaux .30ha, 21,000 bottles; Meursault La Barre .10ha, 600 bottles; Puligny-Montrachet Les Grands Champs .30ha, 1,800 bottles; Puligny-Montrachet Corvées des Vignes .20ha, 900 bottles; St-Romain Clos Sous le Château 1ha, 4,500 bottles.

An impeccably run small domain with a man at the helm who really knows how to make fine white Côte de Beaune wines. There is a "hand-made" quality about the enterprise, with a very old press, but new oak barrels for ageing. M. Germain is not a devotee of unnecessarily high alcohol – he likes his wines to be around 12.8%. The wines are bottled at 11–18 months. They are fruity and supple when quite young, but last beautifully due to the perfect techniques of *élevage*. Jean Germain is also a négociant and exports under the name of the Société l'Elevage et Conditionnement des Vins Fins. In this instance the wines really merit the term *fins*!

Soc. des Domaines Bernard & Louis Glantenay

Volnay, 21190 Meursault. 7.2ha. Mostly Volnay (3ha) and Pommard 'Village' (1.2ha). Also Volnay 1er Cru 3ha and some Bourgogne, Passe-Tout-Grains and Aligoté.

Domaine Elmerich Gouachon

21700 Nuits-St-Georges. 4.8ha *monopole* Nuits 1er Cru Clos des Corvées.

Michel Goubard

Bassevelle, 71390 St-Désert. 12ha. 3,600 Aligoté vines – 3,000 bottles; 12,000 Chardonnay vines – 8,500 bottles; 4,500 Gamay vines, 90,000 Pinot Noir vines – 65,000 bottles; Passe-Tout-Grains 4,800 bottles.

The Goubards have been on the Côte Chalonnaise since 1600. Two-thirds of the vineyards they now have are on marked slopes, beautifully facing southeast for maximum sun exposure. The Bourgogne Rouge is fruity and charming, made by a semi-carbonic maceration method and meant for relatively young drinking. Half the production is sold direct, while half is exported. Good value burgundy drinking for those who like to buy their wine and drink it right away.

Domaine Goud de Beaupuis

Château des Moutots, 21200 Chorey-lès-Beaune. 10ha, mostly among the 1er Crus of Pommard, Beaune, Aloxe-Corton, Savigny and Chorey-lès-Beaune. Pinot Noir: Pommard Epenots, Pommard la Chanière, Beaune Grèves 1er Cru (tête de cuvée), Beaune Clos St-Anne des Theurons 1er Cru, Savigny-Vergelesses 1er Cru, Aloxe-Corton Valozières 1er Cru, Aloxe-Corton, Chorey-lès-Beaune, Bourgogne Château des Moutots. Chardonnay: Beaune Clos des Vignes Franches 1er Cru (Aligoté) Bourgogne Aligoté. 25–30hl/ha. 20,000–30,000 bottles for the domaine as a whole.

A family domain since 1787, there seems to be a thriving direct sale business to the public, although the wines are also exported and sold to restaurants in France. They believe in the virtue of old vines to "assure quality". Vinification is in oak *cuves* with slow maceration in order to develop aromas. The grapes are destalked and the wines are aged in oak barrels for two years before bottling. I have not found the wines to my taste, as the alcohol seems to be all-dominant, masking appellation character.

Domaine Henri Gouges

7 rue du Moulin, 21700 Nuits-St-Georges. 8ha, all in Premiers Crus, incl. all of Clos des Porrets. Also holds land in Les St-Georges (1ha), Les Pruliers (1.8ha) and Les Vaucrains (1ha).

Jean Grivot

Vosne-Romanée, 21700 Nuits-St-Georges. 10ha in small parcels. Clos Vougeot 1.8ha, Vosne-Romanée 4ha, incl. .9ha in 1er Cru Beaumonts, and some land in Suchots and Brulées, 2ha Nuits 1ers Crus and 1.6ha Chambolle-Musigny.

Domaine Jean Gros

Vosne-Romanée, 21700 Nuits St-Georges. 15.50ha (.50ha *en métayage*). Vosne-Romanée Richebourg .60ha, 2,000–2,200 bottles; Vosne Clos des Réas 2.12ha, 10,000 bottles; Vosne-Romanée 2.72ha, 14,000 bottles; Nuits-St-Georges 1.10ha, 4,000 bottles; Clos Vougeot .20ha; Bourgogne (appellation régionale) 3.40ha, 20,000 bottles; Hautes Côtes de Nuits 5ha, 30,000 bottles.

An excellent domain, where one's expectations of grand names are fulfilled. Inevitably, the vineyards have been split up between the family, in true Burgundian fashion, but the Clos des Réas is solely owned by Jean Gros. The most recent development is the Hautes Côtes de Nuits vineyard, planted 15 years ago, some of which is sold under the label of Jean's son, Michel Gros. Traditional methods are followed, with new oak barrels for the Grands and Premiers Crus. Bottling takes place after 18 months to two years. Try to obtain some Gros wines, as they will not disappoint.

M. Pierre Guillemot

21000 Savigny-lès-Beaune. 1er Cru Aux Serpentières. Very good wines with a pure Savigny taste of strawberries. M. Guillemot really knows what his appellation should represent.

Domaine Antonin Guyon

21420 Savigny-lès-Beaune. 48ha. Gevrey-Chambertin 2.60ha; Chambolle-Musigny 3.50ha; Aloxe-Corton 1er Cru 2.50ha; Grands Corton (Corton-Renardes, Bressandes, Clos du Roi) 2.15ha; Savigny-lès-Beaune 2.20ha; Pernand-Vergelesses 1er Cru (red) 2.20ha; (white) 1ha; Beaune 1.90ha; Meursault-Charmes .80ha; Corton-Charlemagne .75ha; Chorey-lès-Beaune .80ha; Volnay Clos des Chênes .87ha; Hautes Côtes des Nuits 23ha; Bourgogne Aligoté 1ha; Bourgogne Rouge 2.50ha; Charmes-Chambertin .10ha. 240,000 bottles per annum for the domain as a whole.

A very important domain, in all senses of the word. Destalking, then traditional vinification for 10–12 days in wooden vats at about 30°C so that the wines have body and good colour. *Elevage* is in oak barrels (one-third new) for 18 months before bottling. The white wines are fermented at 18°C, to gain maximum bouquet, and bottled at 12 months. All the production is bottled at the domain and sold direct, 90% exported and 10% in France, 80% of which to some of the country's grandest restaurants. The reds have finesse and a satiny quality, with fruit and structure perfectly balanced. Wonderful 1978, 1983 and 1979.

Jaboulet-Vercherre

5 rue Colbert, 21200 Beaune. 15ha including Pommard 1er Cru Clos de la Commaraine, and Beaune 1er Cru Clos de l'Ecu. 35–40hl/ha. Négociants and domain owners.

I find it difficult to identify appellation character in their *négoce* wines – a case of house style dominating the nuances.

Paul & Henri Jacqueson

71150 Rully. 11ha (6ha currently in production: Mercurey 4.50ha, Rully 1.50ha). Rully 1er Cru Les Clouds 1.30ha, 1er Cru Les Grésigny .75ha, Les Chaponnières 1.30ha; Mercurey 1er Cru Naugues .65ha; Mercurey .70ha; Bourgogne Aligoté .50ha, Passe-Tout-Grains .50ha. 25,000–30,000 bottles (5,000–6,000 bottles white).

A small, meticulously run domain, created by Henri Jacqueson and now run by him and his son Paul. The family is of Welsh origin as, in the 15th century, the personal guard of Marguerite de Bourgogne was Welsh, and the Jacquesons descend from this line. Exports account for 65% of sales, with private customers also an important element. The predominantly red wines are made with grapes which have not been destalked, with treading morning and evening to keep the skins in contact with the juice – the vinification lasts from 15 to 22 days and the wines are intended for keeping. The whole white grapes are pressed immediately in horizontal presses (for two hours), then the juice clarifies naturally in tank (*débourbage*) for 8–10 hours before fermentation at cold temperature. *Elevage* is in oak barrels, with 30% new each year, and bottling at the end of September.

Maison Louis Jadot

5 rue Samuel Legay, 21200 Beaune. Approx. 20ha, all Grands and Premiers Crus. Aloxe-Corton: Corton-Pougets, Corton-Charlemagne; Pernand-Vergelesses; Beaune: Beaune Theurons, Clos des Couchereaux, Vignes Franches, Bressandes, Clos des Ursules, Chouacheux, Boucherottes; Puligny-Montrachet: Chevalier-Montrachet Les Demoiselles, Puligny-Montrachet Les Folatières.

A very important négociant business, which has been sold to its American importer Kobrand. But M. André Gagey remains to manage, which is a good thing for everyone. The Jadot family also own plots in some very prestigious vineyards of the Côte de Beaune. The white wines are fermented in oak barrels and aged similarly for 12–18 months. The red wines are traditionally vinified in open wooden vats with floating *chapeau* of skins, *pigeage*, or treading, by human feet, and ageing in oak barrels for 18 months to 2 years. The wines are exported around the world, as well as sold in France. The standard is high and the wines age gracefully. The grandest names are much sought after, and justifiably, but I have a particular weakness for their Beaune Boucherottes and the Chouacheux. The whites are consistently fine.

Maison Jaffelin

Caves du Chapitre, 2 rue Paradis, 21200 Beaune.

An old-established négociant, which was bought by Joseph Drouhin in 1969, but which still runs its business separately. They own a small slice of Clos Vougeot, 2.50ha of Beaune Les Bressandes and .50ha in Les Avaux.

Château de Javernand

69115 Chiroubles. 30ha (20ha *en métayage*). 300,000 vines; 200,000 bottles.

M. Philippe Fourneau, owner of the Château de Javernand, is President of the Syndicat du Cru Chiroubles, and a winemaker worthy of this post. The wine has all the airy charm of the appellation, and is utterly irresistible when drunk young, as Chiroubles should be. There is no magic formula – just normal Beaujolais vinification procedure. One can understand why Georges Duboeuf has made it one of his selections and bottles it for sale in France and around the world.

Domaine Henri Jayer

21000 Vosne-Romanée.

Domaine Jacqueline Jayer

21000 Vosne-Romanée.

Philippe Joliet (Domaine de la Perrière)

21220 Fixin, Gevrey-Chambertin. 5.18ha. Fixin Clos de la Perrière. 25,000 bottles.

Both the Manoir and the Clos de la Perrière vineyard were created by the monks of the Abbey of Citeaux in the 12th century. Methods are traditional, with partial destalking according to the year (20% to 60%). Long vatting (18 to 20 days) produces wines which keep, certainly the case with the 1983 and the 1981. 35% of the production is sold to the négociants, 35% on the export markets and 30% goes in direct sales. You will not find delicacy here at Fixin, but certainly a wine to be drunk in cold weather from big glasses.

Domaine Jean Joliot & Fils

Nantoux, 21190 Meursault. 11.50ha (owned). Meursault 1.90ha, 9,000 bottles; Pommard 1.20ha, 4,800 bottles; Beaune aux Boucherottes .42ha, 1,700 bottles; Hautes Côtes de Beaune 7ha, 35,000 bottles; Passe-Tout-Grains .50ha, 2,500 bottles; also .50ha of Aligoté, 2,600 bottles.

A highly regarded domain in the Hautes Côtes de Beaune – the Joliot family have always had vines: "le souvenir se perd dans la nuit des temps", as they say. Apart from the Hautes Côtes wines, there are also small slices of grander appellations, but there is no doubt that the more modest wines are very good value, with the authentic taste of burgundy. Traditional methods are the order of the day, but modified each year according to the quality of the vintage. The aim is to make wines of perfume and finesse allied to reasonable body, maintaining a balance between alcohol, tannin and acidity so that the wines can age according to their place in the hierarchy, i.e. you would keep a Pommard longer than a Hautes Côtes de Beaune.

Claude & Michelle Joubert

Lantignié, 69430 Beaujeu. 13ha (3ha *en fermage*). Beaujolais-Villages 6.50ha, 35,000 bottles; Juliénas 6.50ha, 30,000 bottles.

This is a very reliable domain which has been lovingly built up by Claude and Michelle Joubert. They have created a band of faithful customers in France, many of them buying for their own cellars. The average age of the vines undoubtedly contributes to the full, deep fruit of the wines. The Beaujolais-Villages is made with whole grapes and a semi-carbonic maceration fermentation lasting 4–6 days, while the Juliénas receives a traditional vatting of 8–10 days. There are stainless steel vats which make temperature control easy. The Jouberts were first known for their Villages, but the Juliénas is rapidly catching up.

Domaine Michel Juillot

71640 Mercurey. 25ha (10ha *en fermage*, 5ha *en métayage*). Mercurey: (red) 12ha, (white) 1.50ha, Clos des Barraults 1ha, Clos Tonnerre 3ha, Clos l'Eveque 1ha, Champs Martins 1ha; Corton-Perrières Grand Cru 1ha; Aloxe-Corton 1er Cru .50ha; Bourgogne Rouge 1.50ha; Bourgogne Blanc .50ha. Average production 40hl/ha.

There is a wealth of experience behind the skills of Michel Juillot – his family have been *vignerons* since 1404, and his grandfather became a master grafter of vines at national level, something much needed following the phylloxera. Vinification is in open *cuves*, after total destalking. There is always a third new wood in the cellars, and no barrel is more than three years old. Bottling is carried out after 18-24 months of *élevage*. There is often a scent of ripe, wild fruits in the reds. A small amount of interesting white wine is made.

Domaine de la Juvinière

Clos de Langres, Corgoloin, 21700 Nuits-St-Georges. Owned by La Reine Pédauque, Beaune négociants. 24ha.

Labouré-Roi

21700 Nuits-St-Georges.

A négociant and small domain owner. I have been impressed by the wines of the René Manuel estate, which they distribute. The Meursault is oaky and rich, and the unusual red Meursault has a gamey, fruity character to it. They also usually have a good white Auxey-Duresses, an appellation which is worth finding when Meursault and Puligny look too expensive.

Maurice Labruyère (Président de l'Union des Viticulteurs du Moulin-à-Vent)

Les Thorins, 71720 Romanèche-Thorins. 9.50ha. Moulin-à-Vent Clos du Carquelin 1er Grand Cru Classé.

The Clos du Carquelin is a renowned name in Moulin-à-Vent. Maurice Labruyère is the fourth generation of his family to produce the wine here and he is also President of the Union des Viticulteurs du Moulin-à-Vent. Two-thirds of the harvest each year is sold to Switzerland.

Château de Lacarelle

69460 St-Etienne-des-Oullières. 150ha (100ha currently planted in the communes of St-Etienne-des-Oullières and St-Etienne-La-Varenne. *Vins primeurs* and *vins de garde* 300,000 bottles.

This is a very large domain, situated in the heart of the Beaujolais-Villages terrain, with the vineyards on coarse, sandy soils which resulted from the gradual decomposition of granite. The family of the Comte Durieu de Lacarelle has been making wine here for more than two hundred years. They make aromatic and supple wines which are delicious to drink when young. The installations are of the most modern, with the uncrushed grapes reaching the vats by means of a kind of aerial monorail device, but after fermentation the wine is stored in vaulted, underground cellars.

Domaine Michel Lafarge

Volnay, 21190 Meursault. 9.35ha. Volnay 2.50ha, 11,500 bottles; Clos des Chènes .90ha, 3,500 bottles; 1er Cru 1ha, 4,500 bottles; Beaune Grèves .40ha, 1,800 bottles; Meursault 1ha, 5,200 bottles; Bourgogne 1.25ha, 6,300 bottles; Aligoté .80ha, 4,500 bottles; Passe-Tout-Grains 1.50ha, 10,000 bottles.

This is a meticulous family domain, making wine with both care and intelligence. Complete destalking is practised, and rigorous selection of the grapes if there is an element of rot in the vintage. Vinification lasts approximately 10 days and the wine is aged in oak *pièces* for 18 months – about a third of the crop goes into new barrels. Connoisseurs of fine burgundy around the world now know that a Volnay from Michel Lafarge is a treat indeed – but then, this family has been domain bottling for 50 years.

Domaine des Comtes Lafon

Clos de la Barre, 21190 Meursault. 13ha, 30,000 bottles. Meursault: Clos de la Barre 6,000 bottles; Désirée 900 bottles; La Goutte d'Or 600 bottles, Charmes 4,500 bottles; Genevrières 1,000 bottles; Perrières 1,800 bottles, Montrachet 600 bottles; Volnay Santenots du Milieu 7,500–9,000 bottles; Volnay Clos des Chênes 1,000 bottles; Volnay Champans 600–750 bottles.

A superb domain, making the kind of burgundy I like. At the moment, the property is worked *en métayage*, but this will revert to the Lafon family in a year or two, so their production will double, i.e. they will keep the whole of the crop. Both red and white wines usually need years to be at their best.

Domaine Laleure Piot

Pernand-Vergelesses, 21420 Savigny-lès-Beaune. 8ha. Produce Pernand-Vergelesses and some Grand Cru Corton Bressandes, and 1er Cru Vergelesses from Savigny and Pernand.

Domaine Lamarche

Vosne-Romanée, 21700 Nuits-St-Georges. 8ha of vines situated in Vosne-Romanée, Flagey-Echézeaux and Vougeot. 30–35hl/ha.

This is a remarkable estate, with some "golden" land: they are the sole owners of La Grande Rue, sandwiched between La Tâche and the Romanées, and they also have Grands Echézeaux, Echézeaux and the Premier Cru Les Malconsorts. The objective of the domain is to make wines which keep, wherever possible. Some of them appear somewhat rustic and alcoholic when young, but I have had fine old bottles from this domain.

Lamblin & Fils

Maligny, 89800 Chablis. 10.4ha owned. Also buys in wine from others. Domain wines include Grands Crus Valmur .8ha, Les Clos 1ha, 1ers Crus 4.8ha. Produces Chablis, Bourgogne Blanc, Aligoté.

Hubert Lamy

St-Aubin, 21190 Meursault. 12ha. (Aligoté) 10,500 vines at St-Aubin; (Chardonnay) 7,500 vines at St-Aubin 1er Cru; 11,600 at Puligny-Montrachet; 465 vines at Criots-Bâtard-Montrachet; (Pinot Noir) 21,000 vines at Chassagne-Montrachet; 41,000 St-Aubin and St-Aubin 1er Cru; 28,000 Appellation Bourgogne. 45,000–65,000 bottles.

The Lamy family have been vignerons since 1640, and in this case experience has really resulted in knowledge of subject. They know that St-Aubin is ignored by many, so are committed to "reducing quantity to increase quality". In this they succeed quite admirably, whether it is in the wines of the village or in the grander appellations. The whites have a stylish, acacia-like quality, while the reds are tannic when young, maturing to become a delicious mouthful. The red grapes are not destalked, and vatting lasts for 10–15 days, so you can safely lay down some bottles. The domain sells to private customers in France, Belgium and Switzerland, but England and the USA are also now the happy recipients of some of these wines.

Domaine Lamy-Pillot

Route de Santenay, Chassagne-Montrachet, 21190 Meursault. 17ha (7ha owned, 10ha *en fermage* or *métayage*) in St-Aubin, Santenay, Meursault, Chassagne-Montrachet, including St-Aubin 1er Cru Les Castets, St-Aubin Les Pucelles, St-Aubin Les Argilliers, Santenay Les Charrons, Blagny 1er Cru La Pièce Sous le Bois, Chassagne-Montrachet 1er Cru Morgeot, 1er Cru Boudriotte, 1er Cru Clos St-Jean, Bourgogne, Bourgogne Aligoté, Côte de Beaune Villages and Bâtard-Montrachet. Average production 40hl/ha.

René Lamy has built up this domain via a succession of plots scattered over a wide variety of appellations. A third of the production is sold in bulk to local négociants, with two-thirds (60,000 bottles) sold direct (and half of that in France). The grapes are not destalked and *pigeage* is practised to extract colour and tannin. Some of the wines are rather hard when young and need ageing. There could be a problem with barrels here, which would explain some rather "off" odours. But other wines have been successful, and there are old vines in the Boudriotte.

Domaine Laroche

10 rue Auxerroise, 89800 Chablis. 86ha. Chablis Grand Cru 6ha, 36,000 bottles (Les Clos 1.10ha, 6,000 bottles; Bougerots. 30ha, 2,000 bottles; Blanchots 4.60ha, 28,000 bottles); Chablis 1er Cru 28ha, 174,000 bottles (Vaudevey 11ha, 70,000 bottles; Fourchaume 8ha, 50,000 bottles; Vaillons 7ha, 42,000 bottles; Montmain 1ha, 6,000 bottles; Beauroy 1ha, 6,000 bottles); Chablis 50ha, 325,000 bottles; Petit Chablis 2ha, 13,000 bottles.

Michel Laroche now runs the domain and the négociant business of Bacheroy-Josselin, and certainly the sheer size of the whole empire makes the wines highly visible on all markets of the world and in French restaurants. Equipment is very modern, with pneumatic presses, centrifuges (for clarifying the must) and controlled fermentation temperatures. Some new oak is used in the ageing of Premiers and Grands Crus. Laroche wines usually keep well. In 1985 Michel Laroche extended his activities, becoming manager of an Australian group which acquired the Château de Puligny-Montrachet from Roland Thévenin and the vineyard belonging to M. André Ropiteau.

Maison Louis Latour

18 rue des Tonneliers, 21204 Beaune. 50ha (43ha currently in production). Aloxe-Corton: Les Chaillots, Les Fournières, 1er Cru, Aloxe-Corton 6ha – 24,000 bottles; Pernand Ile des Vergelesses, Pernand-Vergelesses 2.30ha – 9,000 bottles; Beaune: Vignes Franches, Perrières, Cras, Clos du Roi, Grèves 5.50ha – 22,000 bottles; Volnay-Mittants, Volnay .70ha –

3,000 bottles; Pommard-Epenots .50ha – 2,000 bottles; Corton: Bressandes, Clos de la Vigne au Saint, Chaumes, Pougets, Perrières, Clos du Roi, Grèves, 17ha – 67,000 bottles; Corton-Charlemagne 9ha – 36,000 bottles; Chevalier-Montrachet .50ha – 2,000 bottles; Chambertin .80ha – 3,000 bottles; Romanée-St-Vivant .80ha – 3,000 bottles.

A négociant and a domain owner of excellent reputation, dedicated to producing fine bottles of burgundy for the French market and around the world. Their methods have not changed with the times: the grapes are still harvested and transported in traditional wicker baskets, the vinification of the reds takes place in open wooden vats with treading of the floating cap, and they are aged for approximately 18 months in oak barrels. The whites are fermented and aged in oak barrels and bottled after approximately 12 months. But if the methods are traditional, all the modern techniques of oenological analysis are also called upon. Apart from the illustrious domain wines, Côte d'Or red wines are bought young, in barrel, while the whites are bought as grapes and vinified by the firm. The *élevage* of these wines then takes place in Latour's cellars, side-by-side with the wines of the domain. The white wines are superlative, and the reds are often very good indeed, which tends to be the pattern throughout Burgundy given the tricky weather. The firm has pasteurized its red wines since the early part of this century. I think it is worth commenting that I have tasted many Burgundian wines which were *not* pasteurized but which were also perfectly disgusting! On the other hand, I wonder if pasteurization is really necessary, and would find it very interesting to make a study of similar wines, made with and without the process, tasting them over a number of years to monitor their development.

Domaine Launay
21000 Pommard.

Domaine Leflaive
Puligny-Montrachet, 21190 Meursault. 20.23ha. Bâtard-Montrachet 2.02ha, Chevalier-Montrachet 2.02ha, Bienvenues-Bâtard 1.01ha, Puligny 1er Cru Les Pucelles 3.03ha, Clavoillon 4.04ha, Combettes .80ha; Puligny Village 3.64ha and a patch of Blagny.

This is a splendid old family domain, whose reputation has never been higher. Vincent Leflaive considers absolute cleanliness in the cellar one of the most vital parts of white winemaking. The wines are bottled after about 18 months following an *élevage* in oak *pièces* and small stainless steel vats. Let yourself be seduced by the honeyed smoothness of the wines from this domain – that is, if you have not already succumbed to the heady bouquet!

M. Jacky Legou-Olivier
Concoeur, 21000 Nuits-St-Georges.

GFA Le Logis (Yvonne Couibes)
Le Vivier, 69820 Fleurie. 5ha *en métayage*: Moulin-à-Vent 1.50ha, Fleurie 3.50ha, both AC.
A carefully tended property, the wine being sold to Loron. The density of planting is approximately 7,800 vines per ha, according to the shape and situation of the vineyard plot, the drainage and the configuration of the site.

Domaine Lequin Roussot (René & Louis Lequin Frères)
21590 Santenay. 16ha (14ha in production, 2ha young vines and fallow land). Bourgogne .55ha, 4,000 bottles; Santenay 6.17ha, 40,000 bottles; Santenay: Clos du Haut Village 1.27ha, 7,500 bottles; Le Passe Temps 1er Cru 1.07ha, 6,000 bottles; La Comme 1er Cru 1.67ha, 10,000 bottles; Chassagne-Montrachet Morgeot 1er Cru 1ha, 5,000 bottles; Nuits-St-Georges .30ha, 1,500 bottles; Pommard .14ha, 700 bottles; Corton Les Languettes .37ha, 1,500 bottles; Chassagne-Montrachet (white) .59ha, 3,500 bottles; Chassagne-Montrachet (white) 1er Cru Morgeot and Cailleret .39ha, 2,400 bottles; Bâtard-Montrachet .11ha, 600 bottles.

This is a classic example of a fragmented Burgundian vineyard – the Lequins have to rush up and down the Côte at vintage time. But they make fine wines, and that is quite a feat. Fermentations are relatively long, with *foulages* and *remontages*. The *élevage* is in oak barrels, a fifth of which are new. The wines have plenty of verve and keep well, and their AC character is not masked by an excess of oak. They sell half of their crop to négociants, and the rest is sold in bottle in France as well as on the export markets.

Maison Leroy

Auxey-Duresses, 21190 Meursault. 4.27ha. Meursault, Auxey-Duresses, Pommard, Chambertin, Musigny, Clos de Vougeot.

A small property, but an important négociant, specializing in *vins de garde* and high stocks. Leroy wines are always powerful, massively so in some cases, which can obliterate appellation character. I certainly could not have divined the origin of a Volnay-Santenots 1955 tasted recently – it just seemed alcoholic and "big".

Domaine Lucien Jacob Leroy

Echevronne, 21420 Savigny-lès-Beaune. 18ha, half of which is in Savigny, Pernand and Aloxe-Corton, the other half is in the Hautes Côtes de Beaune.

Domaine Georges Lignier

21000 Morey-St-Denis.

Domaine Hubert Lignier

21740 Morey-St-Denis.

Morey-St-Denis of quality, with excellent Clos de la Roche.

Long-Depaquit

45 rue Auxerroise, 89800 Chablis. Over 40ha: Chablis 19.2ha, 1ers Crus 12ha, Grands Crus 8ha, incl. 2.6ha of Vaudésir.

Loron & Fils

Pontanevaux, 71570 La Chapelle-de-Guinchay. A large family business formerly selling mainly in bulk, but now more and more in bottle under various brand names. Both domain wines (some very good) and non-appellation *vins de marque*.

Lupé-Cholet

21700 Nuits-St-Georges. 6ha. 1er Cru Nuits-St-Georges Monopole Château Gris 3ha; Bourgogne Rouge Monopole Clos de Lupé 3ha.

Lupé-Cholet is a négociant, now merged with the huge Bichot of Beaune, the largest exporter of Burgundy. But they also own two Monopoles on the Côte de Nuits, although one only carries the Bourgogne Rouge appellation. Methods are traditional, with fermentations in wood *cuves* and storage in new oak barrels. The Château Gris is an enclave in the Premier Cru Aux Crots, not a Grand Cru as stated on some of the older labels. The new wood is very evident in recent vintages, but the wines should age well. The négociant wines seem most honourable, and their Savigny selections appear particularly successful.

Lycée Agricole et Viticole

16, avenue Charles Jaffelin, 21200 Beaune. 20.47ha, of which 16.53ha are currently in production. (10.94ha *en fermage*, 1ha *en métayage*). Beaune 1er Cru 6.97ha, Beaune 2.32ha, Côte de Beaune 1ha, Bourgogne Hautes Côtes 1.29ha, Bourgogne Passe-Tout-Grains 1.30ha, (white) Puligny-Montrachet 1ha, Beaune .40ha, Côte de Beaune .86ha, Bourgogne Aligoté .51ha, Bourgogne .88ha. 80,000 bottles produced in 1984.

These are the wines made by the future guardians of the reputation of Burgundy, because so many growers' sons study here. The standard is high and great care is taken. They sell direct by mail order in France, and a little is exported to Belgium and Switzerland, but some goes *en vrac* (in bulk) to the local *négoce*. They make excellent Beaune 1er Cru, such as Champimonts, Perrières and Montée Rouge. The Lycée Agricole et Viticole was founded in 1884.

Domaine Machard du Gramont

6 rue Gassendi, 21700 Nuits-St-Georges. 19ha (7ha *en fermage*). Chambolle-Musigny; Nuits-St-Georges 1er Cru: Les Damodes, Les Hauts Pruliers, Les Vallerots; Nuits-St-Georges: en la Perrière Noblot, Les Argillats, Les Hauts Poirets, Les Poulettes; Aloxe-Corton; Savigny-lès-Beaune 1er Cru Les Guettes; Savigny-lès-Beaune; Chorey-lès-Beaune Les Beaumonts; Savigny Les Vergelesses; Beaune les Epenottes; Beaune 1er Cru les Chouacheux; Pommard les Vaumuriens; Pommard 1er Cru Le Clos Blanc, Bourgogne Rouge; Bourgogne Blanc; Puligny-Montrachet. Three-quarters of crop goes into bottle after vigorous selection.

A comparatively new domain, which has gone through all the vicissitudes of Burgundian family troubles. But what remains of the estate is hardly insignificant, and the wines are models of what burgundy should be all about. The emphasis is on fruit rather than acquired weight, and consequently there is always lovely Pinot Noir bouquet, not overwhelmed by alcohol. Vattings are long, with ageing in oak barrels, part of which are new. The cellars are in Prissey, and the wines are widely exported.

Domaine du Duc de Magenta

Abbaye de Morgeot, Chassagne-Montrachet, 21190 Meursault. 12ha. 4.4ha Clos de la Chapelle. 2ha 1er Cru Clos de la Garenne in Puligny, 3.2ha in Auxey-Duresses and .8ha in Meursault Meix Chavaux. Sole owner of the former monastic vineyard of Clos de la Chapelle beside the old abbey of Morgeot. The red Morgeot can last well but there are patchy bottles from this domaine.

Domaine de la Maladière

14 rue Jules Rathier, 89800 Chablis. 42ha. Chablis Grand Cru: Bougros 6.40ha, Les Clos 3.50ha, Les Preuses 2.50ha, Valmur 1.80ha, Vaudésir 1.20ha, Grenouilles .60ha – 16ha total producing 100,000 bottles; Chablis 1er Cru (Vaulorent, Montée de Tonnerre 12.50ha, 80,000 bottles; Chablis 13.50ha, 100,000 bottles.

William Fèvre runs this domain with formidable efficiency and it is certainly enviable to be able to produce about as much Grand Cru as straight Chablis. Vinification is traditional in oak barrels, a quarter of which are renewed every year. M. Fèvre is convinced that this produces wines which ultimately are deeper and richer in bouquet and taste as they age in bottle. Some wines destined for earlier drinking are fermented in tank. Grands Crus are usually bottled in May after the vintage. The domain is associated with another grower, thus increasing sales capacity to the equivalent of a vineyard of 50ha. The USA takes the greatest part of the production, followed by the UK, Germany, France and Japan. M. Fèvre is clearly a man of enormous organizational capacity and ability who would have done well in any field – luckily for us, winemaking is his chief occupation.

GAEC du Domaine Michel Mallard & Fils

21550 Ladoix-Serrigny. Ladoix 1er Cru, Corton Les Maréchaudes.

Château de la Maltroye

Chassagne-Montrachet, 21190 Meursault. 12.8ha incl. a small bit of Bâtard-Montrachet and some land in Chassagne Clos St-Jean and Santenay La Comme.

Proprietor André Cournot makes some good white wines, including the *monopole* Clos du Château de la Maltroye. Some disappointments.

P. De Marcilly Frères

21200 Beaune.

A négociant, with small holdings in Chassagne-Montrachet and Beaune. Their best wines are the modest Appellation Bourgogne Marcilly Première and Marcilly Réserve, which are usually velvety and oaky.

Jean Maréchal

71640 Mercurey. 9ha AC vines (owned). Clos Barrault, Clos L'Evêque, Les Crées, Les Naugues, Champs-Martin, Les Byots. 45,000 bottles.

This is a much respected domain, with its 9ha facing south on clay-limestone slopes. There is partial destalking and *foulage* three times a day. Vatting lasts from 10 to 12 days. The aim is to produce wines which have the ability to age, with good colour and deep bouquet. *Elevage* is in oak barrels, a part of which is new, for a period of 15 months. The family goes back to 1570, and finally became owners of 9ha of vines in the best *crus*.

Domaine Marquis-d'Angerville

Volnay, 21190 Meursault. 12.92ha. Volnay 1er Cru: Clos des Ducs, en Champans, les Caillerets, Fremiet; Meursault Santenots 1er Cru; Pommard; Volnay; Bourgogne. 30,000–60,000 bottles.

This was one of the first great Burgundy estates to domain bottle and their standards have never slipped. The emphasis is on finesse and elegance, and the wines usually have a long, lingering finish. They are made in wooden vats and matured in oak barrels which are renewed every five years. Exports account for 65% of turnover, to all the traditional markets. The d'Angerville family has contributed enormously to both quality and authenticity in wine production in Burgundy, and for that burgundy lovers must always be grateful. The Marquis d'Angerville is the sole owner of the Clos des Ducs.

Domaine Joseph Matrot et Pierre Matrot

21190 Meursault. 18ha. Meursault-Perrières .53ha; Meursault-Charmes 1.12ha; Meursault-Blagny 1.78ha; Meursault 4.43ha; Puligny-Montrachet Les Chalumeaux 1.31ha; Puligny-Montrachet Les Combettes 0.31ha; Auxey-Duresses .57ha; Blagny la Pièce sous le Bois 2.34ha; Volnay-Santenots 1.38ha; Bourgogne 1.20ha; Bourgogne Aligoté 2.06ha. Average production figures over the last five years: 40hl/ha for white wines, 30hl/ha for red wines.

A typically Burgundian fragmented domain, with the biggest parcel in straight Meursault, but the red Blagny La Pièce sous le Bois is also made in significant quantity, and is well worth finding. The red grapes are destalked, varying between 60%–100% according to the year. Vatting lasts for 6–10 days in enamel-lined *cuves* for the reds and the wines are matured in oak barrels (with no new wood). The reds are fined with albumen and the whites with bentonite, and are filtered before bottling.

Sales in bottle are to private customers and restaurants in France, the USA, England, Belgium, Germany, Holland, Switzerland, etc. The wines do not show great breed, but often have full flavour and character.

Maison Prosper Maufoux

21590 Santenay. Négociants-éleveurs only.

This is a family firm of négociants-éleveurs based in Santenay. Although the head of the firm, Pierre Maufoux, jointly runs the Domaine St-Michel with Michel Gutrin, he is also dedicated to selecting and maturing fine wines from all over the Côte d'Or. A firm believer in wood-ageing, he matures his white wines in oak barrels for 12–15 months, and the reds for a minimum of 18 months. Sales of red and white wines are equally divided – both last well, and some of the whites are gloriously rich. Maufoux wines are found throughout the world, and they also appear under the name of Marcel Amance.

Domaine Maume

21220 Gevrey-Chambertin.

Big wines, sometimes rather inky and tannic, but they should last well, especially the top *crus* of Gevrey-Chambertin Lavaux St-Jacques and Mazis-Chambertin.

Domaine Mazilly Père & Fils

Meloisey, 21190 Meursault. 11.35ha. Beaune 1er Cru: Les Vignes Franches .35ha, 1,500 bottles; Les Montrevenots .40ha, 2,000 bottles; Les Cent Vignes .20ha, 1,200 bottles; Bourgogne Hautes Côtes de Beaune 6.50ha, 27,000 bottles; Pommard Les Poutures .80ha, 4,000 bottles; Pommard .80ha, 4,000 bottles; Meursault .80ha, 4,000 bottles; Bourgogne Passe-Tout-Grains 1.50ha, 10,000 bottles.

This is principally a Hautes Côtes de Beaune domain, with small parcels in grander appellations. Vinification is long and the wines are tannic when young. The *élevage* lasts from 12 to 18 months, with the wines stored in barrels or bigger oak *foudres*. There have been generations of Mazillys owning vineyards and making wine here, only now they export half of their production. Some of the Hautes Côtes wines are *tastevinés* and are very pleasant at 2–3 years of age.

Domaine du Meix-Foulot (Paul & Yves de Launay)

Clos du Château de Montaigu, 71640 Mercurey. 13ha (1.50ha *en fermage*, 4ha *en métayage*). Vineyard holdings include Mercurey 1.30ha, Clos du Château de Montaigü 2ha, Les Veleys 1.50ha. 30,000–35,000 bottles.

A family domain planted around the ruins of the medieval Château de Montaigü. The grapes are destalked, and vatting lasts from 8–10 days with treading. The wines are left in vats for six months, with no heating of the cellars, so that the malolactic fermentation can take its own time. Ageing is in oak barrels, where the wines stay for six months to a year, depending on the character of the vintage and the *cuvée* – thus, some wines are bottled just before the following harvest, but more often between March and June of the next year, which gives a total ageing of 18 months. The wines are often not filtered. Both red and the small amount of white wine can keep well. If you are passing through Mercurey and decide that you want to visit the domain, it is as well to ask for careful directions, as it is somewhat hidden, isolated amid the vine-covered slopes.

Domaine Prince Florent de Mérode

Serrigny, 21550 Ladoix-Serrigny. 11.38ha. Corton Clos du Roi .57ha, Corton Bressandes 1.19ha, Corton Renardes .51ha, Corton Maréchaudes 1.53ha, total 11,000–12,000 bottles; Aloxe-Corton 1er Cru .69ha, 2,300 bottles; Pommard Clos de la Platière 3.73ha, 10,000 bottles; Ladoix Rouge Les Chaillots 2.84ha, 9,000 bottles; Ladoix Blanc 1er Cru Les Hautes Mourottes .31ha, 1,000 bottles.

There are certainly some "prime sites" in this domain. It was a *maison forte* in the time of the Ducs de Bourgogne; the Château de Serrigny was rebuilt in 1700 by Pierre Brunet, president of the Chambre des Comptes in Paris. Since then it has always been inherited, never sold. The grapes are sorted on arrival, eliminating anything that does not come up to standard, and partially destalked. The domain itself considers that the wines should not be drunk before 4–5 years. In France and Belgium the wines are sold only through the Savour Club, a powerful force in mail-order sales, as well as being exported to the principal markets. Maybe the wines could be more impressive. Consistency is often a Burgundian problem but is more serious when associated with a great domain.

Mestre Père & Fils

Place du Jet d'Eau, 21590 Santenay. 19.59ha (1.96ha *en fermage*). Red wines: Santenay 3ha, 5,000 bottles; Santenay 1ers Crus: Les Gravières 2.20ha, 9,000 bottles; Clos de Tavannes .31ha, Passetemps 1.74ha, 5,000 bottles; La Comme 1.97ha, 7,000 bottles; Clos Faubard 1.60ha, 5,000 bottles; Chassagne-Montrachet .66ha, Chassagne-Montrachet Morgeot .18ha, 1,200 bottles; Cheilly les Maranges 1ha, Ladoix 2.93ha, 5,000 bottles; Aloxe-Corton 2.58ha, 5,000 bottles; Corton Grand Cru .63ha 1,200 bottles; White wines: Santenay Passetemps 1er Cru .55ha, 1,800 bottles; Chassagne-Montrachet Tonton Marcel 1er Cru Monopole .24ha, 1,500 bottles.

An important Santenay domain, built up by the fifth generation of a family of vignerons. It is particularly strong on Premiers Crus. Vinification lasts 8–10 days with quite high temperatures and *remontages* twice a day. Ageing lasts from 12 to 24 months in oak barrels, some of which are new. They particularly stress the fact that they bottle in strictly controlled clean conditions, an imperative with all wines, but the Burgundian grape varieties are noticeably vulnerable to sloppy handling. Half of the crop is sold in bulk to local négociants, and half is now sold in bottle, divided between sales to the home market and export sales. Recently some of the wines have appeared rather dry and tired at an early stage with a marked lack of colour.

Domaine du Château de Meursault
21190 Meursault. 43ha. Château de Meursault, Clos du Château, Volnay Clos des Chênes, Pommard Clos des Epenots, Beaune-Cent-Vignes, Beaune Grèves, and other 1ers Crus, Savigny.

This great domain is now owned by Patriarche, the very large Beaune négociants. But the estate side of things seems, to me, to be on a different level from the *négoce* business, and the standard is impressive. They combine the modern (stainless steel, the latest presses) with the traditional (maturing in new oak casks). The white grapes are pressed and then fermented in new barrels (hence the stylish sheen to them) and the red grapes are crushed, partially destalked, fermented for 8–12 days and then aged in new oak barrels. The domain sells direct, including to all those who visit the beautiful *caves*, or cellars, to restaurants and on the export market. Wherever one is, in far-flung countries or even on an airline (1st class!), a bottle of Château de Meursault is always rewarding to drink. In 1975, a park of 8ha was replanted to vines, as it was two centuries ago, and now a Chardonnay white wine is produced, Clos du Château, AC Bourgogne.

Domaine Louis Michel & Fils
11, Bd. de Ferrières, 89800 Chablis. 20ha. Average total production: 137,000 bottles per annum. Chablis Grand Crus: Les Clos .50ha, Vaudésir 1.20ha, Grenouilles .55ha, 14,000 bottles; Chablis 1ers Crus 13.80ha, 100,000 bottles; Chablis 4ha, 23,000 bottles.

This is a very fine, fourth-generation domain founded in 1870. The must goes through *débourbage* and fining in order to work with absolutely clean material. Fermentation takes place in vats at low temperature (18–20°C), and the malolactic fermentation is prolonged as long as possible, i.e. no measures are taken to speed it up. The wines are bottled in September. There is no wood in the process, but the slow, natural winemaking, plus yields which are not exaggerated, mean that the wines remain young, fresh, and full of bouquet for years, always with that yellowy-green light to them which is so reminiscent of Chablis. 80% of the production is exported, with the remaining 20% going to private clients and restaurants in France.

Domaine Michelot-Buisson
31 rue de la Velle, 21190 Meursault. 20ha in the best sites in Meursault (Genevrières, Charmes, Perrières), Puligny, Pommard etc.

GAEC René & Christian Miolane
Le Cellier, 69460 Salles-en-Beaujolais. 16ha (4ha *en métayage*), all in Beaujolais-Villages, producing 100,000 bottles: 10,000 are a *cuvée spéciale*, Cuvée de la Côtabras, 1,500 bottles are Marc de Beaujolais and several thousand bottles are Beaujolais Rosé.

The Miolanes have had vineyards on the same slope for three centuries, which gives a pleasant sense of continuity. René Miolane now runs the property, with his son, his daughter and his son-in-law. The wines are solid for a Villages and are not of the ephemeral, here-this-minute-gone-the-next variety. They sell across the board to private clients and wholesalers, but exports account for 60–70% of the total volume.

Moillard-Grivot
2 rue F. Mignotte, 21700 Nuits-St-Georges. 38.90ha (2.20ha *en métayage*). Grands Crus: Chambertin and Chambertin Clos de Bèze .29ha, 1,200 bottles, Romanée St-Vivant .68ha, 2,400 bottles, Clos de Vougeot .60ha, 2,600 bottles, Bonnes Mares 15ha, 600 bottles, Corton Clos du Roi .84ha, 3,000 bottles; 1ers Crus: Vosne-Romanée Les Malconsorts 3.42ha, 12,000 bottles, Vosne-Romanée les Beaux Monts .93ha, 4,000 bottles; Nuits-St-Georges Clos de Thorey 4.12ha, 18,000 bottles; Clos des Grandes Vignes 2.12ha, 10,000 bottles; Les Richemones .89ha 4,000 bottles; Les Murgers .17ha, 900 bottles; Les Porêts .54ha, 2,500 bottles; 2èmes Crus: Nuits-St-Georges Les Charmottes .75ha, 7,500 bottles; Les Grandes Vignes .54ha, 5,000 bottles; Les St-Julien .58ha, 5,000 bottles; Beaune Les Grèves 1er Cru 2.20ha, 10,000 bottles; Hautes Côtes de Nuits (red) 1.71ha, (white) 2.64ha; Corton Charlemagne Grand Cru .23ha, 1,000 bottles.

This is a large négociant firm as well as an important domain. The names of Moillard and Moillard-Grivot are interchangeable, although there is now a tendency to label the top domain wines Moillard-Grivot. The Thomas family is the fifth generation in charge today. Fermentations are carried out partly in enamel-lined steel *cuves* and partly in stainless steel rotating *cuves* with automatic *pigeage*; they last from 5 to 11 days, according to the type of *cuve*. The wines are subsequently stocked in a warm cellar to facilitate the malolactic fermentation. Flash-pasteurization has been practised since the first part of this century, although there are now experiments with non-pasteurized wines. There is a large business in buying grapes and vinifying. I have not been very impressed by the *négoce* wines, but there seems to be distinct improvement in the domain wines, some of which combine structure with fat in quite a majestic way. Moillard wines are exported to 43 countries, as well as sales on the French market.

Mommessin-Clos de Tart

21 Morey-St-Denis. 7.43ha Grand Cru Clos de Tart, 30,000 bottles.

Mommessin are first and foremost important négociants dealing in wines from the Mâconnais and the Beaujolais, as well as *vins de marque*. But the proverbial jewel in the crown is the Morey-St-Denis Grand Cru Clos de Tart, which they have owned since 1932. It was founded in the 12th century by the Benedictines de Tart le Haut and is the only Clos in Burgundy which has never been divided since its foundation. Fermentations are carried out with the *chapeau immergé* system, which means that the skins are permanently in contact with the must – this is a rarity for Burgundy and results in big wines. Clos de Tart can age magnificently, with heady tastes and aromas. In the Beaujolais and the Mâconnais, Mommessin either own or distribute a number of domains, such as the Domaine Bellenand in Pouilly-Fuissé and the Domaine de Champ de Cour in Moulin-à-Vent. Sometimes I find that a lighter touch here would be more attractive, as the fruit can be smothered by alcohol.

Mongeard-Mugneret

21670 Vosne-Romanee. 14.8ha estate making Vosne Les Suchots, Echézeaux, Grands-Echézeaux, Vougeot etc.

Domaine Jean Monnier & Fils

20 rue du 11 novembre, 21190 Meursault. 16ha. Pommard: Les Argillières, Les Epenots Clos de Citeaux 4ha; Puligny Montrachet Les Petits Nosroyes 1ha; Beaune Les Montrevenots 1ha; Meursault: Les Charmes 1er Cru, Les Genevrières 1er Cru, Les Malpoiriers 6ha; Bourgogne (Rouge, Blanc and Aligoté). 100,000 bottles.

An impeccably run domain, which has been increasing gradually through the acquisition of small parcels. In 1950, Jean Monnier bought the Clos de Citeaux in Pommard Epenots – the 3ha which once belonged to the monks of Citeaux. Tradition is followed in the vinification, and all the wines, even the *petites appellations*, are aged in oak barrels, with a certain proportion of new *fûts*. The result is wines which have immense finesse and style – it is always a treat to come upon a bottle from this estate. They are sold in some of the best restaurants in France – 25% of the production is sold in this way, 30% goes to the export markets, and 45% to discerning private customers, who obviously know a good thing when they find one.

Domaine René Monnier

6 rue du Docteur Rolland, 21190 Meursault. 18ha *en métayage* (7ha 1ers Crus). Meursault Charmes 1er Cru Dessous 1.19ha, 7,000 bottles; Meursault Limozin .86ha, 5,000 bottles; Meursault Chevalières 2.72ha, 16,000 bottles; Puligny-Montrachet .22ha, 750 bottles; Puligny-Montrachet Folatières 1er Cru 1.01ha, 6,000 bottles; Volnay 1er Cru Clos des Chênes .73ha, 3,500 bottles; Beaune 1er Cru Les Cents Vignes 1.69ha, 9,000 bottles; Beaune 1er Cru Toussaints .80ha, 4,000 bottles; Pommard les Vignots .77ha, 3,500 bottles; Santenay Les Charmes .25ha, 1,300 bottles; Côte de Beaune Villages .96ha, 6,000 bottles; Bourgogne Blanc 1.26ha, 8,000 bottles; Bourgogne Rouge 1.82ha, 11,000 bottles; Bourgogne Aligoté 1.83ha, 13,000 bottles; Bourgogne Passe-Tout-Grains 2,000 bottles. 1.85ha of vines have been uprooted for replanting.

This domain has been wisely built up through the acquisitions of each generation of Monniers. White wines are vinified and aged in barrels of three origins: Allier, Vosges and Nevers, with one-third new barrels for each *cuvée*. The wines are bottled around June. The reds undergo 12–14 days of fermentation, after about two-thirds of the stalks are removed, varying with the year. Treading takes place twice a day, after the must has started to ferment, with *remontages* which cause the yeasts to multiply through the process of oxygenation. The wines are then stocked in Limousin oak barrels until the end of the malolactic fermentation. Exports are to 16 countries, with the UK, USA and Switzerland the most important, and the wines are also to be found in a number of starred restaurants.

Domaine Monrozier

Les Moriers, 69820 Fleurie. 8.50ha (6ha *en métayage*). The domain borders the *cru* of Moulin-à-Vent, north of the commune of Fleurie. 2,000 bottles per annum of Fleurie, the rest exported in bulk.

This is a property which makes Fleurie designed to keep for a few years, as opposed to instant drinking. A Swiss négociant takes a good chunk of the production.

GAEC J. & B. Monternot (H. Monternot & Fils)

69460 Blacé en Beaujolais. 8.79ha (*en fermage*). Beaujolais AC 2.79ha; Beaujolais-Villages 6.39ha. 3,000–4,000 bottles.

The Beaujolais-Villages from this domain is very good indeed, coming from slopes to the northwest of Villefranche sur Saône near the "border" with the appellation of Brouilly. Négociants at the moment take about 20% of the annual crop, but bottle sales are going up. The length of the vatting varies according to the age of the vines, but lies between five and nine days. They are looking for high fruit and the ability to age for several years, if the client likes to drink his Villages at this stage – some find it irresistible from the first year. The two Monternot brothers divide all the work between them; vineyard, vinification, sales and administration – their father was one of the pioneers of direct sales in bottle in the Beaujolais 35 years ago.

Domaine de Montille

Volnay, 21190 Meursault. 7.2ha scattered among the Premiers Crus of Volnay (Champans, Taillepieds, Mitans) and Pommard (Epenots, Rugiens, Pézerolles).

J. Moreau & Fils

Route d'Auxerre, 89800 Chablis. 75ha. Chablis Grands Crus: Clos des Hospices 2.14ha, Les Clos 5ha, Valmur 2ha, Vaudésir 1ha, Blanchot .20ha, Chablis 1er Cru Vaillons 10ha, Chablis Domaine de Biéville 55ha. 45hl/ha.

This remarkable domain is family owned, although half of the important négociant business is owned by Hiram Walker; Moreau are both the largest négociants and the largest vineyard proprietors in Chablis. Wood has no part in the vinification, and after the fermentations, the wines are kept for between three and six weeks on healthy lees before being racked. The pride of the pack is the Chablis Grand Cru Clos des Hospices (within Les Clos) which, they say, combines on the bouquet hazelnuts, a steely or flinty quality which comes from the soil and a vanilla or lemony nose coming from the Chardonnay – and there is no wood to influence these aromas. I thought their 1978s were wonderful although, interestingly, they place both the great 1975s and the 1976s higher. 99% of the production is exported, with the USA, Great Britain and Canada the top markets.

Albert Morey & Fils

Chassagne-Montrachet, 21190 Meursault. 12ha, mostly in Chassagne. Red and white wines. Best known white is 1er Cru les Embrasées (1ha). Also Caillerets .8ha, Morgeot .4ha, Les Champs-Gain .4ha, and some Bâtard-Montrachet. .8ha Santenay for red and .8ha Beaune Grèves rented.

Albert Morot
Château de la Creusotte, 21200 Beaune. 7ha. Beaune 1ers Crus: Teurons, Bressandes, Grèves, Toussaints, Cent-Vignes, Marconnets 5.20ha; Savigny-Vergelesses Clos la Bataillère 1.80ha. 25,000–30,000 bottles.

The house of Albert Morot is both négociant and domain owner, as is often the case in Beaune, only this négociant business is on a very small scale. There is no departure from the vinification in oak vats/*élevage* in oak barrels formula. The cellars, on two levels, are beside the vineyard. They are particularly proud of their Beaune-Bressandes 1979. Although the domain does export, there is a strong clientele of private customers.

Mugneret-Gibourg (Georges Mugneret)
Vosne-Romanée, 21700 Nuits-St-Georges. 9ha. Bourgogne 1ha; Vosne-Romanée 3.50ha; Nuits-St-Georges 1er Cru Chaignots and Vignesrondes 1.70ha; Echézeaux 1.30ha; Chambolle-Musigny 1er Cru Feusselotte .40ha; Ruchottes Chambertin .70ha; Clos Vougeot .35ha. 20–40hl/ha, 20,000–25,000 bottles.

There are six families called Mugneret at Vosne-Romanée, all wine-producers, so this becomes complicated. The names of Mugneret-Gibourg and Georges Mugneret are both associated with the same domain, however, and the wine is made by Georges Mugneret, who has given up his activities as a doctor. Methods owe nothing to modernization – open *cuves*, vattings of about 15 days, first racking after the malolactic fermentation, then two others before bottling at 18 months to two years – *élevage* is in oak barrels, one-third new. Fining is with white of egg (six egg whites for a barrel of 228 litres). M. Mugneret is well aware that the Côte de Nuits has a reputation to keep up and he is certainly honouring his end of the bargain. He has many private clients and also sells to restaurants, négociants and on the export markets.

Charles Noëllat
Vosne-Romanée, 21700 Nuits-St-Georges. 14ha (owned). Romanée St-Vivant 1.49ha; Richebourg .77ha; Clos Vougeot 1.70ha; Vosne-Romanée: Beaumonts 2.90ha; Genevrières 1.23ha; Nuits-St-Georges: Boudots 1.49ha; 1er Cru .38ha; Les Lavières .68ha; Nuits-St-Georges .66ha; Vosne-Romanée .49ha; Savigny Les Narbantons .81ha. Grands Crus 20hl/ha, 1ers Crus 30–35hl/ha.

This is a fragmented domain, as most are, with some splendid sites. M. Noëllat considers that the quality of the wine is above all decided by the amount of sun in the last weeks before the harvest rather than by the vinification. The wines are kept some years before being released – in 1985, the vintages up to and including 1980 were being sold. I have never had a great bottle from this domain – somehow, the wines seem too rustic and not completely clean-tasting.

Hospices de Nuits-St-Georges
rue Henri Challand, 21700 Nuits-St-Georges. 12.4ha. Nuits 1er Cru 5.6ha, Nuits Village 2.2ha. Remainder Bourgogne and Bourgogne Grand Ordinaire.

Domaine Parent
21630 Pommard. 16ha (7ha *en fermage*). Bourgogne, Côtes de Beaune, Pommard, Pommard 1er Cru (includes Epenots, Chaponnières), Beaune 1er Cru, Corton 1er Cru. 70,000–80,000 bottles.

There are no departures from traditional methods here, as befits a former supplier of Thomas Jefferson. The wines are usually perfect examples of their appellation and an exercise in the charms of the Pinot Noir. Just occasionally, when the year has given high yields, there is a lack of definition (especially vexing at high prices), but their Pommard Epenots and Clos Micault always give great pleasure.

Domaine Jean Pascal & Fils
Puligny-Montrachet, 21190 Meursault. Family domain, 7.6ha. Speciality is Puligny-Montrachet of which 4ha is owned (Premier Cru 1.8ha). Also Pommard .8ha, Volnay .4ha.

Pasquier-Desvignes
St-Lager, 69220 Belleville. Volume firm for Beaujolais and Mâconnais wines. Produces the Beaujolais brand of Le Marquisat.

Patriarche Père & Fils
Couvent des Visitandines, 21200 Beaune. 40.46ha. Château de Meursault and Beaune 1ers Crus 40.46ha.

A huge concern, fuelled by the sales of a non-appellation sparkling wine. But they are also the owners of the magnificent estate of the Château de Meursault, where quality is high. Some of the négociant wines have been pleasant, especially the whites.

Pavelot Père & Fils
21420 Savigny-lès-Beaune. Growers in Savigny since 1640. 10ha – half in the Premier Cru vineyards of the slopes.

Maurice & Gilles Perroud
Château du Basty, Lantignié, 69430 Beaujeu. 15ha (4ha *en métayage*). Beaujolais-Villages Château du Basty 80,000 bottles.

This property is very well placed, in one parcel, 4km from Beaujeu and 3km to the north of Villié-Morgon. They do not make Primeur but Beaujolais-Villages which can be kept for a few years. They sell all their own production, 50% abroad. The Perrouds are the 15th generation on this domain, which has come down by direct descent since 1482. The family motto is *Sans Tromperie*, which should inspire confidence in prospective customers.

Piat
71570 La Chapelle-de-Guinchay. A large, quality firm.

Château de Pommard (Jean-Louis Laplanche)
21630 Pommard. 20ha (owned). The largest domain in one single parcel in the Côte d'Or producing 60,000 bottles per annum; the best barrels are kept back after tasting and sold under the exclusive label of the Château de Pommard.

An impressive property, with the Château in the middle of the vineyard, which is entirely surrounded by walls. Traditional vinification, with two years' ageing in new oak casks before bottling. The wines are big, tannic and beefy, much beloved by the general public (mostly French, Swiss, German and Belgian), who buy direct. M. Laplanche says a good winemaker should be able to make good wine in any year. The bottle and label are very beautiful.

Maison Pierre Ponnelle
Abbaye St-Martin, 53 avenue de l'Aigue, 21200 Beaune. 4.86ha. Parts of Musigny, Bonnes Mares, Charmes-Chambertin, Clos Vougeot, Corton Clos du Roi, Beaune Grèves.

A négociant with a small domain. There used to be some fairly good old wines, but I tend to find more recent vintages on the anonymous side.

Domaine Ponsot
Morey-St-Denis, 21220 Gevrey-Chambertin. 8ha all in Morey-St-Denis (except for a small part of Latricières-Chambertin). Clos de la Roche is half the total.

M. Virgile Pothier
21000 Vosne-Romanée.

Henri Potinet
Monthélie, 21190 Meursault. 8ha. Puligny-Montrachet .25ha, Meursault Perrières .35ha, Charmes .45ha, Meursault 2ha; Bourgogne Pinot Blanc .25ha, Bourgogne Aligoté .35ha, 1er Cru Pommard Pézerolles .50ha, 1er Cru Volnay Clos des Chênes .60ha, 1er Cru Auxey-Duresses Les Duresses .15ha, Monthélie 2.50ha, 1er Cru Monthélie Champsfulliot .25ha. 5,000hl/ha.

These wines are sold under the Potinet-Ampeau label. The aim is to make really long-lasting wines, so there are no short-cuts, no heating at any stage of the vinification and bottling two years after the harvest – bottles in their cellars prove that this policy works. There are direct sales to private customers and exports to traditional markets nearby, such as Switzerland and Belgium, as well as more far-flung countries such as the USA and Japan.

Poulet Père & Fils

12 rue Chaumergy, 21200 Beaune.
Négociant house founded in 1747.

Domaine de la Poulette

Grande Rue à Corgoloin, 21700 Nuits-St-Georges. 15ha (2ha *en métayage*). 66,400 bottles. Nuits-St-Georges 1er Cru: Les St-Georges .65ha, 3,500 bottles; Les Vaucrains 1.32ha, 5,800 bottles; Les Poulettes 1ha, 4,500 bottles; Les Chaboeufs .61ha, 3,600 bottles; Les Vallerots .35ha, 1,600 bottles; Nuits-St-Georges Les Brûlées 1.22ha, 5,000 bottles; Vosne-Romanée 1er Cru Les Suchots .25ha, 1,000 bottles; Côte de Nuits-Villages (red) 7.10ha, 28,000 bottles; (white) .12ha, 500 bottles; Bourgogne Rouge 1.20ha, 4,000 bottles; Bourgogne Aligoté .31ha, 3,300 bottles; Bourgogne Passe-Tout-Grains .75ha, 4,000 bottles; Bourgogne Rosé 1,200 bottles.

A domain where all the traditions are followed, including treading (after the treaders have showered, says M. Lucien Audidier!). But modern innovations of improved presses and temperature control are also in evidence, as befits the cellars of a distinguished Ingénieur Agronome. There is a strong following for these wines in France, but Switzerland is also an important market. The domain dates back to the 18th century and has been in the family since that time.

Société Civile du Domaine de la Pousse d'Or

Volnay, 21190 Meursault. 12.57ha. Volnay 1er Cru: Clos de la Bousse d'Or 2.14ha, 9,600 bottles; Caillerets Clos des 60 Ouvrées 2.39ha, 10,700 bottles; En Caillerets 2.27ha, 10,100 bottles; Clos d'Audignac .80ha, 3,600 bottles; Pommard 1er Cru les Jarollières 1.04ha, 4,800 bottles; Santenay 1er Crus: Clos Tavannes 2.1ha, 9,400 bottles; Les Gravières 1.83ha, 8,200 bottles.

Gérard Potel, an Ingénieur Agronome and oenologist, runs this domain with admirable precision; the principal proprietor, M. Jean Ferté, is a noted connoisseur of fine wine and food. There is little destalking, vinification in open vats, with *pigeage* every day and a vatting of 10 to 15 days. *Elevage* takes place in oak barrels with about 20–30% new wood. 70% of the production is exported around the world, with the 30% sales to the French market being divided between private customers and top restaurants. The wines combine fruit and appellation character together with a long, emphatic aftertaste. The top *crus* from this domain last beautifully in bottle.

Domaine Jacques Prieur

21190 Meursault. 15ha. Gevrey Chambertin: Chambertin .83ha; Chambertin Clos de Bèze .13ha; Musigny .84ha; Clos de Vougeot 1.28ha; Beaune Clos de la Féguine 1.90ha; Volnay Clos des Santenots 1.20ha; Volnay Santenots .80ha; Bourgogne (red) 1ha; Meursault Clos de Mazeray (red) 1.60ha, (white) 1.60ha; Meursault-Perrières .30ha; Puligny-Montrachet les Combettes 1.50ha; Chevalier-Montrachet .13ha; Le Montrachet .60ha. 60,000–100,000 bottles.

This is a famous domain, with excellent vineyards on both the Côte de Nuits and the Côte de Beaune. The children of Jacques Prieur are now the shareholders of this family company, and the domain is managed by his son, Jean Prieur, while his son-in-law, Pierre Poupon, the reputed author, helps in tastings during the vinification and *élevage*. All the wines are made at Meursault. The intention is to produce wines which keep, and I have had some remarkable bottles, but recently there have been a few disappointments – perhaps I have been unlucky. About 85% of the wines produced by the domain is exported, to all the usual Burgundy markets of our days.

Domaine du Prieuré (Armand Monassier)
Rully, 71150 Chagny. 9ha. Rully Rouge 2.40ha, Rully Rouge 1er Cru (Mont Palais and Préau) 2ha, 20,000 bottles; Rully Blanc and Rully Blanc 1er Cru (Mont Palais and Grésigny) 2.50ha, 12,000 bottles; for Crémant: Aligoté .50ha, Pinot Noir .75ha, 10,000 bottles; Mercurey (Rouge) .64ha, 2,300 bottles.

Armand Monassier created the Domaine du Prieuré in 1959, buying vines and undertaking new plantings. The red grapes are almost entirely destalked and vatting lasts for 8 to 10 days (the *vin de presse* is not added, but distilled into Fine de Bourgogne). Ageing takes place in oak barrels, a quarter of which are renewed each year. White vinification is classic, with a part of the crop kept in oak barrels. 45% of production is sold to restaurants (perhaps because M. Monassier was once himself a Paris restaurateur), 30% is sold to private clients, and the remaining 25% is exported.

Domaine Maurice Protheau & Fils
Le Clos l'Evêque, 71640 Mercurey. 45ha (17ha *en métayage*). Mercurey Rouge, 26.30ha 40hl/ha: Clos l'Evêque 6.25ha, Clos des Corvées 4ha, La Fauconnière 4.50ha, Les Vellées 2ha, Mercurey Rouge 9.55ha; Mercurey Blanc les Ormeaux 2.50ha, 40hl/ha; Rully 10.40ha, 40hl/ha; Rully Blanc 1er Cru les Grésigny 1.30ha; Bourgogne Rouge Vigne de Champrenard 4.50ha, 50hl/ha; Crémant de Bourgogne 875kg/ha.

This is an important Côte Chalonnaise domain, with the wines distributed by the négociant François Protheau et Fils. The Protheau family have been growers in Mercurey since 1720, but created a new vineyard in Rully in 1976. The red grapes are completely destalked, vatted for 8–10 days and aged in oak barrels for 12–14 months. Clos l'Evêque and Clos des Corvées are treated to new oak. The reds tend to be tannic and slow maturing. The white Mercurey attains richness with age. Switzerland is the leading client for these wines.

Charles Quillardet
18 route de Dijon, 21220 Gevrey-Chambertin. Gevrey-Chambertin 1er Cru Les Champeaux, Chambertin, Fixin, Gevrey-Chambertin, Rosé de Marsannay, Bourgogne Les Grandes Vignes, Bourgogne Montre Cul, Côte de Nuits-Villages. Average annual production for whole domain is 100,000 bottles.

This is something of a puzzling domain. Occasionally there are good wines with liquorice and cassis overtones, but at other times one is really disappointed, with clumsy, coarse wines which lack Pinot Noir frankness. M. Quillardet says he vinifies *à l'ancienne*, with partial destalking according to the vintage.

Half of the production is exported, half is sold direct, which must be easy, as the domain is right on the Route Nationale. There is also a Bourgogne Rouge, called Montre Cul, produced at Larrey in the suburbs of Dijon. The label is in execrable taste, but apparently it is a traditional name for the site – the slope is so steep that the *vendangeuses* showed more than they perhaps should have. It would be better if they wore jeans for picking, one would think.

Ramonet-Prudhon
Chassagne-Montrachet, 21190 Meursault. 13.6ha, half white incl. Bâtard- and Bienvenues-Bâtard-Montrachet, Chassagne Premier Cru Les Ruchottes, Chassagne Village; half red incl. Clos de la Boudriotte, Clos St-Jean, Chassagne Village.
Very fine wines, some of them under the label of André Ramonet.

Rapet Père & Fils
Pernand-Vergelesses, 21420 Savigny-lès-Beaune. 12ha including parcels of Corton-Charlemagne, Corton Grand Cru (red), Pernand-Vergelesses 1er Cru, Bourgogne (red and white).

Château de Raousset
69115 Chiroubles. 45ha (*en métayage*). Chiroubles 20ha, Fleurie 12ha, Morgon 13ha.

A very important property, producing fine wines. 65% of the production is sold in bulk, 35% in bottle – Duboeuf does a bottling of the Chiroubles at the Château. There is semi-carbonic maceration with a vatting of 6–7 days. They look for a balance between a wine which can keep for a few years and one destined for very young drinking, making their choice according to the intrinsic potential of the vintage. They regard temperature control as paramount to the development of aromas and bouquet.

François Raveneau

rue de Chichée, 89800 Chablis. 7.2ha in Grands Crus Valmurs, Les Clos, Blanchots, and 1ers Crus.

A. Regnard & Fils/Albert Pic/Michel Rémon

89800 Chablis. Négociants specializing in 1er Cru Fourchaume, Grands Crus Vaudésir, Valmur.

Domaine de la Reine Pédauque-Clos des Langres

Corgoloin, 21700 Nuits-St-Georges. 38ha (plus fermage). Clos Vougeot Grand Cru 1.10ha, 6,000 bottles; Clos des Langres 3.15ha, 12,000 bottles; Corton Renardes 4ha; Corton Pougets Grand Cru 1.46ha, 6,000 bottles; Corton Combes Grand Cru .60ha, 2,160 bottles; Aloxe-Corton 1.10ha, 6,000 bottles; Aloxe-Corton 1er Cru 2.50ha, 11,400 bottles; Savigny-lès-Beaune 1er Cru Les Guettes 2.50ha, 14,400 bottles; Savigny-lès-Beaune 1er Cru Les Peuillets 4.20ha, 24,000 bottles; Savigny 1er Cru Les Clous 3.50ha, 21,000 bottles; Savigny-lès-Beaune 3.50ha, 22,800 bottles; Ladoix (red) 3.50ha, 21,000 bottles; Corton Charlemagne (Grand Cru) 1.50ha, 6,000 bottles; Bourgogne (red) 6.50ha, 42,000 bottles; Bourgogne Aligoté 2.50ha, 18,000 bottles.

This is both domain and large négociant-éleveur, owned by Pierre André, another name under which they trade. I am afraid I find their red wines to be somewhat jammy and burnt-tasting, right across the range, but the whites are more palatable. The reds go through the *chapeau immergé* method of vinification, a rare occurrence in Burgundy, for 10 days and the *grands vins* are matured in oak barrels, a third of which are renewed each year. The Corton-Charlemagne is vinified in new oak barrels. They bottle early as they believe this conserves the maximum of fruit.

Remoissenet Père & Fils

21200 Beaune. 2.40ha Beaune 1er Cru (including Grèves and Toussaints).

Both domain owner and important négociant. I tend to prefer the top white wines to the more patchy reds.

Henri Remoriquet & Fils

25 rue de Charmois, 21700 Nuits-St-Georges. 5.51ha. Bourgogne Hautes Côtes de Nuits 1.26ha, 6,000 bottles; Nuits-St-Georges 2.26ha, 3,000 bottles, the rest sold in bulk to the local négociants; Nuits-St-Georges Les Allots .73ha, 3,200 bottles; Nuits-St-Georges 1ers Crus: Les Damodes .36ha, 1,500 bottles, Aux Bousselots .32ha, sold in bulk to the local négociants; Rue de Chaux .40ha, 1,700 bottles; Les St-Georges .18ha, 750 bottles.

This is a small domain which has been slowly built up this century and where the wines are made with great care and respect for true taste and flavour. The grapes are half destalked and vatting is quite lengthy. *Elevage* is in oak barrels renewed "as often as possible". Bottling takes place at 22 months, after a fining with white of egg. There seems to be a preponderance of fruit in these wines.

Domaine D. Rion

Prémeaux, 21000 Nuits-St-Georges.

Domaine de la Romanée-Conti

Vosne-Romanée, 21700 Nuits-St-Georges. 20ha. La Romanée-Conti 1.80ha, 7,000 bottles; La Tâche 6ha, 24,000 bottles; Richebourg 3.48ha, 14,000 bottles; Grands-Echézeaux 3.52ha, 14,000 bottles; Echézeaux 4.65ha, 18,500 bottles; Romanée-St-Vivant rented *en fermage* from the Domaine Marey-Monge; Le Montrachet .67ha, 2,500 bottles.

I have been temporarily forbidden entry to the domain because of my "quasi systematic denigration" of its wines, which seems somewhat oversensitive as I have only occasionally criticized some of its vintages. However, having never believed in sacred cows, be they in wine, politics, or the arts, I am not in the least deterred, especially as the co-proprietors, M. Aubert de Villaine and Mme Bize-Leroy, cannot prevent me from seeing the wines!

The vineyard holdings are fabulous, some of the best sites in Burgundy. The policy is late picking in order to achieve maximum possible ripeness, even if this means that the weather breaks. The domain says it always practises rigorous grape selection in years where there is rot. Partial destalking according to the vintage, and very long fermentations are also features of DRC practice. There is, naturally, the finance to use new oak barrels every year and racking and filtrations are kept to a minimum. The domain aims for great longevity in its wines.

When one aspires to be amongst the best, at astronomic prices, expectations run high. Sometimes these expectations are more than satisfied by splendid, heady wines of exotic richness. At other times, there are disappointing bottles, poor colours and unstable characteristics – even burnt flavours and an excess of alcohol. Everyone would agree that it is impossible to produce great red wines every year in Burgundy; perhaps it might be better not to bottle under an illustrious name in poor years. One hates to think of a monied, relative newcomer to wine paying a great deal for very little – would he remain a customer for life? But when domain wines are performing well, from fine vintages, a treasure-trove of tastes awaits the lucky drinker. There are some marvellous old bottles, when La Tâche and Romanée-Conti vie for top place. These are instances when the Emperor is most certainly wearing all his clothes!

Ropiteau Frères

21190 Meursault. 21.06ha. Vineyard holdings: 1ers Crus in Genevrières, Perrières and 4 other *climats* 4.86ha, Village 12.96ha, 1er Cru Puligny 1.61ha, Monthélie 1.61ha; small parts in Volnay, Monthélie, Pommard, Beaune (Grèves), Clos Vougeot, Echézeaux and Chambolle-Musigny.

A négociant house with some estate wines. They have always been known for their range of Meursault, but at the last tasting they did not seem to be as good as before: slightly unbalanced wines with wood and fruit in mild disarray.

Domaine Rottiers/Clothilde

rue Auxerroise, 89800 Chablis. 4ha in production, 10ha more planted. 8.8ha producing 1ers Crus, incl. Fourchaume and Montmains. 1ha Grand Cru Vaudésir, producing a *vin de garde*.

Joseph Roty

21220 Gevrey-Chambertin. Charmes-Chambertin, Gevrey 1er Cru and Villages. Small but good grower. Prices positively at "boutique" level and sales mostly to restaurants and private clients. The wines are particularly appreciated in Belgium and Luxembourg.

Domaine Guy Roulot

1 rue Charles Giraud, 21190 Meursault. 12ha (4ha *en métayage*). Meursault: 5.30ha (Les Perrières, Les Charmes, Les Tessons, Les Luchets, Les Meix Chavaux). Auxey-Duresses 1.30ha; Beaune 1ha; Bourgogne Chardonnay, Rouge, Aligoté, Gamay 4.40ha.

This is an admirable domain, ably managed by Madame Guy Roulot, with the wines now made by a young nephew. They were amongst the first growers in Meursault to vinify the different *lieux dits* separately. Guy Roulot, who so sadly died in November 1982, developed the domain to what it is today. For me, these are wines of finesse and breed. Vinification is in oak barrels with a proportion of new wood, varying between one-third and one-quarter for the Meursaults. Bottling takes place, on average, after 10–11 months. They aim to do as little *pompage* as possible, moving wine or must by means of a pump, a tiring process. The results have texture and length on the palate. Wines from the Roulot domain are to be found in restaurants in France as well as outside France on the export markets.

Domaine G. Roumier

Chambolle-Musigny, 21220 Gevrey-Chambertin. 14ha; Chambolle-Musigny 7.2ha, Morey-St-Denis 2.4ha, Bonnes Mares 2.4ha, Clos de Vougeot 1ha, Le Musigny .4ha, Les Amoureuses .4ha.

Domaine Roux Père & Fils

St-Aubin, 21190 Meursault. 20ha. Santenay 1er Cru 2ha, 10,000 bottles; Chassagne-Montrachet (white) 1ha, 5,000 bottles, (red) 1ha, 5,000 bottles; Chassagne 1er Cru .66ha, 4,000 bottles; Puligny-Montrachet Enseignères .33ha, 2,000 bottles; Meursault 1er Cru Poruzots .33ha, 2,000 bottles; St-Aubin La Pucelle 1ha, 5,300 bottles; St-Aubin 1er Cru (white) 2ha, 10,000 bottles (red), 3ha, 17,000 bottles; Bourgogne (red and white) 4.50ha, 15,000 bottles; Bourgogne Aligoté 3.50ha, 20,000 bottles; Bourgogne Passe-Tout-Grains 1ha, 5,500 bottles.

A very good domain; the Roux family also started a négociant business two years ago. There is no destalking and the *élevage* is done in oak barrels which are renewed by one-third every three years. The wines are perfect examples of their different appellations.

Domaine PBI Sarrau

69840 Juliénas. 6ha. Fleurie Grand Pré 4ha, 25,000 bottles; Morgon Château Gaillard 2ha, 13,000 bottles.

These two properties are owned by Pierre, Bernard and Isabelle Sarrau. The wines are bottled at the domain and sold through the firm of Sarrau – an exercise in keeping it in the family! 65% is exported, 35% sold in France. Same style and vinification methods as other properties in the Sarrau group.

Domaine Etienne Sauzet

Puligny-Montrachet, 21190 Meursault. 12.4ha. Puligny 1ers Crus 5.2ha, Combettes 1.6ha, Champ-Canet 1.6ha. Also Puligny 3.2ha, Chassagne .8ha, and small parcels of Bâtard- and Bienvenues-Bâtard-Montrachet.

Domaine Savoye (Pierre Savoye)

"Sur la Côte du Py", 69910 Villié-Morgon. 13.50ha (*en métayage*). Morgon Côte du Py, Morgon, Chiroubles, Beaujolais 13.50ha, 60,000 bottles.

This is a splendid domain, principally on the Côte du Py, where the schistous rock is called *pierre bleue*, which in effect becomes ochre in colour as it decomposes and gives that elusive quality to a wine – *un vin qui "morgonne"*. Vinification for the Côte du Py will last from 7 to 10 days, so the wine will have depth and keeping potential. The most solid wines are kept some months in oak barrels and bottled towards the end of the year following the vintage. They are an experience for all those who wish to taste "true" Morgon.

Domaine Seguin (distributed by Seguin-Manuel)

Rue Paul Maldant, 21420 Savigny-lès-Beaune. 6ha. Savigny 3ha, 20,000 bottles, Beaune 3ha.

Pierre Seguin (whose grandfather invented the *wagon-citerne*, or road tanker) is both a domain owner and a négociant. The domain wines are fermented in oak *cuves* in a 14th-century Cistercian *cuverie*, and the aim is to make wines which will keep well. But that does not mean heaviness – the wines have bouquet and supple fruit. The Seguin family have owned the house, cellars, *cuverie* and the vineyards since the 18th century.

Domaine Daniel Senard

21420 Aloxe-Corton. 8ha (owned). Corton Clos du Roi .64ha, 3,200 bottles; Corton Bressandes .63ha, 3,200 bottles; Corton Clos des Meix 2.11ha, 10,000 bottles; Corton .83ha, 6,000 bottles; Aloxe 1er Cru .70ha, 3,500 bottles; Aloxe-Corton (red) 2.39ha, 8,000 bottles; Aloxe-Corton (white) .21ha, 900 bottles; Beaune 1er Cru .29ha, 900 bottles; Chorey-lès-Beaune .51ha, 4,500 bottles; Aligoté (white) .20ha.

Philippe Senard now makes the wines, the fourth generation of vignerons. The 14th-century cellars were built by the monks of the Abbaye de Ste-

Marguerite and were forgotten for several centuries. Methods are traditional, but with great emphasis on automatic temperature control at the time of fermentation/vatting. There are both wooden *cuves* and enamel-lined steel vats, and *élevage* is in oak barrels, with 10–12% new wood. These are nearly always wines for long keeping, bottled after two years, and tannic, even rustic when young. Sometimes the "lesser" wines seem more balanced. There is a most unusual Aloxe-Corton Blanc made from the Pinot Beurot, or Pinot Gris – powerful stuff. 80% of sales is exported.

Simonnet-Febvre

9 avenue d'Oberwesel, 89800 Chablis. 5ha. Chablis Grand Cru les Preuses, Chablis 1er Cru Mont de Milieu, Chablis.

This is a small domain, but Simonnet-Febvre is an important négociant-éleveur who buys in must and vinifies it for young bottling. The house was founded in 1840 and Jean-Claude Simonnet is the fifth-generation member of the family now in charge. The firm also make a speciality of other Yonne wines, such as Irancy and Coulanges. The wine is bottled under several other labels.

Pierre Siraudin

Château de St-Amour, St-Amour Bellevue, 71570 La Chapelle-de-Guinchay. 13ha (8ha *en métayage*). St-Amour 7ha (of which 4ha *en métayage*), Beaujolais-Villages St-Vérand Rouge 6ha (of which 4ha *en métayage*) 9,000–10,000 bottles.

The Château de St-Amour is an excellent example of the appellation. It is fermented for 7 to 10 days, according to the nature of the year, and keeps well. The Beaujolais-Villages from St. Vérand ferments for between six to eight days, again, in order to make a wine which is not ephemeral. For 25 years part of the crop has been sold to Piat, but there is also direct selling in bottle from the Château.

Société Civile d'Exploitation de Romanèche-Thorins (SCERT) Château des Jacques

71720 Romanèche-Thorins. 52ha. Moulin-à-Vent Château des Jacques 40ha (36ha currently in production), 1,800hl (young wines sold in bulk) 150,000–180,000 bottles; Beaujolais Blanc Château de Loyse 12ha (9ha in production), 450–500hl/60,000 bottles.

The Château des Jacques is a famous name in Moulin-à-Vent, and I have had bottles which were 30 years old and still a force to be reckoned with, albeit more resembling something from the Côte d'Or than the Beaujolais. The aim is still to make wines which keep, and fermentation lasts from 10 to 12 days, but I have found recent vintages rather alcoholic, eclipsing the fruit. The Beaujolais Blanc Château de Loyse is vinified at about 18°C and stocked in stainless steel under nitrogen to conserve freshness. Apart from sales in France, exports of the Château des Jacques, particularly to distant countries, are effected through the firm of Thorin which is based at Pontanevaux.

Paul Spay

Domaine de la Cave Lamartine, 71570 St-Amour-Bellevue. 13.50ha (7ha *en métayage*). St-Amour: Clos du Chapitre, 2.50ha, Vers l'Eglise 5.55ha, 40,000 bottles; St-Amour (white): Clos de la Cure, Vers l'Eglise 2ha, 12,000 bottles; Juliénas Côte de Bessay 3.45ha, 10,000 bottles.

This domain possesses good sites, facing south and southeast. They are increasing their bottle sales and their exports to all the usual markets. Their vinification is classic, their aim to make wines with regional character and fruit which are delicious for two to three years after the harvest. But Paul Spay is against laying down these *crus* – "leave that to the Côte d'Or and Bordeaux"!

Domaine St-Michel (Michel Gutrin)

21590 Santenay. 30ha on the Côte d'Or. Santenay (Santenay Commes 1er Cru, Clos Rousseau 1er Cru), Chassagne-Montrachet, Puligny-Montrachet, Bourgogne.

The domain was founded in 1972 by Michel Gutrin, a grower, and Pierre Maufoux of the well-known négociant firm at Santenay. Much of the crop is sold in bulk to different négociants, but bottle sales are increasing, and already there are private customers in France and exports to Germany and Switzerland. Traditional vinification in wood *cuves* and maturing for two years in oak barrels for those wines bottled at the domain. The Santenay wines are strong and marked with appellation character, and show significant tannin.

Louis Tête

St-Didier-sur-Beaujeu, 69430 Beaujeu. 3.50ha. Beaujolais-Villages 3ha, 23,000 bottles; Moulin-à-Vent .50ha, 4,000 bottles.

This is the small family property of Louis Tête, the highly respected négociant in Beaujolais wines, whose selections are always prime examples of their kind. The wines are made at low temperature to conserve maximum fruit, but so that the finished bottles have good structure too.

Domaine Tollot-Beaut & Fils

Chorey-lès-Beaune, 21200 Beaune. 22ha (3.50ha *en fermage*). Corton Charlemagne .25ha, 1,500 bottles; Corton Bressandes .92ha, 4,500 bottles; Corton .62ha, 3,000 bottles; Aloxe-Corton 3.50ha, 20,000 bottles; Beaune Grèves .60ha, 3,300 bottles; Beaune Clos du Roi 1.10ha, 6,000 bottles; Beaune Blanches Fleurs .29ha, 1,600 bottles; Savigny Lavières 1.32ha, 7,200 bottles; Savigny Champ Chevrey 1.48ha, 7,800 bottles; Savigny-lès-Beaune .28ha, 1,500 bottles; Chorey-lès-Beaune 7.90ha, 45,000 bottles; Bourgogne Rouge 1.75ha, 12,600 bottles; Bourgogne Blanc .70ha, 4,800 bottles; Bourgogne Aligoté 1.30ha, 12,300 bottles.

This is a renowned family domain – the first vines were bought in 1880 and now the fifth generation is starting to work. The age old Burgundian formula is followed here – vinification in open wood *cuves* with a floating *chapeau* of skins, constantly in contact with the fermenting must, all with the aim of producing wines of good colour, aromatic in their bouquet and with real potential for longevity. In the main, Tollot-Beaut succeed admirably, with some gloriously heady wines. The Chorey-lès-Beaune is a wine with a good *rapport qualité/prix*, a distinct asset to those on a budget. Two-thirds of the production is exported.

Domaine Tollot-Voarick

21200 Chorey-lès-Beaune. Especially good Pinot Blanc.

Domaine Tortochot

12 rue de l'Eglise, 21220 Gevrey-Chambertin. 10ha (owned). Morey-St-Denis 2,000 bottles, Gevrey-Chambertin 30,000 bottles, 1er Cru Lavaux St-Jacques 3,000 bottles, 1er Cru Les Champeaux 4,000 bottles, Mazis-Chambertin 2,000 bottles, Charmes-Chambertin 3,000 bottles, Chambertin 1,500 bottles, Clos Vougeot 600 bottles.

A well-respected domain, run by M. Gabriel Tortochot. Half of the production is sold to local négociants in barrel, half in bottle direct from the domain – Switzerland and Belgium are good customers, and private clients calling in are given a warm welcome. Grapes are destalked, and fermentations are long, up to 14 days. One-tenth new barrels are bought each year. The wines tend to be big, sometimes slightly rustic. But there are grand bottles when aged.

Roland Thévenin

Domaine du Château, Haut de Santenay, 21590 Santenay. 19.50ha. Puligny-Montrachet 4ha, Meursault 1ha, Auxey-Duresses 5.90ha, St-Romain 5ha, Pommard 1.24ha, Beaune .41ha. 35hl/ha.

M. Roland Thévenin has always been a tremendous supporter of "his" village of Saint-Romain (*mon village* appears on the labels) and his Domaine du Château de Puligny-Montrachet has an excellent reputation. At Auxey-Duresses there is the Clos du Moulin aux Moines. In the latter part of 1985, an Australian group bought the Château de Puligny-Montrachet and M. Michel Laroche of Chablis was appointed as the manager.

Domaine Roy-Thévenin

Château de la Saule, Montagny-les-Buxy, 71390 Buxy. 11.80ha. Chardonnay 8.60ha, Aligoté .88ha, Gamay 1ha, Pinot Noir 1.30ha. 49,000 bottles.

This is a very reliable domain, with labels under the names of both Alain and Marcel Roy-Thévenin. The grapes for the Montagny are pressed rapidly and then the clarified must ferments in *foudres* (wooden vats), enamel-lined tanks and a part in oak barrels. The wines are then racked in March/April for an early bottling. The result is fresh and youthful, and always in balance. The Aligoté is very worthy too. The wines are now nicely spread in France and on the export markets.

René Thévenin-Monthélie & Fils

St-Romain, 21190 Meursault. 15ha. St-Romain (red and white), Auxey-Duresses (red and white), Meursault, Monthélie, Beaune, Savigny-lès-Beaune 1er Cru, Savigny-lès-Beaune, Volnay Clos des Chênes 50,000–100,000 bottles.

This domain is principally known for its white St-Romain, which is a more than honourable wine, deserving to be better known. It is, as they say, for those "in the know".

Domaine Thevenot-le-Brun & Fils

Marey-les-Fussey, 21700 Nuits-St-Georges. 25ha (5ha *en fermage*). Hautes Côtes de Nuits: Aligoté 4.70ha, Gamay 3ha, Pinot Blanc 1.30ha, Chardonnay 1.90ha, Pinot Beurot .80ha, Pinot Noir 13.30ha, (Clos du Vignon 6.60ha). Production: Bourgogne Aligoté 20,000 bottles, Bourgogne Passe-Tout-Grains 15,000 bottles, Clos du Vignon Rouge 20,000 bottles, Clos du Vignon Blanc 7,000 bottles, Hautes Côtes de Nuits Rouge 25,000 bottles, Hautes Côtes de Nuits Blanc 5,000 bottles.

Father and two sons work this property, and they are particularly proud of their Clos du Vignon, which the family revived after the vines had been completely abandoned. I have liked the red better than the white. There is rather a special Bourgogne Aligoté, Perles d'Or, which is bottled straight off the lees to give some fresh *pétillance*.

Thorin

Pontanevaux, 71570 La Chapelle-de-Guinchay. Owns Château des Jacques in Moulin-à-Vent and Château de Loyse. Also sells under the name of Faye in supermarkets. Not my favourite Beaujolais.

Domaine Louis Trapet

53 route de Beaune, 21220 Gevrey-Chambertin. 61.8ha. Chambertin 3.6ha, Latricières and Chapelle-Chambertin 2ha, Gevrey 1ers Crus 2ha, Gevrey Village 6.8ha.

Société Civile du Domaine des Varoilles (J-P. Naigeon)

11 rue de l'Ancien Hôpital, 21220 Gevrey-Chambertin. 11.90ha (2ha *en métayage*). Gevrey-Chambertin .40ha, 1,800 bottles; Clos du Couvent .40ha, 1,800 bottles; Clos Prieur .32ha, 1,200 bottles; Clos du Meix des Ouches 1.05ha, 4,000 bottles; Champonnets 1er Cru .70ha, 2,500 bottles; La Romanée 1er Cru 1.06ha, 4,500 bottles; Clos des Varoilles 1er Cru 6ha, 17,000 bottles; Charmes-Chambertin and Mazoyères-Chambertin .78ha, 2,800 bottles; Bonnes Mares .50ha, 1,500 bottles; Clos Vougeot 2.60ha, 7,000 bottles.

Jean-Pierre Naigeon is co-owner and winemaker at this domain, and his high standards show in the majestic evolution of the wines. They often start life with more body and structure than some others, due largely to a policy of old vines and rigorous selection. The cellars are also very cold, so early development is slow. An interesting technique involving cables across the vats keeps the fermenting must in contact with the *chapeau* of skins. There is both fat and tannin in the wines, the perfect ingredients for successful ageing in bottle. For those who say that all "modern" burgundy is made for early drinking, this is a lesson – although, of course, years like 1982 are more early-maturing. Many wines from this domain are *tastevinés*. M. Naigeon also runs the Naigeon-Chauveau négociant business.

Charles Viénot

5 quai Dumorey, 21700 Nuits-St-Georges. .30ha Pinot Noir in Nuits-St-Georges Clos des Corvées Pagets (1er Cru), 1,700 bottles.

Traditional methods produce full, slightly sweet wines. Charles Viénot is also a négociant-éleveur in Nuits, and I have liked the firm's Côte de Nuits-Villages. Viénot belongs to Jean-Claude Boisset.

A & P de Villaine

Bouzeron, 71150 Chagny. 17.50ha (2.50ha *en métayage/fermage*). Bourgogne Aligoté Bouzeron 6.5ha, 35,000 bottles; Bourgogne Blanc Les Clous 4ha, 26,000 bottles; Bourgogne Rouge La Digoine 7ha, 35,000 bottles; Bourgogne Rosé de Pinot Noir 6,000 bottles.

A very well-run property, making wines which are a good introduction to the tastes of burgundy. The Aligoté and the Rosé de Pinot Noir are given a very light pressing and are vinified at 21°C maximum in concrete vats, but above all, in large oak *foudres*. The Chardonnay is partly vinified in oak vats and partly in oak barrels. The red wines are vinified in wooden *cuves*, with frequent *pigeages*, and *élevage* in barrels. In years when more concentration is desired, some juice is drawn off to get a better ratio of matter to fermenting must. 20% of the production is sold in bulk to négociants, but the rest is sold in bottle in France and around the world.

Henri de Villamont

rue du Docteur Guyot, 21420 Savigny-lès-Beaune. 10.10ha. Savigny Domaine Marthenot 6.06ha, Chambolle-Musigny Domaine Modot 4.04ha, Grands-Echézeaux.

An important Swiss-owned négociant. Their Savigny wines can sometimes be most pleasant. In 1969 they bought the Barolet business, but of course the recent wines have nothing to do with the great collection of wines built up by the late Dr. Barolet which are now, unfortunately, mostly happy memories.

Domaine Michel Voarick

21420 Aloxe-Corton. 13ha (6.50ha *en métayage*). Corton-Charlemagne 1.50ha, Aloxe-Corton 4ha, Corton Crus 4.50ha, Côte de Nuits Crus .66ha, Pernand-Vergelesses 2ha. Production: Villages 20,000 bottles; Crus (red) 15,000 bottles, (white) 5,000 bottles.

Amongst the vines tended by this domain, is the famous 2.5ha Hospices de Beaune vineyard, Cuvée Corton Docteur Peste. The old Burgundian rules are followed to the letter here, including a policy of no destalking. The wines which result usually last very well and make fine, sturdy bottles. It is now a label which is seen in a number of countries.

Robert Vocoret

rue d'Avallon, 89800 Chablis, 30.4ha. 4ha in Grands Crus Les Clos, Valmur, Blanchots, 13.2ha in 1ers Crus and 13.2ha Chablis.

Joseph Voillot

Volnay, 21190 Meursault. 10ha. (1.50ha *en métayage*). Volnay, Volnay 1er Cru 4ha; Pommard, Pommard 1er Cru 3.50ha; Meursault 1er Cru .40ha; AC Bourgogne 2.10ha 37hl/ha.

The Voillot family have been vignerons in Volnay since the 14th century, which certainly displays fidelity to one's origins! They are supporters of warm fermentations. One-third new oak barrels are used for the wines which are domain bottled – two-thirds of the production is sold in bulk, either to Beaunois or Swiss négociants.

CHABLIS

Chablis produces stupendous wines and contentious people. They can never quite agree amongst themselves which villages and slopes should fall within the appellation and which should not, whether Portlandian limestone is as good as Kimmeridgian, whether or not to use wood in the *élevage* of the wines, and even whether the aspersion method of frost protection (spraying the vines to give a protective coat of ice) is ultimately beneficial – the man who, in my view, makes the best Chablis today has serious reservations about the practice.

The one aspect of the Chablis saga which has never been in dispute is the status of the Grands Crus, which have remained inviolate since the creation of the AC in 1938. The seven Grands Crus are all on the slopes of the huge hill over the little Serein river from Chablis itself. They are:

Blanchot	*11.65ha*
Bougros	*15.85ha*
Les Clos	*25.81ha*
Grenouilles	*9.68ha*
Preuses	*11.10ha*
Valmur	*13.20ha*
Vaudésir	*16.19ha*

The name La Moutonne is used for wine from a 2.35ha parcel of Preuses and Vaudésir, so it is considered as a Grand Cru.

The Premiers Crus area is currently being expanded, and here there is serious contention. It is difficult to judge these new plantings until the vines are older, although interested parties already think the quality is of sufficient standard. The nomenclature of Premiers Crus in Chablis has always been complicated, with a mass of alternative names, but now the majority are gathered under the main vineyards, which certainly makes for ease of marketing. They stand as follows, but it is worth remembering that Chablisien spelling is notoriously idiosyncratic:

Premiers Crus	Vineyards
Fourchaume:	*Fourchaume, Vaupulent, Côte de Fontenay, Vaulorent, L'Homme Mort*
Montée de Tonnerre:	*Montée de Tonnerre, Chapelot, Pied d'Aloup*
Mont de Milieu	
Beauroy:	*Beauroy, Troesmes (or Troême)*
Les Fourneaux:	*Les Fourneaux, Morein, Côte des Près-Girots*
Côte de Léchet	
Vaucoupin (or Vaucoupain)	
Vaillons:	*Vaillons, Châtains, Séchet (or Séché), Beugnon, Les Lys*
Vosgros:	*Vosgros, Vaugiraut*
Mélinots:	*Mélinots, Roncières, Les Epinottes*
Montmains:	*Montmains, Forêts, Butteaux*
Vaudevey	

Naturally, there is far greater disparity of quality between the Premiers Crus than between the Grands Crus, which are in another category as far as richness and concentration are concerned. The Premiers Crus are scattered over a clutch of villages, some of them outlying. These villages include Fyé, Fleys, La Chapelle-Vaupelteigne, Poinchy, Fontenay, Maligny, Milly, Chichée and Beines, as well as the town of Chablis itself. Vaudevey in the commune of Beines is, in fact, a new Premier Cru.

The villages which stand to gain most from the extension of the vineyard area are Maligny, Lignorelles and Villy; at Maligny, particularly, much vineyard area hitherto defined as Petit Chablis has been upgraded to Chablis, contributing to the decline of the former name. While most people with some knowledge of soil types would agree with the Institut National des Appellations d'Origine that Kimmeridgian and Portlandian clay are very similar, the importance of microclimate and site of a vineyard are vital, especially in a viticultural area as far north as Chablis, with its constant problems of frost and ripeness.

The danger of spring frost exists from the end of March until the middle of May. Two main methods of protection are now in use: aspersion, or spraying the vines to give a protective coat of ice, and burners in the vineyard. The timing of spraying must be perfect, starting the moment when the temperature reaches zero, and it must be uninterrupted, continuing until the temperature rises above zero again – a blocked sprinkler can be disastrous. Wind, also, can blow the water off course. The installation of such a system is expensive, but labour costs are low. Spraying equipment can easily be seen on the hill of the Grands Crus and over large parts of Fourchaume, but the two methods of protection often exist side by side. The oil burners can now be filled automatically but they still have to be lit manually, so fuel and labour costs are the main disadvantages here. In both cases, efficacy is increased by accurate frost forecasts from the nearest Station Météorologique – the most dangerous moments are usually in the early hours of the morning.

The risk of frost has also been lessened by the use of weedkillers (fewer weeds mean less humidity and therefore less frost and, as the soil does not need to be worked, it exudes less humidity). Also, there are not so many isolated vineyards as in the past – both frost and birds seem to

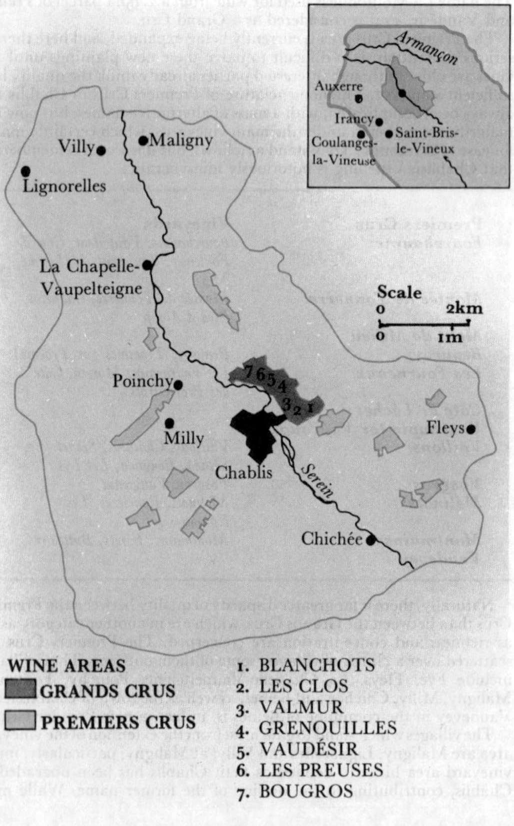

descend with greater frequency when vines are interspersed with uncultivated land. But no one would pretend that frost in Chablis has been conquered; its effects have, however, been mitigated. To people who knew the region in the 1950s, the change is nothing less than dramatic.

Most growers now ferment in stainless steel or lined cement vats, but opinion varies as to the best material for ageing Chablis. There are advocates of both new and old oak, and others who prefer that their wine sees no wood at all. In general, it appears to me that Grands Crus and Premiers Crus from ripe years, particularly the former, benefit enormously from some wood ageing (and the age of the wood seems, on tasting, to matter less than the absolute cleanliness of the casks), while straight Chablis can be delicious bottled younger and straight from the vat. Some more traditional winemakers keep their wine in vat until the spring following the vintage, when it should have finished its malolactic fermentation, and then age the wine in barrel for about a year. These casks, now, are more likely to be 225 litre *pièces* than the traditional smaller Chablis *feuillettes* of 132 litres. Naturally, new oak barrels are expensive, but that should probably not be a consideration where Grands Crus are concerned. However, care should be taken that no oxidation occurs when ageing in wood, which entails rigorous topping up, or *ouillage*, and that the wine does not take on too strong a taste of oak. Chablis supports this much less than a richer, fatter Meursault or California Chardonnay – even in a Grand Cru from Chablis there should be some underlying "nerve" or steel, the true appellation character.

Fresh, youthful straight Chablis need not see any wood – this is the kind of delicious *grande brasserie* wine one chooses with a dozen oysters. But just as winemakers should guard against over-heavy Chablis, they should also take care not to produce wines that are too neutral and that fade away a year or two after their birth. As with most things, a judicious mixture of the two methods, a winemaking compromise, probably produces the most memorable Chablis.

Commercially, the most significant change in Chablis has been in the greater control of its own destiny apparent during the last 20 years. Although Chablisiens still like to blame the négociant houses of Beaune for the wild fluctuations in price and the unsatisfactory balance between supply and demand too frequently encountered in the region, the fact remains that they now have more control over their own affairs than ever before. Outside négociant houses sell about half of the Chablis produced, while the Chablis négociants sell between 35–40% and the growers are left with 10-15%. And as the producers of Chablis have a commodity which is in worldwide demand, they can very much call the tune as to the prices they charge. Obviously, it is difficult to have a stable situation when annual production figures vary as much as they do in Chablis, but the region has always been known for allowing prices to soar when there is little wine to sell, of whatever quality, and for selling its wine too quickly and too cheaply when there is a prolific vintage, such as 1982. If only some of the stock could be sensibly blocked until the result of the following vintage is known, and the sale spread over a longer period of time. Many people shunned the wonderful 1978s because the prices were too high initially, whereas in 1985 there is a critical stock and price situation which is almost bound to spill over into 1986. Chablis has always made a speciality of lurching from one crisis to another!

As an indication of the unreliable nature of the yields in Chablis, either due to frost or poor flowering, it is worth looking at the figures for recent years:

YIELDS OF CHABLIS *(in Hectolitres)*

Year	Grand Cru	Premier Cru	Chablis	Petit Chablis	Total
1978	3,850	17,731	25,179	2,332	49,092
1979	6,124	33,988	66,126	7,989	114,227
1980	5,113	25,491	46,601	5,359	82,564
1981	2,864	15,686	22,749	1,723	43,022
1982	6,075	33,775	69,682	7,375	116,907
1983	6,772	41,359	83,260	8,724	140,115
1984	5,617	35,603	68,129	5,161	114,510

As an illustration of how the number of hectares under vine is increasing, here are the comparable figures for 1982, 1983 and 1984:

	1982 *hectares*	**1983** *hectares*	**1984** *hectares*
Chablis Grand Cru	92.13	95.09	98.08
Chablis Premier Cru	476.94	536.50	581.08
Chablis	989.11	1,093.76	1,182.12
Petit Chablis	109.48	115.96	121.23

A Personal Selection of Chablis Producers

Domaine René Dauvissat
Wines of great beauty, perfectly balanced, with just the right amount of oak. Luscious Preuses and Les Clos, elegant Forêts and Vaillons. The epitome of all that Chablis should be about.

Domaine Paul Droin & Fils
Pretty, flowery wines, especially the Premiers Crus which see no wood, while the Grands Crus have a year's ageing in old oak.

Joseph Drouhin
The firm of Drouhin is both owner in Chablis and négociant in Beaune. The wines are splendid, very influenced by wood, and often fat and concentrated. Consequently, they last very well in bottle.

Domaine Jean Durup
A large estate, greatly increased by new plantings, but including a goodly chunk of Fourchaume. The wines can be labelled Château de Maligny, Domaine de l'Eglantière, Domaine de Paulière and Domaine de Valéry. The wines are flowery and pretty, without a strong finish but with attractive fruit, totally uninfluenced by oak.

Domaine William Fèvre/Domaine de la Maladière
A very important domain, with more Grand Cru Chablis than any other grower. The wines have finesse and style, lanolin smooth from the ageing in new oak barrels.

Domaine Alain Geoffroy
Some very stylish wines which never see oak. Even in 1983, which produced heavier, more alcoholic wines than is usual for the appellation, the true Chablis character was much in evidence, including that straw-like, newly mown grass bouquet.

Lamblin & Fils
Négociants and vineyard owners, with all the trappings of modern vinification. Clean wines, but perhaps a touch too neutral.

Henri Laroche
This is now a big operation, with over 80ha of vines as well as the négociant business of Bacheroy Josselin. There is also the Domaine Laroche and its *sous marque* Domaine La Jouchère. The winemaking is of the most modern, with centrifuging of the must, cultured yeasts for the fermentation and only some limited new oak for the Grands Crus. There are some separate bottlings of *Vieilles Vignes*, such as Fourchaumes and Les Blanchots – the Fourchaumes 1983 was remarkable, but some of the wines seem a mite too neutral in comparison with the very best.

Domaine A. Long Depaquit
The Beaune négociants Bichot are behind this well-run domain, which has a large part of La Moutonne, Grands and Premiers Crus as well as straight Chablis – some of the latter is bottled in Beaune.

Domaine Louis Michel/Domaine de la Tour Vaubourg
There is a fine array of elegant, fruity Premiers Crus, wines almost with a sheen to them, as well as some Grands Crus and straight Chablis. The balance is achieved with ageing in stainless steel not wood.

J. Moreau & Fils
This is high-powered business, the largest négociant of Chablis, who sells his wines young, straight from concrete or stainless steel. The family-owned Grands Crus, however, can be very serious wines indeed. The *vin de table* Moreau Blanc has nothing to do

with Chablis but, as with Mouton Cadet, there is sometimes confusion in the public mind, not helped by the fact that the labels are so similar.

Société Civile de la Moutonne

Bichot own most of the Société Civile. La Moutonne is majestic wine, enormously concentrated in great years.

Domaine François Raveneau

Classic Grands and Premiers Crus, wood-aged and built for long life in bottle. They have style and great interest.

A. Régnard & Fils

This purely négociant house is run by M. Michel Rémon, who also sells his wines under his own name and that of Albert Pic. The wines are impeccable, with very little oak ageing but a later bottling than some. The complete range of Chablis is covered by this house, and if you tasted no other, you would have a very good idea of the appellation.

Simonnet-Febvre

Owning only a few hectares of vines, Simonnet-Febvre is an important négociant-éleveur who buys in must. The wines are mostly bottled young and are pleasantly balanced.

Domaine Philippe Testut

Philippe Testut had virtually to begin all over again, after his family had sold nearly all its large estate. However, a small part of Grenouilles was kept and the domain also has fine Premiers Crus and straight Chablis. The wines are archetypal Chablis, with both vat and barrel ageing preserving harmony, fruit and balance.

Domaine Gérard Tremblay/Domaine des Iles

Rather full, broad wines, some of which are wood-aged.

Domaine de Vauroux

Jean-Pierre Tricon specializes in straight Chablis, but he also has some Montmains and Montée de Tonnerre and a small chunk of Bougros. Fruity wines with attractive definition and pure Chablis character.

Domaine Robert Vocoret

Here, the more usual process is reversed, because the wines are fermented in large oak barrels but aged in stainless steel vats. The wines are textured and full, and there is a generous span of them in all categories.

La Chablisienne

This is the somewhat coy name for the omnipresent cooperative at Chablis. It has great influence on the pricing policy each year, for it swallows nearly a third of the total production of the appellation and has just under 200 *adhérents* who bring must, not grapes, to the cellars. The policy of sometimes using the growers' names on the labels is criticized in some quarters, as it gives the impression of being domain wine when it came out of a cooperative vat. But La Chablisienne also sells in bulk to négociants in Chablis and Beaune, as well as abroad in both bulk and bottle. As with any cooperative, selection is the key to buying success, but there is no doubt that some of the top wines are excellent, including some memorable Grands Crus.

OTHER WINES OF THE YONNE

No one would pretend that these wines are much sought after on export markets, but they are fun to track down while on holiday in the area and rewarding to drink in local restaurants at some of the most modest prices in the whole of Burgundy.

Irancy

By far the best known of the Yonne red wines, it has had its own appellation since 1977 and is now mostly made of Pinot Noir, with small quantities of César. Undoubtedly, the Pinot Noir contributes finesse, while the César is more rustic. The soil is Kimmeridgian, and the vineyard area is prey to the twin dangers of frost and hail, although Irancy has a favoured micro-climate. Some Bourgogne Rosé is also produced here. The individual vineyard Palotte is, in fact, in the neighbouring village of Cravant and therefore can only be called Bourgogne Rouge; it is the same for the wines from the commune of Vincelottes. The best growers are Léon Bienvenu, Bernard Cantin, André and Roger Delaloge, Gabriel Delaloge and Jean Renaud. Much Irancy goes to the Chablis négociants, with Simonnet-Febvre making a speciality of the appellation. There is also the Domaine de Pérignon, run by the Nuits-St-Georges firm of Chauvenet, which produces Passe-Tout-Grains from Pinot Noir and Gamay.

Coulanges-la-Vineuse

Wine from Coulanges is only classed as Bourgogne but, rather strangely, Coulanges-la-Vineuse may appear on the label. The wine is similar to Irancy, although usually lighter, and it is made entirely from the Pinot Noir. The principal growers are Raymond Dupuis, Serge Hugot, André Martin & Fils and Pierre Vigreux, while the Chablis négociants of Bacheroy Josselin and Simonnet-Febvre also sell Coulanges.

Saint Bris-le-Vineux

Although it is the Sauvignon de St-Bris which has the regional denomination *Vin Délimité de Qualité Supérieure*, the Aligoté is really the better wine and the one with the more optimistic future. Pinot Noir, Gamay, a little César, Chardonnay and Sacy are also grown, which gives scope for the production of Bourgogne Rouge and Blanc, Passe-Tout-Grains, Bourgogne Grand Ordinaire and Crémant de Bourgogne. The best growers, whose wines can also sometimes be seen abroad, are Louis Bersan & Fils, now run by the two sons, Jean Brocard, Robert Defrance, Michel Esclavy and André Sorin.

Chitry-le-Fort

Chitry has the same array of grape varieties as St-Bris, with especially good Aligoté, and Bourgogne Blanc made from Chardonnay, which shares the Kimmeridgian soil of Chablis and some of its characteristics. Very good Aligoté Côtes de Chitry comes from Léon Berthelot, Jean-Claude Biot, Paul Colbois (much better than his Sauvignon) and Gilbert Giraudon. Joel Griffe and Roland Viré are other reliable names. Many of the growers of Chitry and St-Bris belong to the agricultural collective of the SICAVA, which makes Crémant de Bourgogne. Wine is also made at Tonnerre, Epineuil and Vézelay.

VIEWS ON VINTAGES

The relative merits of each vintage are much discussed in Burgundy, as elsewhere. It is interesting, however, to note that there is one point on which the Burgundians seemed to be in accord in late 1985, when this book was being written: 1978 was the greatest vintage for red wines in recent years. Producers were almost unanimous in their praise for this vintage. Vintage assessments for white wines were more mixed, but many Chablis producers felt that 1975 was a classic year for the region.

At time of going to press, the 1985 vintage in Burgundy looked very good indeed. The superb weather throughout September and into October gave grapes in excellent condition and hopes are high. The only shadow on the horizon was the small quantity in Chablis, due to the winter freeze.

●○ COTE CHALONNAISE

The region known as the Côte Chalonnaise stretches from the valley of the Dheune near Chagny in the north to St-Gengoux-le-National, southwest of Châlon-sur-Saône, in the south. Vines cluster on propitious slopes, but it is by no means an uninterrupted viticultural landscape. The basic soil types are limestone or calcareous clay, although variations between the villages and appellations are based more on subtleties of microclimate than of soil. However, the Chardonnay should ideally be planted where there is high limestone content, and the Pinot Noir where there is more clay, as this helps provide stronger colour. Often the calcareous matter has a tendency to fall to the foot of the slopes. The Pinot Noir is the most important grape variety on the Côte Chalonnaise, with 67% of the vineyard area, while the Gamay covers 13.5%, the Chardonnay 10% and the Aligoté 9.5%. The best vineyard sites face east, southeast or south, but they can be planted up to a height of 350 metres (1,150 feet), which means later picking than on the Côte d'Or. This, coupled with the fact that it can be slightly cooler here in the summer months than around Dijon, means that in less than perfect years, ripeness can be a problem. But when fate is kind, the wines of the Côte Chalonnaise are not just mini-replicas of the Côte d'Or – they have real regional character and a great deal to say for themselves.

●○ BOUZERON

The Aligoté wine produced in this village close to Chagny and Rully had long been appreciated as something exceptional, and in 1979 the Appellation Bourgogne Aligoté de Bouzeron was created. The wines are often richer, spicier and fuller than elsewhere and make a very worthwhile bottle for those who can be lured away to something less usual. Bouchard Père & Fils own about two-thirds of the vineyard area at Bouzeron and so this wine is quite a speciality of theirs. Other very good domains for Aligoté de Bouzeron are those of Aubert and Pamela de Villaine and the Clos de la Fortune of Chanzy Frères. Delorme, also, are known for their well-made Aligoté.

●○ RULLY

1983 production: Rully blanc *3,031 hectolitres*
Rully rouge *2,957 hectolitres*

Premiers Crus: Margotey, Grésigny, Vauvry, Mont-Palais, Meix-Caillet, Les Pierres, La Bressande, Champ-Clou, La Renarde, Pillot, Cloux, Raclot, Raboursay, Ecloseaux, Marissou, La Fosse, Chapitre, Préau, Moulesne.

The white wines of Rully are particularly known for their finesse and straw-like quality, often with a taste which is half floral, half the contents of the spice shelf, perhaps with a preponderance of cinnamon.

The reds are pure Pinot, never very dark in colour, sometimes violetty, sometimes more raspberries, with a nicely balanced kernel of flavour to them – the results are so much better in Rully when the vines have a bit of age to them.

A Personal Selection of Rully Producers

Domaine Belleville
White wine with a lovely nose, but a slightly more vulgar finish.

Domaine Pierre Cogny
Good red and white Rully, slightly rustic.

Domaine Jean Coulon
Rully Blanc Grésigny of real interest.

Domaine de la Folie
The red Clos de Bellecroix of M. Noël-Bouton can be both fruity and gamey. The white Clos St-Jacques has elegance and charm.

Domaine du Prieuré
M. Armand Monassier has made strawberryish Sous Mont-Palais, but recently the wines have looked dirty.

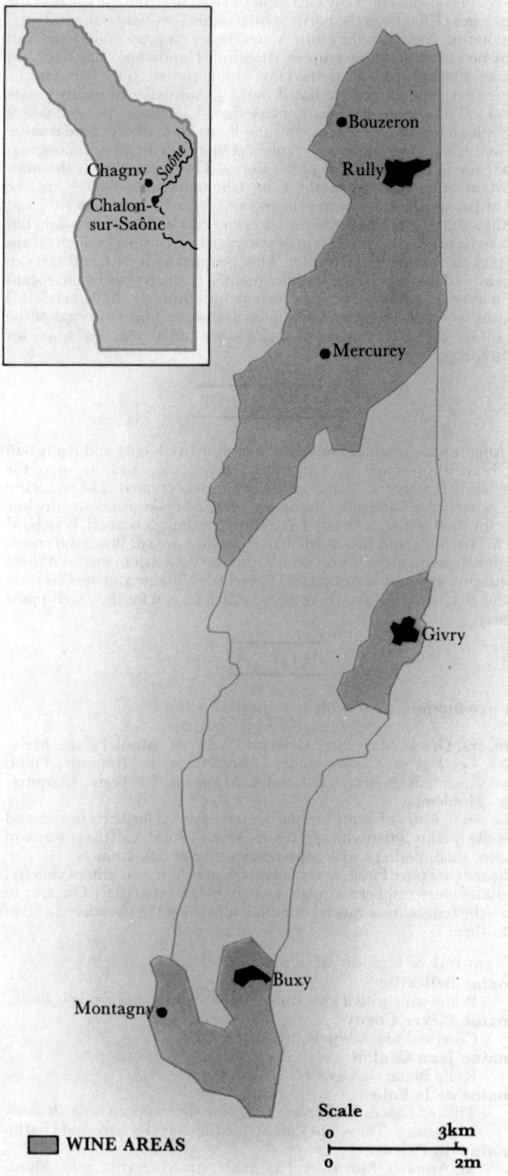
Chagny
Saône
Chalon-sur-Saône
Bouzeron
Rully
Mercurey
Givry
Buxy
Montagny
Scale
0 3km
0 2m
WINE AREAS

Domaine de la Renarde

Jean-François Delorme has built up a very important domain at Rully owning, amongst other things, all of the 18-hectare Varot vineyard which produces elegant white wine with a scent of newly mown grass. What is unusual in Burgundy is to have 18 hectares in one parcel, rather than in scattered plots. The red Rully has greatly improved as the vines have aged and now both raspberries and strawberries spring to mind when tasting.

● ○ MERCUREY

1983 production: Mercurey rouge *20,116 hectolitres*
Mercurey blanc *1,205 hectolitres*

Premiers Crus: Clos-du-Roi, Clos-Voyen or Les Voyens, Clos-Marcilly, Clos-des-Fourneaux, Clos-des-Montaigus.

Mercurey produces wines which are almost entirely red and they are the biggest, most structured wines of the Côte Chalonnaise. They can sometimes be solid and quite earthy, and certainly they last longer than the red wines of the other appellations. Sometimes there is more than a hint of *terroir* in the taste, derived from the marl and limestone soil which predominates here. At their best, the wines are robust, frank, with an attractive "wet earth" bouquet, at their worst, they are dry and rustic.

A Personal Selection of Mercurey Producers

Domaine Michel Juillot

White Mercurey with a *goût de terroir* and a touch of liquorice. Excellent red, benefiting from about a third new barrels in the cellar, scented, fruity and well made.

Domaine Marceau

Another well-regarded domain.

Domaine Maréchal

Wines with a high reputation.

Domaine du Marquis de Jouennes d'Herville

Château de Chamirey that can be pleasantly fruity on the nose, but with rather a soapy finish. The white is ripe and flowery, with hints of mayblossom. The wines are distributed by the firm of Antonin Rodet.

Domaine du Prieuré

Clos de la Vigne De Devant with creditable fruit.

Domaine François Protheau & Fils

Clos l'Evêque, La Fauconnière and Clos des Corvées which show good regional character and often make solid older bottles.

Domaine Saier

Champs Martins which is lovely young drinking.

Domaine de Suremain

Wine with scent and regional character. The straight Mercurey often has a taste of cherries, while the Clos-Voyen is bigger, firmer and shows more length on the palate.

● ○ GIVRY

1983 production: Givry rouge *5,438 hectolitres*
Givry blanc *493 hectolitres*

There are no official Premiers Crus, but the following vineyards appear on labels: La Barande, Bois-Chevaux, Cellier aux Moines, Clos Saint-Paul, Clos Saint-Pierre, Clos Salomon, and Champ Poureau for white wine.

Known, somewhat strangely, on some labels as the "preferred wine of King Henri IV", when we all thought he was more closely associated with Jurançon in the Pyrenean foothills of southwest France, Givry can have a lovely fragrance and a delicious, lingering Pinot Noir charm. The wines do not have the body of Mercurey, but boast a more delicate flavour. But if, as it is rumoured, the King's mistress *did* have a vineyard at Givry, that is all as it should be.

A Personal Selection of Givry Producers

Domaine Jean Chofflet

Smoky Pinot fruit on nose, with a touch of violets. Earthy, raw truffles flavour – very frank Pinot without having the style of the classiest Givry.

Domaine Michel Derain

Good white Givry and traditionally vinified reds.

Propriété Desvignes

Correct red Givry.

Domaine du Gardin

This historic estate produces Clos Salomon of subtlety, charm and fruit.

Domaine Ragot

Very interesting white Givry, yellow in colour, with a nose of anise, and traces of it on the palate too, finishing rich and nutty. Agreeable, pleasant red.

Domaine de la Renarde

Red Clos du Cellier aux Moines which can have a fascinating nose of toasted bread; at other times it smells of all the herbs of Provence. The taste is always very Pinot and long-lingering.

Domaine Thénard

The wine from the old vines is very good. Known for its Clos Saint-Pierre.

MONTAGNY

1983 production: Montagny (blanc) *4,434 hectolitres*
Premiers Crus: All the vineyards in the area have the right to the appellation Premier Cru, provided that the wines reach 11.5% alcohol before chaptalization.

The vineyards of the appellation Montagny are spread over the villages of Montagny itself, Buxy, Saint-Vallerin and Jully-les-Buxy. The wine was meant to be that preferred by the monks of Cluny, as opposed to royalty. It is also said that it keeps the mouth fresh and the head clear. Be that as it may, cool, white Montagny is absolutely delicious. It is a mite fuller and fatter, sometimes broader, than white Rully, which can have more breed and elegance. There is more almondy honey in Montagny, and more straw and cinnamon in Rully. It is interesting to note that there is Kimmeridgian limestone at Buxy.

A Personal Selection of Montagny Producers

Cave des Vignerons de Buxy

This large cooperative is the source of supply for many people, both in the French and the British trade. Naturally, there is variation amongst the *cuves*, but the best are most worthy of the name of Montagny. The cooperative also makes red and white Bourgogne, Passe-Tout-Grains and Aligoté, generic appellations commonly produced on the Côte Chalonnaise.

Château de Davenay (*bottled and distributed by Moillard*)

The proprietors are the Héritiers Gilardoni, and the wine is full, nutty, even spicy. Good, without being imbued with breed.

B. and J.-M. Delaunay

This house produces very fine Montagny selections.

Domaine Lucien Denizot

Frank, fruity Bourgogne Rouge, redolent of cherries and cassis. One was *Chante-Flûté*, which is the Côte Chalonnaise version of *Tasteviné*. (A jury selects a high-quality wine which is then given a numbered label, bearing the name of the producer, the vintage and the words *Chante-Flûté*.)

Domaine Michel Goubard

This domain, at St-Désert near Buxy, makes Bourgogne Rouge from Pinot Noir by a semi-*macération carbonique* method; thus the wines are light and fruity, delicious when young.

Louis Latour

This famed Beaune shipper always makes superb selections of Montagny.

Château de la Saule

Alain Roy-Thevenin makes delicious, frank Premier Cru, lanolin textured and fresh, managing to avoid excessive alcohol even in 1983. Also good Aligoté wine is produced under the label of Marcel Roy-Thevenin.

●○◕ THE MACONNAIS

Geologists love the Mâconnais, because there are some fascinating cliff formations in the southern part, and visitors love it no less for the pretty green countryside and the wealth of Romanesque churches. If one can tear oneself away from the fruit and nut trees, the small brown goats and the white cattle dappling the hillsides, the wines are very rewarding as well.

The whole district covers about 50 kilometres (31 miles) from north to south but is only 15 kilometres (9 miles) wide. The area is determined to the east and west by the two valleys of the Saône and the Grosne, but the line of hills runs from north-north-east to south-south-west. The site and altitude of the vineyard is critical to ultimate quality, because although the summers can be very hot in the Mâconnais, the winters are cold, with frost a danger until the four days (May 12–15) of the Ice Saints are past.

There are two main soil types: low-acid, calcareous soil for the Chardonnay, an excellent combination for making fine white wine; and more acid, clay, sand or siliceous soil for white wines destined for very young drinking and for the Gamay for Mâcon Rouge. The most impressive slopes, magnificently exposed to the sun (hence the frequent high natural alcohols), are in the southern part of the region, the hills of Pouilly, Solutré and Vergisson. Indeed, the last two are really cliffs, formed by the same Jurassic strata found in the Côte d'Or, but in rather more dramatic shape. The Chardonnay dominates in the Mâconnais, covering 67% of the vineyard area, with the Gamay occupying 25%, the Pinot Noir 7.5% and 0.5% planted to Aligoté. The grape variety proportions reflect the fact that it is far easier to sell white Mâcon than red. In the Mâconnais, there are 5,800ha of AC vineyard.

Most Mâcon Blanc is made without seeing any wood – it is kept in vat and bottled young. Of course, there are individual growers who bottle their wines, especially in Pouilly-Fuissé, and here there are hogsheads and even wooden vats in the cellars, but as the cooperatives handle about 85% of the white wine, logistics demand modern methods. About 20% less red wine goes through the cooperatives, but that is still a significant quantity. Much Mâcon Rouge is made by the *macération carbonique* method (for description of this, see Beaujolais chapter), which is an attractive way of treating the Gamay if the wine is not intended for keeping. The Pinot Noir can be made into Bourgogne Rouge or be included in Passe-Tout-Grains, and it is sometimes vinified by a semi-*macération carbonique* process, which means that the wine should be drunk young.

I somehow feel that the Mâconnais is the proverbial "gateway to the south" – the grey north gives way to the ochre Midi. The houses are covered with warm-coloured, curvy tiles, reminiscent of Provence, and they have verandahs running the length of them, indicating sunny days. That might be difficult to believe in the grip of a glacial winter, but the summer gives you France in all its rural splendour.

○ POUILLY-FUISSE

1983 production: *42,509 hectolitres*

There are no Premiers Crus, but sometimes a vineyard name is added to the wine label, particularly when a site has become known, over the years, for producing fine wine. The villages which produce Pouilly-Fuissé are Pouilly, Fuissé, Solutré, Vergisson and Chaintré. There are nuances in taste between the villages, with Pouilly making a bid for top position and Solutré for the wines with more body, but probably the hand of the wine-maker, and maybe the age of the vines, is of more importance.

The actual rock of Solutré is somewhat menacing, especially when one knows that at its feet lies nearly a hectare of the bones of wild horses driven over the cliff by "Solutréen" Man 15,000–12,000 BC. It is quite a surprise to see the escapades of this creature so well documented on the other side of France, in the Museum of Prehistory at Les Eyzies in the Dordogne. But the wine of Solutré singularly lacks menace. It is a rich, full, even earthy Chardonnay, not infrequently attaining 13–14% alcohol naturally. There is not the steeliness and "nerve" of Chablis, nor the finesse or breed of, say, Puligny-Montrachet, but there is plenty of flavour.

A Personal Selection of Pouilly-Fuissé Producers

Domaine de l'Arillière

Stylish and fruity, rather than rich and full.

Domaine Roger Cordier

Finesse and complexity on the nose, taste good but not quite as exciting as the bouquet.

Domaine Corsin

Very reliable, down-the-line Pouilly-Fuissé and St-Véran.

Château Fuissé

M. Vincent's famous wine has attained record price levels, but it is an experience in intense flavour. The apogee is attained with the Vieilles Vignes in a really ripe year – positively mind-blowing.

Domaine Roger Luquet

Clos du Bourg which is full and broad, lacking real class, but a good wine.

Domaine Jean-Paul Paquet

Complexity of bouquet, but same broad style as above – both are from Fuissé.

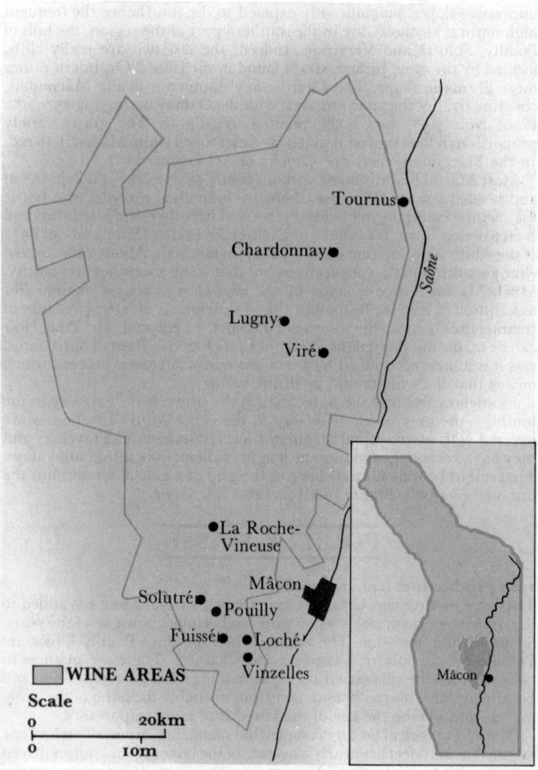

POUILLY-VINZELLES AND POUILLY-LOCHE

1983 production: *3,961 hectolitres*
These two "satellite" appellations would make a good alternative to the expensive Pouilly-Fuissé if the quantity produced were more significant. They can be slightly more earthy than the very best Pouilly-Fuissé, but the best wines have both definition and character and they make interesting bottles.

A Personal Selection of Pouilly-Vinzelles and Pouilly-Loché Producers

Caves des Grands Crus Blancs
Some full, luscious Pouilly-Loché, and others disappointingly oxidized, which shows just how careful winemakers must be when handling Chardonnay.

Domaine Jean Mathias
Fine, fruity Pouilly-Vinzelles.

Excellent selections of Pouilly-Vinzelles are made by Georges Duboeuf and B. & J-M. Delaunay.

ST-VERAN

1983 production: *16,656 hectolitres*
An appellation created in 1971, this virtually replaced Beaujolais Blanc (Louis Jadot is one of the few houses which still makes a speciality of this). Confusingly, the village of St-Vérand is within the appellation St-Véran, as are Chânes, Chasselas, Davayé, Leynes, Prissé, St-Amour and part of Solutré.

Although maturing slightly more quickly than Pouilly-Fuissé, the wines are nearly always better at two years than one, showing more interest and complexity.

A Personal Selection of St-Véran Producers

Caves des Crus Blancs
Nose of acacia, fruity, well-balanced wines.

Maison Mâconnaise des Vins (*Société Coopérative des Viticulteurs de Saône et Loire*)
Nutty, lanolin wine, good though without great character.

Domaine Michel Paquet
The same nuttiness, the same lanolin, no "sparks", but nice St-Véran.

Producteurs de Prissé
Always a very good example of the appellation.

Domaine Roger Tissier
The elegant Cuvée les Crais gives an indication of the chalky soil.

Domaine Marcel Vincent
Rich and full, everything one would expect from this winemaker – in fact this is now Jacques Vincent.

The following domains are also reliable: Georges Chagny and R. Duperron at Leynes, André Chavet at Davayé, as well as the Lycée Agricole at Davayé. Again, the Duboeuf selections are impeccable.

MACON-BLANC-VILLAGES

1983 production: *100,901 hectolitres*
Here the appellation is Mâcon Villages or Mâcon with one of 43 village names. This might sound baffling, but in practice the following villages are most often seen: Lugny, Viré, Prissé, Clessé, Vinzelles, La Roche-Vineuse and Chardonnay, which may or may not have given its name to the grape variety.

On the whole, these wines are at their best at one to two years old, when all their fruit and blossomy scents are at their most tantalizing. The two enemies of good Mâcon Blanc are lack of freshness and a certain vulgarity, usually brought about by a rustic approach to winemaking. A charming characteristic is a smoky muskiness, which comes from the clone of Chardonnay used in the area.

A Personal Selection of Mâcon-Blanc-Villages Producers

Domaine Bénas Frères
Some muskiness on nose, broad and fat on the palate.

Domaine André Bonhomme
Mâcon-Viré which is floral, nutty and lanolin smooth.

Domaine Jean-Noël Chaland
Lanolin smooth Mâcon-Viré – a good bottle.

Domaine de Chervin
Mâcon-Burgy made by Albert Goyard of the same family as the Domaine de Roally. Delicate, pretty wines of finesse.

Domaine de la Condemine
Véronique and Pierre Janny make good, nutty Mâcon-Villages, when they do not use too much sulphur dioxide.

Château de la Greffière
Messieurs Greuzard make broad Mâcon-Villages with a lovely perfume.

Groupement de Producteurs Lugny-St-Gengoux-de-Scissé
Macon-Lugny, Les Charmes, which is elegant and smoky, with good acidity.

Domaine Adrien Guichard
Mâcon-Villages which is always tempting.

Domaine Henri Lafarge
Wonderful floral, acacia nose and great elegance and balance.

Les Vignerons d'Igé
Mâcon-Villages with a good hawthorn flower nose – taste is sometimes a bit submerged with sulphur when young.

Domaine Pierre Mahuet
Mâcon-La Roche-Vineuse with a nose of almonds – excellent fresh wine.

Domaine Manciat-Poncet
Very perfumed, full, immensely seductive Mâcon-Charnay.

Domaine René Michel
Mâcon-Clessé with a nice nuttiness.

Château de Mirande
Baron Patrice de l'Epine makes elegant, delicious Mâcon-Villages, with a lovely nose of acacia and mayblossom.

Domaine "du Mortier"
Mâcon-Péronne made by Maurice Josserand – a lanolin, "clean laundry" nose, slightly common on the palate.

Domaine de Roally
Henri Goyard makes Mâcon-Viré (and fights the dominance of the Co-op!) and succeeds admirably. Wonderful acacia nose, hazelnuts, excellent fresh wine. On the neck label he says *Raisin Cueilli à la Main* – the grapes were picked by hand.

Domaine Jean Signoret
This Mâcon-Clessé was superb in the 1982 vintage, with full flavour and acacia nose, but the 1983 was a failure – why? One to watch.

Société Coopérative des Viticulteurs de Saône-et-Loire
Nutty wines, full and fat.

Domaine Jean Thévenet
Good, consistent Mâcon-Clessé "Quintaine", always scented and floral.

Domaine de Thurissey – Les Vieux Ceps
Robert Bridon makes scented wines with a big, broad taste.

Other excellent wines:
Mâcon-Lugny Les Genièvres of Louis Latour, Mâcon-Viré of Piat, Mâcon-Prissé of Georges Duboeuf, Mâcon-Viré Clos du Chapitre of Dépagneux, Mâcon-Viré of Louis Jadot, Mâcon-Viré, Château de Viré, owned by Hubert Desbois but distributed by Prosper Maufoux, and Mâcon-Villages Laforêt of Joseph Drouhin.

Mâcon Supérieur Rouge	1983 production:	*58,357 hectolitres*
Mâcon Supérieur Blanc	1983 production:	*8,461 hectolitres*
Mâcon Rouge and Rosé	1983 production:	*2,600 hectolitres*
Mâcon Blanc	1983 production:	*2,652 hectolitres*

White Mâcon, made from Pinot Blanc or Chardonnay, can also be called Pinot-Chardonnay-Mâcon which, in these days of greater accuracy with regard to grape varieties, is slightly old-fashioned.

There is also a small amount of red wine labelled as Mâcon, plus the village name, then *Villages*. The *Supérieur* denotes one per cent more alcohol for both the red and white wines, i.e. the minimum level of alcohol before chaptalization for Mâcon Supérieur Rouge is 10% and for Mâcon Supérieur Blanc, 11%. The white wines of this category can be "declassified" into Bourgogne, providing a valuable source of supply for many a merchant.

I have to say that most Mâcon Rosé wines which have come my way have been very unappealing, with the exception of one from the Maison Mâconnaise des Vins (Société Coopérative des Viticulteurs de Saône-et-Loire).

Good Mâcon Rouge or Mâcon Rouge Supérieur has come from: Groupement de Producteurs de Prissé, Jean-Claude Thévenet, Groupement de Producteurs Lugny-St-Gengoux-de-Scissé, the Domaine des Provenchères of Maurice Gonon, Henri Lafarge, and Mâcon-Serrières from Bénas Frères (this is different soil and the wine is not Beaujolais in type; it is traditional, needing time, becoming more "Pinot Noir" in character with age).

The Cooperatives generally maintain a high standard although, as always, the art is in selection. They are as follows:

Aze, Bissey-sous-Cruchaud, Buxy, Chaintré, Chardonnay, Charnay-Les-Mâcon, Genouilly, Igé, Lugny, Mancey, Prissé, Sennece-Les-Mâcon, Sologny, Verzé, "La Vigne Blanche" at Clessé, Vinzelles, Viré.

LAYING DOWN BURGUNDY

There are two main advantages in cellaring fine burgundy: you can drink the wines when they are showing at their best; and you can buy them when they are first offered, at the keenest possible price. It is a sad fact that when a wine becomes ready to drink, it has frequently disappeared from the market, so judicious buying at an early stage is always to be recommended. Only Grands Crus from top quality vintages should be considered for really long-term cellaring, but Premiers Crus make excellent mid-term drinking. Both the Pinot Noir and the Chardonnay make "fragile" wines which are highly susceptible to temperature fluctuation, so laying down burgundy should only be considered if you have access to a cool cellar – between 10°C and 15°C is ideal.

● ○ ◕ BEAUJOLAIS

About 22,000ha are under the vine in the Beaujolais, in a region which is 55km (34 miles) long and 12–15km (7–9 miles) wide, with an average altitude of 300 metres (984 feet). There are a few large domains, but many small family properties of between 4–5ha (2,429 properties of 1–4ha, 1,376 properties of 4–7ha).

There is also the system of *vigneronnage*, very strong in the Beaujolais, whereby the vigneron cultivates the owner's vineyards, while the owner may provide the vigneron's house, but certainly the vinification equipment, vine plants and treatment materials. The vineyard worker usually provides the vineyard equipment, and he does the work. Normally, the profits on the wine are shared. About 50% of Beaujolais properties are worked by vignerons.

The Gamay noir à jus blanc covers 98% of the Beaujolais vineyard area (Pinot Noir and Chardonnay are included in the remaining 2%). It is interesting to note that the nine Beaujolais *crus* can be declassified into Bourgogne, so if you drink a red burgundy made in these areas, it will be Gamay, and not Pinot Noir, wine, somewhat different from a Bourgogne Rouge from the Côte Chalonnaise.

La taille courte, or *gobelet* pruning, is found in the northern area of the *crus* and of Beaujolais-Villages, while *la taille longue*, simple *Guyot* pruning on wire, is found in Beaujolais Sud. In both cases, there must never be more than 12 buds on a vine, and the density of vine plants must be between 9,000 and 13,000 per hectare.

In red wine vinification, the main difference between the Beaujolais and the rest of Burgundy is that the Gamay is never crushed – there is no *foulage* and the grapes are thus whole. They are put into fermentation vats, which are usually of wood *chez le vigneron*, but often of concrete at the cooperatives. The *cuves* are not completely filled, so that the accumulation of carbonic gas in the empty space can act as a break on the speed of the fermentation and protects against acetic contamination. Vats of 60 hectolitres are ideal, but in cooperatives they tend to be much larger. The weight of the grapes on top causes some juice to run at the bottom of the vat and this is then pumped over, and sometimes warmed, to get the fermentation going. Sugar to increase the alcohol and sulphur dioxide (an anti-oxidant) are added at this time.

Optimum extraction of bouquet (one of the great charms of Gamay vinified in this way) occurs between 25 and 28°C, and the fermentation period lasts from 4–6 days, depending on the ambient temperatures and the way in which the yeasts are working.

In effect, there is a fermentation *within* each whole grape, induced by the CO_2 released by the fermenting juice at the bottom of the vat. This is a variation of a pure carbonic maceration fermentation, when the vat is saturated with added CO_2 and a 10–12 day maceration follows; but the typical Beaujolais procedure described above is both natural and ideally suited to the Gamay. The grapes are pressed to extract the rest of the juice, the wine is put into *cuve* to settle down, and then into *fûts* where a month later the fermentation is usually completed. These casks vary enormously in Beaujolais, from 216 litres, 110 litres, 50–55 litres, to 6 hectolitres or a *foudre* with an average capacity of 50 hectolitres (this can also be made of concrete in a cooperative).

Before bottling, usually in the spring following the vintage where the *crus* are concerned, some wines are put through a flash-pasteurization for total stability. But small growers do not have these facilities, and firms like Duboeuf prefer to use membrane filters and cold sterile bottling in order to preserve maximum fruit.

The worst faults of Beaujolais are usually an excess of alcohol, with the "fumes" masking the lovely fresh, fruit aromas, and the over-bolstered body disguising the frank clean taste. Some of the négociants foster a hard, beefy, strong *négoce* style, while some growers' wines are casky and dirty. In large vintages, some wines are often naturally very pale and weak, as the growers give very short *cuvaisons*, or vattings, due to shortage of space. But today, more than ever before, there are lovely examples of pure, lilting Beaujolais just waiting to be selected by wise wine buyers who recognize good quality.

Beaujolais Nouveau, or Beaujolais Primeur, is a comparatively new phenomenon on the export markets which became increasingly popular during the 1970s. Now, in the mid-1980s, there is evidence that the season for drinking Beaujolais Nouveau is growing ever shorter – the wine is released for sale in shop and wine bar on the third Thursday in November, but by Christmas, most people have lost interest in this vinous diversion, and the signs now are that sales of Nouveau are falling off as December advances.

There are many excellent Nouveau wines each year, and the problems of stability in a wine so rapidly prepared are largely overcome, but it is a pity when good Beaujolais, with the potential to be even better in the following year, is sold and drunk as Nouveau.

Nearly 50% of the production of Beaujolais is exported throughout the world. There could not be a more seductive flagship for French exports than this delectable, lively wine.

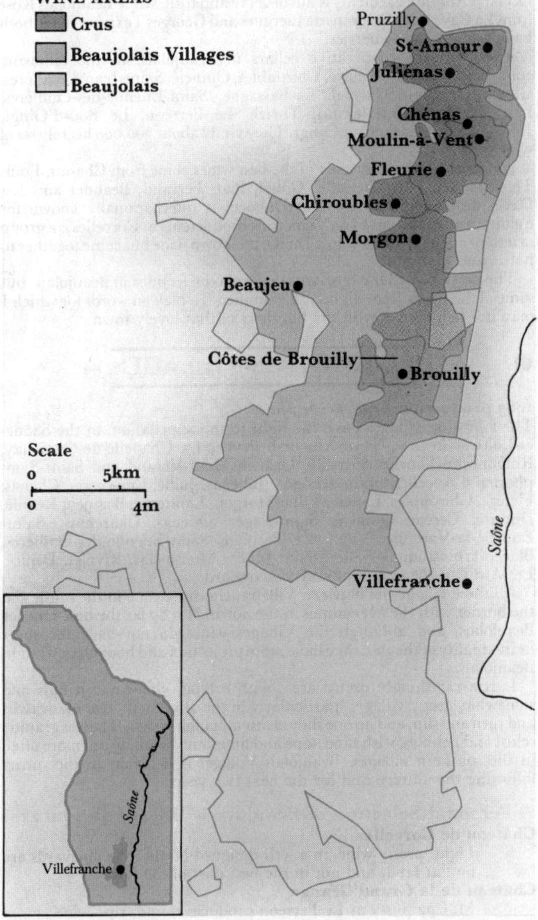

● ○ ◐ BEAUJOLAIS

1983 production: *584,000 hectolitres*
Nearly all Beaujolais is red, although there are very small amounts of white and rosé. Most straight Beaujolais is produced south of Villefranche, on clay and limestone, although it can come from anywhere in the region. Beaujolais Supérieur is rarely seen – it just means that it must have 1% more alcohol than Beaujolais *tout court*. Essentially, simple Beaujolais is best in the year after its birth – then the wise wine drinker moves on to Beaujolais-Villages.

The following growers all produce delicious Beaujolais: Jean-Paul Brun at Charnay, with astonishing, raspberry-flavoured wine, Philippe Jambon at Corcelles, Château de Bel-Air which is made at the Lycée Viticole de Belleville, Château Gaillard of Jacqueline and Jean-Louis Riche at Denicé, René Riottot at Denicé, Pierre Jomard at Fleurieux-sur-l'Arbresle and René Marchand at Cogny. Amongst the cooperatives, the Beaujolais from the Cave Beaujolaise du Beau Vallon at Theizé have been particularly impressive. The Beaujolais Blanc from the Domaine de l'Eclair (Antoine Clement) is full of verve and fruit, while Beaujolais Rosé from La Cave des Vignerons de Liergues and Georges Texier at Blacé both have a hint of strawberries.

There are 18 cooperative cellars in Beaujolais, in the following communes: Chénas, Fleurie, Chiroubles, Quincié, Saint-Jean d'Ardières, Gleizé, Liergues, Sain-Bel, Lachassagne, Saint-Etienne-des-Oullières, Létra, Bully, Saint-Vérand, Theizé, Le Perréon, Le Bois-d'Oingt, Juliénas, Saint-Laurent-d'Oingt. They vinify about 300,000 hectolitres of wine a year.

Amongst négociants, some of the best wines come from Chanut, Louis Tête, Trenel, Fessy/Dessalle, Gobet, Piat, Ferraud, Beaudet and Les Caves de Champclos. Georges Duboeuf is internationally known for quality, and the Éventail de Vignerons Producteurs at Corcelles is a group of independent growers who all make their own wine but come together to bottle and market it.

The best Côte d'Or négociants make good selections in Beaujolais, but some of the wines seem slightly "Beaunified", a play on words for which I may not be popular with the burghers of that lovely town.

● BEAUJOLAIS-VILLAGES

1983 production: *368,000 hectolitres*
The following villages have the right to the appellation: in the Saône-et-Loire – Leynes, Saint-Amour-Bellevue, La Chapelle-de-Guinchay, Romanèche-Thorins, Pruzilly, Chânes, Saint-Vérand and Saint-Symphorien d'Ancelles; in the Rhône – Juliénas, Jullié, Emeringes, Chénas, Fleurie, Chiroubles, Lancié, Villié-Morgon, Lantignié, Beaujeu, Régnié, Durette, Cercié, Quincié, Saint-Lager, Odenas, Charentay, Saint-Etienne-la-Varenne, Vaux, Le Perréon, Saint-Etienne-des-Oullières, Blacé, Arbuissonnas, Salles, Saint-Julien, Montmelas, Rivolet, Denicé, Les Ardillats, Marchampt and Vauxrenard.

All these villages lie between Villefranche-sur-Saône in the south and the border with the Mâconnais in the north. It is by far the best zone for Beaujolais, and although the Villages wines do not have the sheer individuality of the *crus*, they have more projection and body than straight Beaujolais.

It is a ravishingly pretty area, with rolling, vine-covered hills and somewhat sleepy villages, particularly in the afternoon. The roads twist and turn and dip, and no one should attempt high speeds. There is granite, schist and pebbles, with sandstone and limestone breaking out more often in the southern villages. Beaujolais-Villages is delicious in the spring following the vintage and for the next two years.

A Personal Selection of Beaujolais-Villages Producers

Château de Corcelles
Light, pretty wine, in a well-designed bottle. The vineyards are on flat land, and not in the best part of the hills.

Château de la Grand'Grange
M. Chamussy at Le Perréon produces round, ripe wine.

Domaine Joubert
Claude and Michelle Joubert make rich, full Villages at Lantignié.

Château La Tour Bourdon (*bottled at the Château by Duboeuf*)
Old vines, but a wine which is delicious for the summer after the vintage.

Domaine H. Monternot et Fils
This is excellent Villages from Blacé, with fruit, style and body.

Domaine de Montmeron (*bottled at the domain by Duboeuf*)
More old vines give a wine of individuality.
Other Duboeuf Beaujolais-Villages include the Domaine du Colombier, Domaine des Buillats, Domaine du Potet, which ages well, Château de la Tour, Domaine des Trois Coteaux, Château des Vierres and the Domaine de la Treille, again a Villages which can be kept a year or two.

Domaine St-Sorlin
René Jacquet makes wine which finishes with a fruity flourish.

Château Varennes (*distributed by Piat*)
Totally tempting, with a glorious bouquet and a really attractive flavour.

The Eventail de Vignerons Producteurs
The Eventail produces high-quality Beaujolais-Villages with flavour and character from Paul Fortune, André Jaffre, André Depardon, Roger Tissier, Jacques Montange and Jean and Jacques Sangouard.

BROUILLY

1983 production: *70,000 hectolitres*

Brouilly produces much more wine than any of the other nine *crus* and so it inevitably has a high profile in cafés, bistros, and brasseries. Some people say, rather cruelly, that it is just a glorified Beaujolais-Villages, but good Brouilly has more substance and finish, and the more solid examples keep longer than a straight Villages.

The appellation is spread over six communes: Odenas, St-Lager, Cercié, Charentay, Quincié and St-Etienne-la-Varenne. In fact, many producers make both Brouilly and Beaujolais-Villages. Brouilly is a totally legitimate *cru*, because the vines grow on granite and schist, called locally *gore* and *morgon*. Brouilly is frank and without complication, a heady glass of the grape in liquid form.

A Personal Selection of Brouilly Producers

Château du Bluizard (*bottled at the Château by Duboeuf*)
These are round, rich wines, supple and tempting – the Château du Bluizard also produces Beaujolais-Villages.

Château de la Chaize
This is a stunning property, outside the village of Odenas. The wine is no less impressive, sold at a premium price but luscious and full, brimming with Brouilly fruit.

Domaine de la Roche (*bottled at the domain by Duboeuf*)
This vineyard is on steep slopes 420 metres (1,380 feet) high – the yields are small and the work difficult on a mixture of gravel and sand. The wine is relatively light and "floaty", for young drinking. The domain also makes Beaujolais-Villages.

Domaine André Ronzière (*Eventail*)
Really rich Brouilly, no doubt due to a high percentage of old vines.

Domaine Ruet
Jean-Paul Ruet makes most respectable wine.

Domaine Patrick Vermorel
Really wonderful fruit – all that a beautifully handled, frank wine should be. His Beaujolais-Villages maintains the same high standard.

Domaine de Vuril
Georges Dutraive is responsible for very commendable Brouilly.

André Large and the **Verger** family also have fine Brouilly, sold through the Eventail.

COTE DE BROUILLY

1983 production: *17,500 hectolitres*
In the context of the Côte d'Or, anything that is *Côte de* is not as good as the straight name, i.e. Côte de Beaune is not as good as Beaune itself. But Côte de Brouilly is most certainly one up the ladder from plain Brouilly, due to the fact that its vineyards are on the slopes of Mont Brouilly. But, as there is far less Côte de Brouilly than Brouilly, not so many people discover it. It is interesting to note that Côte de Brouilly has a higher minimum alcohol level than the other *crus* – 10.5% instead of 10% – but in all cases, if the name of the *climat* or vineyard is added, it has to be 11%. Mont Brouilly rises to 500 metres (1,640 feet), with the vines on all sides (therefore some sites are better exposed than others), on a base predominantly of granite.

The appellation is spread over the communes of Odenas, St-Lager, Cercié and Quincié. I have seen Mont Brouilly described as a sort of giant mole-hill placed like a lighthouse at the head of Beaujolais – the person who coined that mixed metaphor must have imbibed a good deal of its wine. Côte de Brouilly has tremendous projection of fruit, rich, savoury and grapey.

A Personal Selection of Côte de Brouilly Producers

Domaine de Chavanne
Claudius Geoffray makes excellent wine, with massive fruit on the nose and the impression of crunching grapes as you drink.

Domaine de Conroy (*bottled at the domain by Duboeuf*)
Wine of balance and charm and great drinkability. The vines are right on the *pierre bleue*, which is the porphyry of the old volcano that is now Mont Brouilly.

Domaine André Large (*Eventail*)
Delicious, gulpable wine, usually ready a little earlier than that of Verger.

Domaine du Petit Pressoir
Marcel and Daniel Mathon make juicy, tempting wine.

Château Thivin
Mme Veuve Claude Geoffray is responsible for superb Côte de Brouilly. It has a wonderful gutsy, fruity nose, lovely fruit and no hardness – yet body – on the palate. Terrific wine.

Domaine Lucien and Robert Verger (*Eventail*)
Their L'Ecluse has a nose of violets, which is very marked in this vineyard – another wine of superb fruit. The name is curious, with its evocation of running water, because the vineyard is right on the slopes and there has never been a stream here.

MORGON

1983 production: *58,000 hectolitres*
Morgon makes the most wine, after Brouilly, amongst the nine Beaujolais *crus*. The actual village of Bas-Morgon is not nearly as important as Villié-Morgon, but between the two lies the splendid Mont du Py, from whence come the most exciting wines. The underlying soil is granite, but a distinctive feature of Morgon is the disintegrating schist called *roche pourrie*.

The wines from the best parts of the appellation have such an individual bouquet that they have created a verb – *morgonner*. But this pronounced nose is a product of the best sites and finest winemaking, and needs time to develop, because very young Morgon (for example, in the spring after the vintage) tends to be rather dumb of bouquet in comparison with the other *crus*. However, given time in bottle, the robust, generous, fleshy character of the *cru* really shows its paces. There are rich, fine flavours at two to four years old and, in great years, exotic flavours in wines far older. Descriptions such as wild cherry and sherry are bandied about, but if I ever found a taste of sherry in my mature Morgon (which I have not), I think I would be worried!

The best *climats* are Le Py, La Roche Pilée, Bellevue, Les Pillets and Les Charmes, but frequently the wines are mixed between these favoured sites and others.

A Personal Selection of Morgon Producers

Domaine Georges Brun (*Eventail*)
Excellent colour, terrific bouquet – big, beefy Morgon from Le Clachet.

Domaine de la Chanaise
Dominique Piron emphasizes the fruit in his Morgon, perhaps more than the body.

Domaine de Colonat
Bernard Collonge produces very fruity wine which likes some bottle age to show its paces.

Domaine Jean Descombes (*bottled at the domain by Duboeuf*)
This is, obviously, one of the best Morgons, with three-quarters of the vines more than 30 years old. In 1985, I had the pleasure of tasting in Descombes' cellars, and a bottle of his 1976 was heavenly, all chocolate, truffles and warm cocoa! What a delicious, balanced wine.

Domaine Louis Genillon (*Eventail*)
Fine rich Morgon, which lasts well. *Louis Desvignes* is another member of the *équipe de l'Eventail*, but his Javernières is more supple and ready earlier.

Domaine Lieven
The property is owned by the Princesse de Lieven (Madame Charles Piat) and her delightful, raspberry-scented Morgon Charmes is bottled at the domain by Georges Duboeuf. The wine can also be sold under the Château de Bellevue label.
Another Duboeuf bottling is the solid, full *Domaine des Versauds*.

Domaine des Pillets
Gérard Brisson produces Morgon with a lovely fruity, deep bouquet, and a highly commendable full, juicy taste. In ripe vintages, they are splendid at between three and four years.

Château de Pizay
This is a beautiful property, whose vineyards lie partly in Morgon, partly in Beaujolais-Villages territory. Their Côte du Py is lighter than the wine of Pierre Savoye, but has great finesse. The reason for this is that the Pizay vineyards are on the other side of the Côte, near the foot of the slope – Morgon from St-Joseph is like that too.

Domaine de Ruyère
Paul Collonge makes good Morgon, not ultra flavoursome, but most pleasing.

Domaine Savoye
Pierre Savoye, the son-in-law of Jean Descombes (who could be called the honorary grandfather of Morgon) makes splendid Côte du Py. It has wonderful colour and formidable taste, stamped with the impact of true Morgon. These wines keep. They even *terroitent*, due to the mineral content of the soil.

Sylvain Fessy
The Cuvée André Gauthier displays exemplary crunchy fruit.

Domaine Jacques Trichard
Typical Morgon, with fine fruit, sometimes a bit hard in youth but promising well.

CHIROUBLES

1983 production: *18,000 hectolitres*

This is the most ethereal of all the *crus*, light and fragrant, as airborne as the height of its vineyards. It is the *cru* one drinks first of all the nine – I have nostalgic memories of downing bottles of it in February and March in the Paris bistros where returning skiers met to swap stories of derring-do on the slopes. Chiroubles is ready before all the other *crus*, with developed bouquet and enormous charm when the rest are still at the dumb stage. There is a marvellous viewpoint at La Terrasse de Chiroubles, where from a height of 750 metres (2,460 feet) you can see the whole of Beaujolais, the River Saône and, on the horizon, the Jura topped by the snowy Alps and even Mont Blanc on clear days. The Terrasse and surrounding hills are themselves often dusted with snow in January and February. Although this is the highest in altitude of the *crus*, the vineyards are still firmly based on granite.

A Personal Selection of Chiroubles Producers

Domaine Cheysson-les-Farges
Archetypal Chiroubles, which means it is delicious and *gouleyant* – utterly gulpable.

Domaine Desmures Père & Fils (*bottled by Duboeuf*)
Another jewel in the Duboeuf crown, a triumph of teamwork between a family of growers and winemakers and the perfect technique and cleanliness of professional bottling.

Château de Javernand (*bottled by Duboeuf*)
This property belongs to M. Fourneau, President of the *cru*. It is extraordinarily "Chiroubles", with a "floaty" taste but a lovely kernel of fruit to it. The topsoil is sandy and the slopes steep.

La Maison des Vignerons à Chiroubles
Delicious, light, textbook Chiroubles – quaff it in huge quantities when it is six months to a year old.

Domaine Gérard-Roger Méziat
Delightful Chiroubles, true to the appellation's role as a giver of pleasure.

Domaine Georges Passot (*Eventail*)
Divine, scented Chiroubles nose – a lovely mouthful of ethereal fruit. La Grosse Pierre is always one of the best wines of the appellation.

Château de Raousset (*bottled by Duboeuf at the Château*)
The property possesses 20ha of Chiroubles, as well as 12ha of Fleurie and 13ha of Morgon. Granite-based vineyards, the soil here has a little less clay than at Morgon. The average age of the vines is 25–30 years. The Duboeuf bottling of this well-known property is impeccable, as one would expect.

Domaine René Savoye (*Eventail*)
Another Chiroubles which gives real lift-off. Other excellent examples of the appellation available through the Eventail are those of **Christian Lafay** and **Philippe Gobet.**

All in all, the Chiroublons are very lucky to have such a delicious commodity which "sells itself" so young.

MOULIN-A-VENT

1983 production: *35,500 hectolitres*
This is the grandest of the nine Beaujolais *crus*, the wine, they say, which most resembles a Pinot Noir from the Côte d'Or when it is aged in bottle. Maybe this was true with the 1947s, and perhaps it will be true with the 1983s. Much of the vineyard has a soil of crumbly, pink sand over granite, but the special ingredient is manganese – there is an old mine under Romanèche-Thorins. Whether this contributes to the silky power of the wine is a moot point. But fine Moulin-à-Vent has real breed allied to structure and length. The appellation does not take its name from a village, but from a sail-less windmill perched on the granite hillock of the Poncier in the hamlet of Les Thorins. Don't be surprised if Moulin-à-Vent has little bouquet when a year old – it needs time in bottle to develop.

A Personal Selection of Moulin-à-Vent Producers

Jean Brugne-Le Vivier
Bottled by the Eventail. Straightforward fruit rather than sheer Moulin style.

Domaine des Caves – Famille Delore
The sloping vineyards, facing south-south-east, give a powerful, generous wine, well able to age. Bottled by Duboeuf.

Domaine Louis Champagnon
Consistently excellent wines which have the balance to age well.

Héritiers Finaz Devillaine
Bottled by the Eventail. Fine violets, fruity nose leads to silky, good and frank taste – breed rather than blockbuster type.

Château des Jacques
40ha of vines make this the largest estate of the appellation. It is the pride of the Thorin family and there have been famed older vintages. It seems a bit heavy-handed with the alcohol to me, and I preferred the 1982 to the 1983.

Domaine Jacky Janodet
Very old vines produce rich, solid bottles.

Alphonse Mortet – Les Fargets
Bottled by the Eventail de Vignerons Producteurs. Lovely fresh fruit and no exaggerated chaptalization.

Château du Moulin-à-Vent
Owned by the Bloud family, this is one of the three largest estates in the appellation. Wood ageing. Textbook Moulin-à-Vent, ideal for laying down. Depth and richness.

Clos du Moulin-à-Vent – Domaine des Héritiers Tagent
Right in the shadow of the windmill, this is a Moulin which can age and take on the flavours of Pinot Noir. Bottled by Duboeuf.

Moulin-à-Vent des Hospices
The Bourisset family manage the vineyards of the Hospices de Romanèche and the wine is usually quite hefty.

Château Portier – Michel Gaidon
I have found this rather alcoholic, at least in the 1983 vintage.

Domaine de la Tour du Bief – Comte de Sparre
Georges Duboeuf does a domain bottling of this wine from the commune of Chénas. The soil is sandy, the style is full and robust. The Domaine de la Rochelle is in the same family.

Union des Viticulteurs Romanèche-Thorins at Chénas
Fruity, but tends to be thick style, without real Moulin silkiness.

FLEURIE

1983 production: *44,000 hectolitres*

Fleurie is blessed with the most evocative name of all the nine Beaujolais *crus*, easy to say, even easier to drink. The wines are charming and full of fruit – and there are enough of them to go round. Between Chiroubles and Moulin-à-Vent the underlying granite gives Fleurie its *ampleur* a fine bottle is at its most seductive between 18 months and three years old. Fleurie's perfume and crushed fruit should jump out of the glass at you.

A Personal Selection of Fleurie Producers

Cave des Producteurs de Fleurie
A very well-run cooperative. They make a lovely full, round Cuvée Présidente Marguerite, named after their President, Mademoiselle Marguerite Chabert. Some of their wines remind one of raspberries, others of redcurrants, and the standard is high.

Domaine Michel Chignard
"Les Moriers" is a good wine, full of crunchy fruit.

Domaine de Montgenas (*Eventail de Vignerons Producteurs*)
Really copybook Fleurie, full of ripe fruit and juicy texture.

Domaine du Point du Jour
Guy Depardon makes clean, appellation-character wine.

Domaine des Quatre Vents (*Duboeuf*)
Owned by Dr. Darroze, this exemplary Fleurie is distributed by Duboeuf and a Swiss négociant, but bottled at the property. Other Fleuries bottled and sold by Duboeuf are Château Couhard, Clos de la Pointe du Jour, Château des Déduits, Domaine de Fansotin, Domaine du Haut-Poncié, Clos du Pavillon and "La Madone", an important *climat* of 50ha with 20 owners. It is beautifully sited overlooking the village of Fleurie on sandy topsoil – the statue of the Virgin Mary is perched on a little chapel in view of the whole vineyard. Here, the nose is meant to be of peaches and peonies, but it is true crushed red fruit.

Other Fleurie sites are La Chapelle des Bois and La Roilette. Mostly the wines are very good (such as Sylvain Fessy's La Roilette), but sometimes they are spoilt by excessive alcohol, as if the winemakers have sought to gild the lily. This is a pity, as it destroys the essential fruit character of Fleurie, indeed, of all Beaujolais. Perhaps, here as elsewhere, this was noticeable in 1983, when the natural alcohol was of a good level, so there was really no need to be heavy handed with the chaptalization. The Fleuriatons have a fine reputation which is worth guarding against these kinds of vinous aberrations.

CHENAS

1983 production: *13,800 hectolitres*
Chénas produces less wine than any of the other Beaujolais *crus* and so it is the least known. The name comes from *chênes* as this area used to be covered by a forest of oaks, but now the vine has taken over. The vineyards lie on granite between the villages of Chénas and La Chapelle de Guinchay, on either side of the valley of the Mauvaise and to the north-west of Moulin-à-Vent. The wines have pronounced character and repay keeping for a few years in ripe vintages. They share some tasting qualities with Moulin-à-Vent, but do not have the silkiness of the "ultimate" wines of that appellation. However, Chénas is generous and fruity, not quite as robust as Morgon – they say it has a bouquet of peonies, but I have yet to detect that characteristic.

A Personal Selection of Chénas Producers

Château Bonnet
Pierre Perrachon here makes wine with good, fruity, definite bouquet – perhaps even better than the impression on the palate.

Domaine Guy Braillon
Fruity wine, remaining youthful in bottle – lots of body.

Domaine Louis Champagnon
Chénas from Les Brureaux, this is superb wine, deep coloured, full of fruit, all rose petals and crushed grapes.

Château de Chénas (*Eventail de Vignerons Producteurs*)
Lovely crunchy fruit – magnificent taste.

Domaine Michel Crozet
Chénas from the Coteaux des Brureaux, with vibrant fruit, roundness and body.

Manoir des Journets (*Georges Duboeuf*)
Old vines here give a wine that is "a bouquet of flowers lying in a velvet basket", a fanciful description with which I would agree. Basically, it means delightful floral aromas and a velvety texture.

Domaine Hubert Lapierre
Wines with good, fruity bouquet and ripe power, which is not the same as excessive alcohol.

Domaine Jean-Louis Santé
Fruity, bouncy, frank Chénas.

Les Rougemonts is a Chénas site which is much appreciated.

JULIENAS

1983 production: *32,700 hectolitres*
Near St-Amour, the high vineyards of Juliénas give wines which are really the epitome of what Beaujolais *crus* are all about. They are wonderfully sturdy, oozing purple fruit when young, positively crunchy in the mouth, but with a backbone which promises further development if you can only prevent yourself from pulling the cork straightaway. There is granite and schist, and the wines have the *charpente* of the soil. This is the most northerly *cru* of the Rhône department and it includes some vineyards from the villages of Jullié (about 80ha) and Pruzilly. The slopes of Jullié are very steep, comparable to those of Chiroubles – no picking machine is going to venture up this kind of gradient. Some Juliénas has intriguing spicy overtones (cinnamon and cloves) to add to the glossy richness.

A Personal Selection of Juliénas Producers

Château des Capitans
Robust Juliénas which usually lasts well in bottle.

Domaine Gonon
Highly respected wine, which really "delivers the goods".

Château de Juliénas
Owned by M. François Condemine, this is always remarkable wine, with a scented, delicate nose but immense crunch and bite on the palate – even irony. It keeps beautifully.

Domaine Monnet (*Eventail*)
This is part of the Château de Juliénas vineyard – the vines face

south-south-east and therefore attract the best of the sun. The wine is very fruity, with that Juliénas structure behind it.

Domaine André Pelletier (*Eventail*)

Les Envaux which is consistently amongst the best Juliénas of each year, full of fruit and *élan*.

Château des Poupets (*bottled at the Château by Georges Duboeuf*)

Solid wine, *gardé en fûts*, with character and flavour. Duboeuf also bottles the rich wines of the *Domaine des Vignes*.

Domaine de la Seigneurie de Juliénas (*bottled at the domain by Duboeuf*)

This is a domain which is part of the Château de Juliénas and under the same ownership. Not surprisingly, the Condemine-Duboeuf connection produces fine wine, with body and even some tannin (an unusual quality for a Beaujolais), so a few years in bottle suits it admirably.

● ○ ST-AMOUR

1983 production: *15,900 hectolitres*

It may be facetious to say that this is the wine for St-Valentine's Day, but there can be few more pleasurable ways of cementing a relationship than by drinking a bottle of St-Amour *à deux*! It is perhaps best not to go into the reputed origins of the name, since it reflects somewhat badly on the clerics of times past. Suffice it to say that here we are still on a granite base, although it is the only *cru* of the Beaujolais entirely in Saône-et-Loire. In recent years St-Amour had considerable trouble from the outpourings of a factory nearby, which tainted many of the wines – happily, this is now a thing of the past. The white wine made in the commune can be called St-Véran. The wines have a certain sprightliness, which is intriguing, combined with fruit and delicacy – they need sunny years to give them the necessary ripeness. Light vintages can be drunk young, but when conditions are good, a St-Amour of two to three years old is all the more interesting. Unfortunately, there is not a great deal of St-Amour to go around.

A Personal Selection of St-Amour Producers

Domaine Dufour

Highly regarded St-Amour which gives a very good lesson in appellation taste

Domaine Elie Mongénie

St-Amour that keeps well in ripe years.

Domaine de Mongrin

Duc Frères are responsible for this pretty, soft, flowery wine, the epitome of charm in a St-Amour.

Domaine du Paradis (*bottled by Duboeuf*)

Vines of a good age on sandy, gravelly topsoil produce a rich St-Amour of finesse. Other good Duboeuf bottlings in the appellation include the *Domaine des Sablons* and the *Cuvée Poitevin* (this is not a wine which has escaped from the other side of France – M. Poitevin is the vigneron and the vinificateur). This wine is produced from clay-limestone topsoil, balanced and elegant and capable of ageing with grace.

Domaine Guy Patissier (*Eventail*)

Marked by strong regional flavour, this really packs a punch, but through its depth of *taste*, not through its alcohol imbalance.

Domaine Jean Patissier

Has an equally high reputation – lovely wines with bite and attack – as has **Jean-Bernard Patissier** with Les Bonnets.

Domaine Francis Saillant

Very creditable, easy-to-drink St Amour.

Château de St-Amour

M. Siraudin produces one of the top St-Amours, with consistent quality over a number of years.

Index

Wine estates, Domaines etc. and their proprietors are listed in the A–Z of Burgundy Producers (pp. 77–116).